SHEDS ON THE SEASHORE

A TOUR THROUGH BEACH HUT HISTORY

Kathryn Ferry

en Press

© Kathryn Ferry 2009

All paper used in the printing of this book has been made from
wood grown in managed, sustainable forests.

Every attempt has been made to secure the appropriate
permissions for materials reproduced in this book. If
there has been any oversight we will be happy to rectify
the situation and a written submission should be made to
the Publishers.

ISBN13: 978-1-906710-97-2

Printed and bound in the UK

Pen Press is an imprint of
Indepenpress Publishing Limited
25 Eastern Place
Brighton
BN2 1GJ

A catalogue record of this book
is available from the British Library

Cover design by Jacqueline Abromeit

For my parents Mike and Vanessa Ferry
and my Grandma, Doreen Ferry

Acknowledgments

Beach hut history has never really been written before. It is the history of the people who have owned and used beach huts over the past century. Digging in archives revealed some great stories but the best part of my research has been actually speaking to people. Without exception, the 'hutters' I met have been helpful and hospitable; despite my being a stranger to them, numerous people around the English coast invited me into their huts for a cup of tea, if not something stronger! This friendliness is a trademark of beach hut communities and I cannot thank owners enough for their willingness to talk to me.

The following list is incomplete because lots of people chose to remain anonymous but my thanks are due, in geographical order, to: the Royal West Norfolk Golf Club, Bob and Vera Owen, Ann Thornton and Sarah Chapman, Julia and Barry Salmon, Mr and Mrs Robinson of Felixstowe Bowls Club, Mr J. W. Hipkin, Mr and Mrs Watts, Betty Holloway and Mandy Martin, Pat and Geoff Allen, Don and Julia Gordon, Kevin and Lori Doswell, the Formby's of Bexhill, Jack Corke, Julian Martyr, Pauline and Mark Sutton, Ivor and Hazel from Rustington, Malcolm and Lynne at Fareham, Kath, Penny and Marie from Calshot Spit, David Limebear, Jean Cornah, Ann Croxford, Jez Harris.

Some owners went out of their way to give me assistance and it has been my pleasure to keep in touch with them after my big trip. Special thanks therefore go to Graham Last, Olive Pigney, Peter and Joanna Kemp, Tim Baber, Heather and Tony Payne, Jim and Dessie Carnell and Tim Langdon. Yet more people responded to my appeals for beach hut stories and in this regard I am grateful to Pat & Frank Cook, Michelle

Le Bailly, Joyce Maggs, Mickey Sandoe, Denis Green, Rob Townshend, Cath and Tony Lynn, Janet Wingate, Joy Puritz, Sylvia and Stan Lavers, Mr F. L. Pettman and Helen Chagg.

Friends and family made my trip financially possible by providing accommodation and lifts between destinations so, for their invaluable help, I would like to thank Robert, Ania and Lenny Watson, Bev & Sam Smith, Eileen & Chris Wellington, Wendy Bevan-Mogg, Sheila and Ron Rogers.

My thanks also extend to the staff of numerous archives, libraries, museums and Tourist Information centres of whom there are too many to list individually. Special thanks, however, go to Julie Ann Lambert of the Bodleian Library, Oxford; Tony Sharkey, Blackpool Central Library; the staff of Cambridge University Library, the British Library, Brighton Local Studies Library, the East Kent Record Office and Cromer Museum; Bob and Terry at Margate Museum; Roger Kennell, Timewalk Museum at Weymouth, David Buchanan, Scarborough Museum, Bude-Stratton Museum, Andrew Emery of Bournemouth Council, Stefan Ganther of Waveney District Council and to all the Council employees up and down the country who answered my beach hut questionnaire.

The field of seaside history is peopled by a relatively small number of academics and over the course of my research it has been a privilege to have the assistance of Professor John K. Walton, Gary Winter, Allan Brodie, Fred Gray and Sue Berry. For their help in publicising my work I am also hugely grateful to Hagen Rose and Greg Wade. Special thanks are also due to Wayne Hemingway for providing the book's Foreword. Although many, many people have shared their time, knowledge and memories to make this book, any mistakes in it are mine.

Finally, I wish to thank the people who have borne with me through the decade of my beach hut obsession. To Eric Holroyd, who was there at the beginning and didn't think I was mad; to Matthew Slocombe who has given me the love and encouragement to see this project through; and to my parents, Mike and Vanessa Ferry, for their unerring support.

Contents

Foreword

Beaches have something for everyone. They are a place to dream, to escape, to play, to relax, to discover.

Being able to do all these things and escape a sudden downpour, make a cuppa and a cheese and ham Breville in a shed is a concept that Britain has happily bestowed on the world. The media do their annual "A 6 ft by 4 ft beach hut goes for £100,000" incredulous headline, but how can you put a price on the precious coastline? Men have always enjoyed escaping to the shed, but a beach hut, a fishing rod and a gas burner takes shed heaven to new heights. When the little ones are happy then us parents can usually relax; is there anywhere or anytime a small child feels happier than dipping their freshly made toastie into sand? Can there be a better way to spend your retirement than watching the world go round from a deckchair on the decking outside your own mini property by the sea? We often put ourselves down in Britain. But we lead the world when it comes to beach huts and with the return to sustainable local travel our beach huts have an increasingly important role to play in the resurgence of the British seaside holiday

When I was first asked by Bournemouth Council to get involved in the Boscombe Overstrand beachfront regeneration project, as a British designer how could I resist the opportunity to work on the re-imagining of a true British cultural institution, the Beach Hut. The same enthusiasm inspires *Sheds on the Seashore*, a book that celebrates beach huts past and present.

Wayne Hemingway   www.hemingwaydesign.co.uk

Introduction

A perplexed reaction is something I've come to expect when I tell strangers I am writing a book about beach huts. The pause may only be momentary but I am aware of the same question forming in their minds: 'What on earth is there to write about beach huts?' Some are too polite to let the words fall from their lips. Others are not. And yet experience has taught me that nine times out of ten this first thought will quickly be superseded by reference to Aunty Olive, Carol from work or a Mr and Mrs Brown who live down the road; relatives, friends and acquaintances who have a beach hut. Just as often people recall long-dormant memories of their own childhood holidays in which the shelter provided by a beach hut was an essential element. For such simple structures, these seaside buildings have secured a privileged place in the popular imagination.

On the fast train to Newcastle, starting out on my beach hut journey around the English coast in July 2002, I sat opposite a Scottish lady who told me about the wife of one of her cousins.

'They lived in Kings Lynn. It was fifteen years ago or so, I suppose. My cousin's wife was in the supermarket and a whole shelf of tins fell on her.'

'Poor woman!' I sympathised.

'She hurt her ankle and got compensation from the supermarket. She used the money to buy a beach hut. She'd always wanted one, you see, but her husband was a miserly Scot and didn't hold with it. But the money was hers and she bought her beach hut.' The hut didn't get much use, apparently, but that didn't really matter. 'I expect it's worth a fair bit now.'

My Scottish companion had been reading an article in the property section of a Sunday newspaper the previous week.

Over the past decade beach huts have become very fashionable, the ultimate must-have 'des res' with prices soaring as a reflection of increased demand. In some places there are as many names on the waiting list as there are huts and each time a beach hut breaks past price records, journalists head for the coast to write stories of the bygone British seaside being reclaimed by rich city types.

My own fascination, dare I say obsession, with the humble beach hut is easy to date but harder to explain. Although I grew up just seven miles from the seaside in North Devon, my childhood experience of the wide sands at Westward Ho! was more often in Wellington boots and copious layers of clothing than in sunshine and swimming costume. My parents preferred the beach out of season.

I didn't really begin to *notice* beach huts until a November visit to Herne Bay in Kent. Among the thousands of photographs I've since taken of beach huts, it is the one I took that day that stands out. That photo captures the moment when it all began. Elongated shadows stretch away from a row of coloured huts, darkening the shingle foreground in sharply delineated, seaward-pointing arrows. The light is crisp and wintry; the sky softly blue above the mellow shades of painted and stained wooden huts. Stripes of sunlight break through the line of gabled structures and accentuate the uneven ground of pebbles and shells. Looking at that photo now I can hear the sound of my feet crunching along the beach and feel the chill salty air against my cheeks.

From that day I began to make frequent weekend visits to other coastal towns and villages. On day trips from Cambridge I explored the East Anglian seaside and got my first glimpse of Southwold's famous candy-coloured huts. Perhaps I should have begun to suspect the growing strength of my interest when I experienced an uncanny feeling of *déjà vu* at Wells-next-the-Sea; crossing the slipway onto the sand I saw the beach huts resting on stilts that I had dreamt about only days before. The thrill was undeniable.

Because when you start noticing beach huts you start noticing how, at each place, they have their own character. In essence they may be little more than sheds on the seashore but these petite buildings, providing a place to change and brew a pot of tea, are the guardians of happy holiday memories.

Still, I was intrigued by why, in such a peculiarly English way, so many of my compatriots still wished to spend their spare time sitting in a painted shed gazing out across open water; were prepared, in fact, to spend large sums of money to secure the privilege. Even more intriguing was why I found *myself* so very attracted by this proposition. Has any other nation clung so steadfastly to the idea of a holiday dwelling on the seashore in which overnight stays are forbidden, there is no sanitation and which, if the forces of nature should so choose, can be washed away on a high tide? Was it something in the national psyche, I wondered? Was this yearning recordable or definable? Could there be a historical explanation?

In an attempt to find out I spent two months following the coast, south from Seaton Carew in County Durham, then westward along the English Channel recording the presence of more than 20,000 huts and chalets. Using public transport wherever possible, my journey ended on the more familiar beaches of North Devon. Twenty years before me, American travel writer Paul Theroux made a similar trip for his book *Kingdom by the Sea*, in which he described hut residents as sad and old-fashioned symbols of everything that was wrong with the traditional British seaside. I wanted to update his analysis by speaking to modern beach hut owners. And yet my travels only answered half the question. The background to their stories lay in libraries and archives.

I knew that before beach huts there had been wheeled changing rooms called bathing machines. What I hadn't realised was how long these contraptions had been part of the coastal landscape and how we'd exported them around the world. In popular tradition bathing machines have become associated with Victorian prudery, so it was surprising to find they actually had a much lengthier history that included a good helping of nudity. And all of this was inextricably bound to that popular English invention, the seaside. Revealed in the history of the humble beach hut are centuries of changing attitudes toward health, class, morality and public decency.

This is the story of beach huts, how they got here and why they're here to stay.

Chapter One
Inventing the seaside

A century ago, visiting the seaside was a form of mass recreation. Travel back another hundred years and it was an exclusive pastime for the rich. Turn back the clock a full three centuries and few people who didn't live or work by the sea had ever seen it. Whatever the song says, the fact is that we have not always wanted to be beside the seaside. Just like football, the seaside was something we Brits actually had to invent and until we did, there was no such thing as beach huts because no one went to the beach.

In retrospect you could say our colonisation of the beach had an element of phlegmatic inevitability. The shape of the United Kingdom is, after all, determined by more than 11,000 miles of coastline. That's more than twice the distance between the two polar ice caps. Of course, such a statistic would have had little relevance to our more distant ancestors. For them, mileage was not the point. The sea provided food and brought huge profits from a network of foreign markets. It was the scene of epoch-making battles; the navy that 'ruled the waves' was a source of national pride. They didn't need to swim in it to know they were surrounded by it.

In the western world attitudes were conditioned by the Bible and the authors of the Holy book did not go out of their way to paint the sea in a positive light. In the very first verses of Genesis we learn that before the act of God's Creation, all the earth was covered by a raging ocean. On the fifth day, God filled the sea and sky with living beings including great sea-monsters, which He ordered to reproduce along with the fishes and birds. On the sixth day God created human beings and gave them dominion over every other creature. Nowhere did He suggest that Adam and Eve should make friends with the fishes and sea-monsters in their own element. Christian theology characterised the sea as a great abyss, an uncharted liquid mass of unimaginable extent that could be subdued by God's hand or, as in the story of the Flood, turned into an instrument of punishment. In the face of such an apparently vast and volatile element it is hardly surprising early Christians felt little desire to strip off and jump in.

The Romans had different ideas. Ancient writers have left colourful descriptions of Baiae, the capital of fashionable excursion in the Gulf of Naples from where the world's earliest seaside villas once spread out along Mediterranean shores. A general licentiousness was fuelled by the myth that everyone who bathed in the sea at Baiae fell in love. The water had apparently been too chilly for humans until Cupid was made to swim in it by the goddess Venus. A spark fell from his torch into the bay, bursting into flames and warming the water. Seneca found the dissolute lifestyle so contrary to his tastes that he left the day after he arrived but under the Caesars Baiae became even more tightly packed with holiday homes, leading Martial to complain, in an all too familiar manner, about the inflated cost of living. Although little now remains of the pleasure-seekers' palaces, the Neapolitan resort of relaxation and sexual gratification retained its popularity for a remarkable five hundred years, an enviable record compared to modern Brighton or Blackpool.

In addition to the sea, Baiae had its own hot springs, an amenity which the Romans exploited throughout their expanding Empire. Going to the baths, or *thermae*, became a social ritual combining health and beauty with a good workout in the adjoining gymnasium. Fourth century mosaics excavated at one Roman villa even show that female gymnasts exercised in an early version of the bikini. But the collapse of the Roman Empire in A.D. 476 put an end to all this Classical healthiness, ushering in a millennium of suspicious dread and prohibition of anything likely to induce bodily pleasure. The Christian Church considered bathing an immoral habit so hot water took on the taint of sin and wickedness. Knights returning from the Crusades attempted to re-introduce Roman-style baths like the ones they'd seen in Muslim lands but the infidel associations were too strong to permit success. As for sea-bathing, the hedonistic Baiae beach lifestyle had never really travelled north so the practice became just one among many that was rapidly and consciously buried among the ruins of ancient Rome.

From the Italian cradle of the Renaissance a humanist re-evaluation of Classical civilizations had a huge impact upon pan-European standards of taste, stimulating a desire among men of noble birth to visit the sites described by Greek and Roman authors. The aristocratic Grand Tour was to become a prerequisite for lordly education, an intellectual as well as a literal shopping trip. New interpretations of classical architecture inspired reproductions in the English countryside whilst excavated artefacts and skilful copies were purchased as fashionable souvenirs. In 1748 excavations began at the archaeological site of Pompeii with the important by-product of ensuring that more and more Grand Tourists included the Bay of Naples on their itinerary. The beauty of its coastal scenery became legendary and it is no coincidence that resorts as far apart as Weymouth in Dorset and Douglas Bay in the Isle of Man would later offer exaggerated claims of their similarity to this, the most famous stretch of foreign shoreline.

Attitudes were also beginning to change under the influence of natural theology. From the late seventeenth century beaches, dunes, gulfs and bays, which had formerly been seen as harsh reminders of the Biblical Flood, were reassessed as elements in a divinely engineered landscape, the gift of a beneficent God to mankind. In this kinder world view natural harbours existed to provide shelter for ships; even rocks and reefs could be explained as elements in the architecture of human self-defence. And thanks to a concerted period of progress by English oceanographers, between 1660 and 1675 scientific enquiry began to demystify the sea.

If fear of the boundless seas persisted then by the mid-eighteenth century it was being harnessed to a new theory of Romantic aesthetics. In his book *A Philosophical Enquiry into the Origin of our Ideas of the Sublime and Beautiful* (1759), the English writer Edmund Burke described the ocean as 'an object of no small terror'. The difference here was that fear and terror, as passions that robbed the mind of its power to act and reason, were considered to be crucial and even ruling principles of the Sublime. At the root of this new philosophy was the search for personal enlightenment by the use of shock tactics. Like the thrill of riding a rollercoaster at breakneck speed, the Romantics sought an emotional rush from facing their fears head on. 'Greatness of dimension,' wrote Burke, 'is a powerful cause of the sublime.' Depth was more impressive than height, and infinity, where the eye is unable to perceive boundaries, 'has a tendency to fill the mind with that sort of delightful horror, which is the most genuine effect, and truest test of the sublime.' So, if staring out to sea could be judged a test of emotional stamina then how much more effective would it be to face the terror of drowning and actually submit oneself to the oncoming waves?

This re-ordered soul-searching coincided with the medical exhortation to cold water bathing. Instead of superstition, people's lives were increasingly ruled by a belief in science, which meant that advice on health, once dispensed by priests, became the domain of professional physicians. Empirical proof that the sea could serve as a new miracle drug was the necessary first step towards shaping our penchant for beach holidays – early tourists needed a pretty strong reason to travel for days on poor roads to the domain of the fisher-folk. Then fashion took over and the desire to see what all the fuss was about, once stimulated, was assisted by the development of transport networks and rising prosperity, which brought with it a new concept of leisure time.

In the beginning, seaside amusements were modelled upon the precedents set by inland spas like Bath and Tunbridge Wells. In spite of the disinterested neglect of Roman bath complexes around the old

Empire, a popular faith in the benefit of mineral waters had survived. Tales of the miraculous healing power of natural springs were co-opted into the service of Catholic saints and the waters continued to be sites of pilgrimage for medieval health tourists. The reputation of St Ann's Well at Buxton, now tapped by über-brand Nestlé, was so great that specific instructions were given at the Reformation for its closure. Sir William Bassett, willing agent of Thomas Cromwell, reported that he had locked up all the baths and wells in the Peak District town: 'I did not only deface the tabernacles and places where [the images] did stand but did also take away crutches, shirts and shifts...being things that allure the ignorant to the said offering.' Official prohibition and mockery were, nonetheless, unable to halt the rapid build-up of new piles of crutches.

From the late sixteenth century the rising tide of scientific enquiry, combined with the pent-up urge for pleasure released at the Restoration, ensured a renewed demand for mineral spas. Sanctioned by considerations of health, a dip in one of the five healing pools at Bath could mean sharing the thermal waters with gout-ridden judges, scrofulous squires, barren wives and hysterical misses as well as city fops, cuckolds, gamesters and dancing-masters. There was significant potential for riotous behaviour but from the early eighteenth century this was reduced by the appointment of Masters of Ceremony at the most popular inland resorts of Bath, Tunbridge Wells and Buxton. The popularity of these springs demonstrated that people were willing to travel in search of a cure for their maladies whether they were real of imagined. In the 1690s, the gently born but hardy hypochondriac Celia Fiennes rode side-saddle around England 'sipping and dipping' wherever she found water bubbling up through the ground.

As places that catered for visitors staying away from home for an extended period, spa towns were the original holiday resorts. Their success explains why the first ever seaside resort started out as a spa. During a walk along Scarborough beach at some time during the year 1626, an observant lady named Mrs Farrow noticed traces of a rusty-coloured pigmentation where water spilt over rocks at the cliff base. A connoisseur of mineral waters, she proceeded to taste the liquid then got her friends to do the same. Word of the medicinal properties of this chalybeate spring spread into the hinterland but little was made of Scarborough's coastal location. Besides adding a certain saltiness, the sea's presence was a mere geographical fluke. Not until Dr Robert Wittie of Hull suggested, in his 1667 pamphlet, that invalids might wish to consider quaffing sea water or perhaps even take a nice bath in it, was the sea promoted as an optional extra.

At a time when dieticians and the government are trying to curb our national intake of salt, the practice of drinking seawater seems particularly unappealing, if not plain foolhardy. That this tonic was actively promoted as a medical panacea in conjunction with sea-bathing appears absurdly unsophisticated. Yet it demonstrates a fact that remains true to this day; that the human quest for health and well-being is particularly subject to the whims of fashion. New treatments could inspire huge followings but a large part of their appeal relied on novelty. For sea-bathing to compete against the inland spa cure, medical evidence had to be found to prove that cold water was better than hot.

This argument, which focused on the action of temperature, rather than minerals, upon the body, was most influentially set forth by Sir John Floyer, a Lichfield doctor with connections in Buxton. His treatise of 1697 claimed that cold water was divinely sanctioned in the old but abandoned practice of triple immersion baptism. Its substitution with a little pouring or sprinkling was hardly enough to wash away original sin. Furthermore, evidence from northern races including the Muscovites, Tartars, Scots and Irish showed that regular cold plunges from childhood onwards helped the body to acclimatise and toughened the constitution. Four years later he followed this up with an authoritative *History of Cold Bathing* (1701–02). Liberally scattered with references to ancient advocates, it became the textbook for a new trend, going into its fifth edition by 1722.

Writing as one island dweller to his compatriots, Floyer pointed out the obvious; since we 'have the Sea about us, we cannot want an excellent Cold Bath which will preserve our Healths and cure many Diseases, as our Fountains do.' Although he didn't specifically favour *sea*-bathing, Floyer had tried it. His key point, however, was about temperature. The good doctor recommended plunging into water below 10º Fahrenheit as a relief for ailments as diverse as leprosy and corns, gonorrhoea and deafness. That the body would be profoundly shocked by this experience was the therapy's real virtue. After the initial surprise there was a contraction of the 'nervous membrane and tubes', the external senses were enlivened and the more vehement passions suppressed. Whether a man's libido was indecently supercharged or his battery was flat, cold water was offered up as the answer. Indeed, Floyer repeated the popular rhyme that:

Cold bathing has this good alone,
It makes Old John to hug Old Joan,
And gives a sort of resurrection
To buried joys, through lost erection,
And does fresh kindnesses entail
On a wife tasteless, old and stale.

Peddling the eighteenth century equivalent of Viagra among the medicinal benefits of cold water, it is not surprising that Floyer inspired followers in Germany, France and Italy, as well as in England. Claims by quack practitioners became more and more outlandish but the exhortation to drink cold water seems to have been a sensible one, especially as we're now being advised to drink at least eight glasses a day to stay healthy.

It was only a matter of time before advocacy of cold water led to a new concentration on sea water healing. Early on, Dr Wittie had asserted in his 1667 book *Scarborough Spaw* that the sea cured gout, balanced the humours and, in a thankfully unspecified manner, 'killed all manner of worms'. By the 1730s there were a handful of places around

A

DISSERTATION

On the USE of

SEA-WATER

In the DISEASES of the

G L A N D S.

PARTICULARLY

The *Scurvy, Jaundice, King's-Evil, Leprofy*, and the *Glandular Confumption.*

Tranflated from the *Latin* of

RICHARD RUSSEL, M.D.

By an *Eminent Phyfician.*

Θάλασσα κλύζει πάντα τ' ἀνθρώπων κακά
The Sea wafhes away all the Evils of Mankind.
Eurip. Iphig. in Taur. V. 1193.

L O N D O N:
Printed for the TRANSLATOR,
And fold by W. OWEN, at *Homer's* Head, *Temple-Bar*; and R. GOADBY, at *Sherborne.*
MDCCLII.

Title page of Dr Russell's treatise from the English translation of 1752

Frontispiece of Dr Russell's treatise from the English translation of 1752

the coast where people were already testing out these claims. In 1748 a Southampton medic named Dr Richard Frewin recorded how one of his patients made significant progress over a period of three months by drinking sea-water and taking daily dips. The treatment regime began in the middle of November and lasted until early February. It took nearly two weeks worth of daily dips for the young man to get his lost appetite back and though Frewin recorded that he had regained his vigour and liveliness after a further two weeks, he still recommended another month of sea-bathing on the same pattern. After 11 January his prescription was reduced to less frequent immersions and on 8 February he was pronounced fit enough to return home.

There may have been other more publicity-shy pioneers but the best known was Dr Richard Russell who in 1750 published the first (Latin) edition of his *Dissertation on the Use of Sea-Water in Diseases of the Glands, particularly, The Scurvy, Jaundice, King's Evil, Leprosy and the Glandular Consumption*. That Russell was long credited with the invention of sea-bathing illustrates just how influential his work was. An English translation of his ocean-endorsing opus appeared in 1752, prompting Russell to move from Lewes to Brighthelmstone (subsequently shortened to Brighton) in order to supervise the treatment of an increasing number of devoted fans. The cold-water shock remained an essential element of his regimen so patients were advised to get up early, swallow a preparatory half pint of sea-water and bathe before sunrise. After bathing came a second half pint of salt water and, if further invigoration was required, there was the option of a hearty rub-down with freshly collected seaweed. For Russell the sea was equivalent to a modern multi-vitamin, it was a vast God-given mineral soup with natural detergent properties and a saltiness that offered defence against decay and putrefaction.

Among his case studies Russell cited the truly revolting tale of a woman who imbibed twenty-five gallons of sea-water in a continuous course of purging. In all she drank 200 pints, one each morning, which, if her physician is to be believed, resulted in an improvement to her appetite and the reduction of her 'strumous Swellings'. Such a freakishly magnificent effort would be hard to outdo and Russell wrote with some smugness that 'if this vast Quantity of *Sea-Water* drank... does not procure and demonstrate its harmless Virtues; I fear there will never be any Argument strong enough to remove the unjust Prejudices of some People'. Dr Awsiter, his successor at Brighton, was rather more pragmatic about

Dr Richard Russell

the remedy, admitting that many constitutions were too delicate and many stomachs too weak to bear the nausea and sickness produced by drinking sea-water. Even where this 'inconvenience' could be overcome, the doctor recognised the uncomfortable side effect it had of making 'the party very thirsty for the remainder of the day'. Small wonder then that additives were considered a legitimate way of helping the medicine go down. A spoonful of sugar, expensive commodity that it was in the eighteenth century, would have been considered rather too extravagant but in 1768 Dr Awsiter recommended mixing in an equal quantity of new milk to create what he called 'a noble medicine'. He even provided the following recipe with claims that it would help cleanse the blood: 'Take of sea-water and milk, each four ounces, put them over the fire, and when they begin to boil, add a sufficiency of cremortartar, to turn it into whey; strain it from the curd, and, when cool, drink it.' Swallowing sea-water was still being recommended into the 1860s when Spencer Thomson M.D. suggested port wine or beef tea as alternative ways to mask the taste.

The fact that members of the leisured classes got up early and drank these foul-sounding concoctions confirms an impressive degree of faith in the cure. In her diary entry for 20 November 1782, the authoress Fanny

Burney recorded how she and her three friends, the Miss Thrales, bathed at Brighton by moonlight. They woke at six o'clock and went down to the shore where the bathing women were waiting to assist them. It was still dark when they returned to their lodgings to dress by candlelight. From the early nineteenth century, summer rather than winter became the preferred season for coastal excursions but it's noteworthy that, following a 'glorious tumble in the waves' at Ramsgate in August 1819, the poet Samuel Taylor Coleridge complained that the water was not cold enough for his liking!

With the benefit of hindsight, belief in the cold sea-water cure is easy to deride; but for those individuals riddled with leprosy or afflicted by gout and scrofula (the old name for tuberculosis of the lymphatic glands) it was probably just as effective as any other medicine on the market. Besides which, a trip to the sea meant a change of surroundings and the prospect of new company. These were important considerations for the treatment of hypochondria, a malaise with nebulous symptoms and numerous sufferers. Almost endemic among the elite, hypochondria particularly affected women for whom the attentions consequent upon ill health relieved the tedium of days spent in reading, embroidery or music lessons. At a time when divorce was impossible, exaggerating the severity of minor ailments offered distraction from an unhappy marriage; it also gave some distinction to those neglected on the shelf of spinsterhood. Wealth encouraged idleness, an apparently enviable state were it not for the health problems caused by boredom and over-indulgence. A Danish immigrant arriving in London in 1794 described seeing human beings with limbs 'as bulbous as a pumpkin'. These were the characters bulging out of their breeches in the contemporary cartoons of Thomas Rowlandson and George Cruickshank, later exemplified by the corpulent form of the Prince Regent. Obesity may be more pervasive now but it is not a new phenomenon.

Secretly envious of their social inferiors, whose labour lent them vigour, the ruling classes worried that they were being consumed from within. Having distanced themselves from the rhythms of nature, the rich became preoccupied with their neuroses, fearful of their listlessness and their artificial desires. Lacking psycho-therapy or Prozac to nourish their self-indulgence, these men and women responded eagerly to the aesthetics of the Sublime and willingly submitted themselves to the sea-water cure. There was a kind of narcissistic pleasure in the treatment, especially when the rest of the seaside stay could be divided between assembly room, promenade and marine library, comparing notes and competing with fellow patients. Dr Russell considered that a pint of water was 'commonly sufficient in grown persons, to give three or four sharp stools', so we can only hazard a guess at some of the conversations that took place. Exercise and diet were also part of the programme for improved health. In 1779, writer George Keate met a gentleman in a Margate bathing room who was dressed 'in a night-cap, and a gold-laced hat, wrapped in a great coat, with a silk handkerchief tied round his neck'. Questioned about the benefits of a seaside cure, the gentleman described how:

> ...my physician has sent me for three months from London on a fool's errand – and yet he is an honest fellow too, and I follow his rules – but he prohibits me my *morning whet* – denies me *good sauce* and Cayenne *pepper* with my fish – drenches me with salt water and mutton-broth, –and obliges me to sit and walk two hours every morning by the sea-side, and as many after dinner, in order *to smell the sea mud*.

It was the eighteenth century equivalent of a 'detox'.

Overweight urbanites only had to look at the picturesque fisher-folk working along the seashore to observe the advantages of a simpler life. If the rural idyll was a creation of city dwellers, so too was the jolly innocence of Jack Tar and his sea-faring friends whose harbour-side activities provided many a wistful scene for the artists' brush. Their robust health seemed to offer an antidote to the evils of an increasingly industrialised society. Dr Russell, who amassed some twenty years of reflection and experiment in his treatise, drew attention to the way sailors used sea-water as a purgative. The fine teeth and gums of women who made their living gathering shell-fish also suggested that the 'saline particles...dashed out by the breaking of the waves' worked as an effective dentifrice. The real clincher was increased longevity. A guidebook of 1780 claimed that 'several Persons of very advanced Years are now living in and near Margate; and in last April an old Lady was buried there, in her hundredth Year'. According to a turn of the century directory, the inhabitants of Brighton lived reassuringly free from colds. Even the 'men and women who walk kneedeep in the sea to take prawns and shrimps; they who attend upon the bathers; and others who do it for diversion, never catch cold though they keep on their wet shoes and stockings the whole day'. As if that weren't enough, a French doctor advised impotent men to swim in the sea and eat fresh fish regularly as it was these habits that made sailors so 'essentially procreative'.

The sea-water cult rapidly filtered through the social hierarchy, supplementing an established folk-tradition in places like Lancashire. The anonymous author of a 1789 *Description of Blackpool* recounted the histories of several recovering invalids, one of whom gave the following testimony:

> He was a shoemaker from Lancaster, and was drawing towards seventy; that at forty-five his love for the fair sex got the better of his prudence, and he married a girl of eighteen. She soon brought him six children, which had kept him poor to that moment; that he had had a complication of disorders, the most alarming of which was that of being totally blind; that he had resided at Blackpool, in a petty lodging, about six weeks, during which he drank sea water, washed his eyes, and sometimes bathed; that his complaints were removed and his sight so far recovered, as to distinguish an object at two miles distance.

Visiting Blackpool in 1813, the traveller Richard Ayton observed crowds of poor people from the manufacturing hinterland 'who have a high opinion of the efficacy of bathing, maintaining that in the months of August and September there is physic in the sea'. This 'physic' was comprehensive enough to apply no matter what the disease and combined all the myriad properties of 'drugs in the doctor's shop'. For these people the harsh cure began with the long walk to Blackpool and included the morning draught of salt water, which was chased, 'under the notion of fortifying the stomach[,] by an equal quantity of gin and beer'.

The importance of the placebo effect should not be underestimated and resorts were always keen to publicise sensational instances of their success. In September 1789 the Teignmouth correspondent of the *Exeter Flying Post* cited the wondrous recovery of an elderly clergyman who had come to the town after losing the use of both his hands and legs. After just a few weeks of bathing and drinking sea-water, this retired reverend was able to walk with crutches; by the time he went home his movement had been entirely restored. A Margate guide later in the century also claimed the sort of mass jettisoning of crutches, or 'auxiliary legs' as it called them, that had formerly been the exclusive province of inland spas. The author, 'an Inhabitant' whose propaganda suggests a very strong vested interest, also declared that the sick were returned to such rude good health and 'florid countenances that scarcely their most intimate friends can recognise them'. Not everyone was quite so enthusiastic. In 1786 the correspondence columns of one newspaper gave space to the warnings of a writer styling himself 'Caution', who stated the paradoxical belief that once sea-bathing had been begun it could not be stopped without endangering the health. Terminating the practice could lead to headaches, vomiting and nose bleeds. As the writer himself acknowledged, this theory left the urban health tourist in rather an awkward predicament!

For small seaside communities the financial benefits of this new trend were quick to accrue. Indeed, the transformation of such a limitless natural resource into a marketable asset had enormous implications for the reinvigoration of depressed coastal economies. When Daniel Defoe published his first volume of *A Tour Thro' the whole Island of Great Britain* in 1724, he described Brighton as 'a poor fishing town, old built, and on the very edge of the sea'. He fully expected that the encroaching sea, which had already devoured more than a hundred houses, would soon 'eat up the whole town'. Money was being begged for the erection of banks against the water but, Defoe stated, 'the expense...will be eight thousand pounds which if one were to look on the town, would seem to be more than all the houses in it are worth.' In the early years of the eighteenth century Margate was also suffering. The town's fishing industry had fallen into such decay that many fishermen had been forced to sell their boats and much of the once considerable shipping trade had moved to London. For both these early seaside resorts the medical championing of sea-water could not have been more timely – or more necessary for their survival. The example set by Scarborough was an attractive one; a perusal of visitors' lists from the 1740s showed that 'the Earls, the Marquesses, and the Dukes were as thick at that Spa as berries on hedges'. Enterprising inhabitants of other coastal towns were soon putting themselves out to cultivate their own rich berries for the picking.

Encouraging words from a resident physician, especially in published form, could provide a significant boost to emerging resorts. The medic promoters of sea-bathing, who depended for their salaries upon securing the patronage of as many patients as possible, also made sure they profited by stressing the necessity for a qualified intermediary between patient and sea. Weakened by illness or indolence, health-tourists were warned that unregulated exposure to the ocean might actually be dangerous. In Brighton, new patients could be assured of Dr Russell's good reputation by the fact that he lived in the town's most imposing house, built on the proceeds of his book. Whilst he was clearly an astute self-publicist, cynics should not suppose that Russell lacked faith in his cure; he believed in sea-bathing as fervently as Dr Atkins believed in protein. It just so happened that like the celebrity-endorsed diet craze of the early twenty-first century, the popular appeal of sea-water soon proved highly lucrative.

In her unfinished novel *Sanditon*, Jane Austen sent Mr Parker on a wild goose chase over the Sussex Downs in search of a surgeon for his little seaside town. 'He was convinced that the advantage of a medical man at hand would very materially promote the rise and prosperity of the place – would in fact tend to bring a prodigious influx;...He had *strong* reason to believe that *one* family had been deterred last year from trying Sanditon on that account – and probably very many more.' Satirising Regency speculators and the visitors they hoped to attract, Austen cannot have been alone in her scepticism for the sea-water cure. Keen to allay early doubters, Dr Russell stated that he did not 'offer to those who cultivate the Art of Physic, a trifling worthless Remedy, but one that is of great Worth and Efficacy, and doubtless very safe, if it is directed by the Judgement of a skilful Person'. Unfortunately for Russell, his own relocation to the coast came too late to significantly prolong his days; he died in 1759 at the age of seventy-two. A believer to the last, he had the words of Euripides engraved upon his tombstone: 'The sea washes away and cleanses every human stain.'

Around the English coast other doctors sought to make their own names as synonymous with their chosen resorts as that of Russell with Brighton: James Rymer, Surgeon, issued his reflections on cold bathing at Yarmouth in 1777; John Anderson, a Physician to and Director of The General Sea Bathing Infirmary at Margate, published hints on the correct mode of bathing in 1795 while W. Bradfield, Surgeon, talked up the benefits of Southwold in his *Popular Essay* of 1840. One hundred years after Russell's heyday, bathing guidelines on his model were still being produced by local doctors. In the case of Dr Edward William Pritchard, however, sea-water proved an inadequate remedy against the stains of humanity. Author of a guide to Filey, this heavily bearded gentleman sought to make his services indispensable by claiming that sea-bathing could induce brain haemorrhaging if the advice of a professional was not first sought. After six years in the Yorkshire neighbourhood, Dr

A cheeky Edwardian postcard suggests that the health benefits of sea-bathing still had popular currency in the early twentieth century.

Pritchard eventually moved to a practice in Glasgow. By all accounts a selfish and unpleasant lecher, he was convicted in 1865 of poisoning his wife and mother-in-law. A newspaper report of the time claimed that 50,000 people turned up to see him hang in front of Glasgow Gaol.

The potential for quackery was obvious and apparently widely tested but, despite this, people continued to consult seaside practitioners throughout the nineteenth century. As late as July 1883 *The British Medical Journal* considered it worthwhile to reiterate the value of sea-bathing as a preventative and curative medicine. Inspired by the verdict of this professional periodical, the following verses appeared in *Punch*:

> When we go to the Sea, shall we bathe? – that must be
> For all men a practical question;
> For enjoying your dips in the sight of the ships
> Is sure to promote good digestion.
> Now the sound *British Medical Journal* has said,
> From bathing you'll get satisfaction;
> But don't bathe if you're old, or it makes you feel cold,
> And brings on no proper reaction.
> For a child under two no sea-bathing will do,
> It's too great a shock to the system;
> But hard-workers, they say, should take baths every day,
> And won't feel quite right when they've missed 'em.
> So go down to the shore when your labours are o'er,
> Plunge into the waves in commotion,
> For better than pills, as a care for your ills,
> Are the numberless smiles of the Ocean.

Of course, there was a decided problem inherent in the way coastal watering places relied on the sea to attract visitors. It was ultimately very difficult to argue that the essential properties of the sea differed enough to proclaim the health virtues of one place over another. In 1733 Scarborough assertively announced that its particular bit of the

North Sea was, in fact, saltier than any other. An east coast resort might praise its own safe shores in opposition to those of southern competitors, where the swell and surf 'annoys, frightens and *spatters* the bathers exceedingly', but a new and more feasible indicator was soon forthcoming. The entire coastline benefited from sea *air*; as soon as a visitor stepped down from the stagecoach, he or she was already subject to its healing powers. And unlike sea water not all sea air was equal. An anonymous supporter of Blackpool acknowledged this fact in 1789. Stressing the Lancashire town's lack of 'unfriendly soil' and swamps he claimed that as the land was 'without any material hill' and had the 'advantages of sea breezes, just in proportion as westerly winds are more frequent than any other...the air is probably as pure as air can be'. Henceforward, geography and geology would be brought to bear on each case. It was, as Jane Austen's Mr Parker pointed out, the perfect solution: 'The sea air and sea-bathing together were nearly infallible, one or the other of them being a match for every disorder, of the stomach, the lungs or the blood...If the sea breeze failed, the sea bath was the certain corrective; – and where the bathing disagreed, the sea breeze alone was evidently designed by nature for the cure.'

By the twentieth century sea-bathing was well established as a pleasurable activity, having largely shaken off its earlier, more painful associations. For medical efficacy it was superseded by sun-bathing, a craze first introduced by doctors that still informs our relationship with the beach – even if we now know it's not quite the elixir we were promised. The supposed benefits of bracing salt air persisted for longer. On my travels I borrowed a beach hut at Felixstowe, only to find out that it had been purchased on the recommendation of a general practitioner. Julia and Barry Salmon's children, now grown up, used to suffer from repeated bouts of bronchitis and tonsillitis so the hut where I ate my picnic served as their miniature sanatorium as well as a place to keep buckets and spades.

Chapter Two
Birth of the bathing machine

In the course of my research I came across a wonderfully eccentric periodical called *Notes and Queries*. If you were a Victorian with a question it seems you could write into *Notes and Queries* and answers would be supplied by the eager readership. The diversity of trivia covered by this publication was limitless; the small sample I read included discussions on the satellites of Mars, Sir Walter Scott, eel folklore and pronunciation of the word 'golf'. Even egg-cups were not too trifling a subject to elicit replies. I was looking for information on bathing machines and found a kindred spirit in the July 1886 issue. A gentleman signing himself 'F.G.S.' had written to the paper asking if anyone knew 'when these desirable structures came into vogue?' Answers trickled in and were still being published in the December issue. Seven years later another curious reader broached the same subject. It cropped up again in 1904.

From this useful source I learnt about the bathing habits of literary greats; Lord Byron apparently used to bathe in the Thames from a machine at the eastern end of Westminster Bridge while, in Brighton, the eminent Dr Johnson took an unconventional approach. Lodged inside his machine, the author of the first English *Dictionary* would 'roar and bellow Latin hexameters and English heroics' so loudly that he could be heard on the cliff above. There was plentiful evidence to show that bathing machines were becoming a well-established feature of the coastal landscape during the second half of the eighteenth century, but what of the pioneers? What of the carts and carriages that rolled along

Bathing machines became such a well-established feature of the seaside that this Edwardian postcard suggested they were around when the ancient Romans invaded Britain!

the sand and started the craze?

By the 1730s people were already going to bathe in the sea at Whitby, Scarborough, Liverpool, Brighton and Margate, as well as on the Lincolnshire coast. Northern towns were well placed to lead the way because doctors stressed the greater efficacy of really cold salt water, a fact that explains how a tantalising reference to what may have been the earliest form of bathing machine could come from a place now better known as a trading port. Writing in his dairy for August 1721 Nicholas Blundell, master of Little Crosby, recorded that he had escorted an acquaintance 'to Leverpoole & Procured him a Place to lodg at & a Conveniency for Bathing in the Sea'. Unfortunately, Blundell left us no clues as to what this 'conveniency' looked like but the word he chose to describe it certainly implies that it was designed as an aid to the bather.

To get our first glimpse of an early eighteenth century bathing machine we have to move from the northwest to the northeast coast. Scarborough's first attraction was its mineral water, which, according to a guidebook of 1734, could communicate 'a sensible Alacrity and Cheerfulness to the Mind, and Strength and Vigour to the Body'. Access

to the spa was at low tide via the beach, a situation that in 1679 caused
Celia Fiennes to bemoan the brief and changeable promenade hours.
Scarborough was, she decided, a 'dull little town'. This was set to change
and by the time artist John Settrington drew his sweeping panoramic
view of the South Bay in 1735 he was able to depict a much livelier social
concourse. Tall ships navigate into Settrington's harbour with sails
unfurled. On the crescent beach a gentleman doffs his hat and bows to
a lady on horseback; a smart carriage, preceded by six horses, pulls away
from the spa building as other patrons arrive; one man walks with the
assistance of a stick, another cure-seeker is carried in a
sedan chair. There are other walkers, other riders and,
at the water's edge, poised above the lapping waves, a
naked man prepares to step out of a bathing machine.

Settrington's mobile changing hut has four small
wheels and a pyramid roof topped with an ornamental

The first known depiction of a bathing machine (in detail above) in John Settrington's
1735 engraving of Scarborough.

finial. The horse that presumably pulled it to the water has been discharged and the artist gives no indication that this vehicle was meant to enter the sea like later models. It would be helpful to have a written account of how and by whom this early bathing machine was used but no such document exists. Maybe the man emerging in his birthday suit was the owner; a wealthy eccentric in ill health who commissioned his own wheeled 'conveniency'; or perhaps that same bather was simply included to demonstrate the hut's purpose as an un-dressing room for anyone willing to pay? Both explanations are possible and neither can be ruled out by evidence from an engraving made a decade later that shows the same pyramid-roofed vehicle in the sea at Scarborough surrounded by bathing machines of a more recognisable form. In 1745 the vocabulary to describe these carriages was still being formulated so engravers Samuel and Nathanial Buck settled on 'A curious contrivance of Wooden Houses moveable on wheels'.

In the 1730s there were also two *actual* houses on the shore that were designated as a place for ladies 'to retire to for dressing in'. Women wore bathing gowns and had the assistance of guides, whereas it was customary for men to strip off so that every pore could benefit from a plunge made 'much more effectual by the additional Weight of Salt in Sea-Water; an Advantage, which no Spaw in *England* can boast of but *Scarborough!*' Male bathers could hire a twin-keeled Coble in which they would 'go out a little way to Sea...and jump in naked directly'. Settrington depicts a couple of these vessels complete with awnings and a rower in the bow. On the northeast coast these bathing-boats endured into the 1840s but they did rather presuppose that bathers could swim. This sounds obvious but medicinal bathing simply required the patient to take a dip in the sea; his or her feet need never leave the ocean floor and there was certainly no need to travel through the water. Although there may be a bit of proto-backstroke and some progress towards front crawl in Settrington's view, when they first arrived, many health-tourists had little or no experience of swimming beyond the limited manoeuvres possible in the crowded pools of spa towns. Regular visitors must have learnt the skill or there would have been no call for bathing-boats. Nevertheless, this very literal example of being thrown in at the deep end probably did deter some potential participants. And the option of a preliminary paddle can't have been very appealing if it meant walking across the beach in the altogether; the sands were, after all, a social space. For the genuinely infirm a long hike at low tide might not even have been feasible. Hence the need for a dressing room that could move *with* the tide.

Today cars are rarely permitted on our beaches. Their loud engines would disturb our quest for relaxation; their exhaust fumes are only allowed to pollute so near as the Pay and Display car park. Yet in the eighteenth century, the beach acted as a supplementary highway and the firm sands at Scarborough probably offered a smoother ride than most contemporary roads. The earliest wheeled bathing hut seems to have been a logical extension of this horse-drawn traffic, catering to the demands of a new fashion.

Gradually, the idea spread across the country. Richard Pococke, the inquisitive archdeacon of Dublin, travelled through England in the 1750s and noted the new popularity of sea-bathing resorts. Visiting Brighton in September 1754, he remarked how it had been 'greatly improved of late by the concourse of people who come to it to bathe and drink the sea waters, under the persuasion that the water here is better than at other places'. Also noteworthy was the provision of 'carriages for the conveniency of bathing' or, as Dr Russell preferred to call them, 'bathing chariots'. More important to our story, however, were the 'cover'd carriages' described by Pococke at Margate.

It was at Margate that the term 'machine' was first used, specifically describing a more sophisticated bathing vehicle pioneered by local Quaker Benjamin Beale. When it comes to rival claims of precedence, it seems the argument can be reduced to a fine point of nomenclature; in the same way that the brand name Hoover has come to stand for all vacuum cleaners, or that Sellotape is descriptive of all such products, Beale's invention proliferated and was copied to such an extent that the term 'bathing-*machine*' endured as a generic label long after the essential mechanism of its modesty hood had been discarded.

A steady trickle of health seekers had been arriving in Margate since the 1730s. Although the benefits of sea-bathing were proven in 'many Chronical Cases', a resourceful local carpenter by the name of Thomas Barber noticed that due to the lack of 'a convenient and private Bathing Place, many of both Sexes have not cared to expose themselves to the Open Air'. Intent upon removing such a hindrance, Barber advertised his newly built indoor bath in July 1736, stating that it was fed directly by sea-water via a fifteen-foot long canal. He had seen a niche and he filled it. The following year a larger bath was constructed with adjoining lodging and dressing rooms. Still promoting the novelty of his facility in 1740, Barber was aware that he was losing business as a result of a lingering misapprehension that his was an outdoor amenity. 'I have therefore thought it necessary to inform the Publick, that 'tis quite enclos'd, and cover'd by a handsome Dining Room.' Having identified the desire among his potential clientele for privacy in their bathing arrangements, Barber's solution was to bring the sea into a purpose-built room. For Benjamin Beale the answer was to build a room that could be transported into the sea.

In 1756 the merchant and antiquary James Theobald took himself off to Kent on a fact-finding mission. As vice-President of the Society of Antiquaries, he encouraged members to collate parish histories, taking upon himself the task of updating Reverend John Lewis's book on *The history and antiquities, as well ecclesiastical as civil, of the Isle of Thanet*. Theobald's inserts included a detailed drawing and description of the Margate 'Machines or Bathing Waggons' which, at all states of the tide, 'can drive a proper depth into the Sea for the accomodation [sic] of ye Bathers'. According to Theobald's sketch this novel vehicle was so constructed that, when the horse pulling it into the sea was submerged up to the neck, its floor remained above the water. Raised high upon four wheels (the back pair larger than the front), the carriage had a barrel-roof with a folding canvas canopy at the rear. Clearly a noteworthy innovation, Theobald expressly called it 'the Machine to bath with' and gave the following description:

> ...it contains a Room to undress and dress in with Steps to go down into the Sea[,] will hold 5 or 6 People, there are Men and Women Guides who if desired attend[,] the price is 4 Shillings a Week or £1:1: for Six Weeks & yo pay ye Guide for every attendance, they drive into ye Sea till it is about breast high & then lets [sic] down the Screen wch prevents being seen under wch yo go down the Steps into a fine sandy bottom.

Before her death, aged 92, Mr Beale's widow could apparently recall the first family that 'ever resorted to Margate for the purpose of bathing being carried into the sea in a covered cart.' If she was also able to recall the date of this excursion it has not been passed down to posterity nor, unfortunately, do we know if this cart was a design of her husband's or his initial inspiration. Beale's machine was certainly in commercial use by 1753 but early prototypes had probably appeared on the beach in preceding years. Determining the optimal height of the wheels must have necessitated experimental trials, as must the dimensions of its most important feature, the concertina hood.

It was this singular device that transformed a covered carriage into 'the original NEW-INVENTED MACHINE for Bathing in the Sea' advertised at Deal and Broadstairs in 1754. Modern accounts of its conception have tended to view the telescopic awning as an excessively prudish response to the trend for sea-bathing but such an analysis not only fails to recognise the popular demand it met, it also undermines the originality of Beale's contribution. The importance attributed by Margate residents to the birth of the bathing machine on their doorstep was such that a town guidebook of 1785 considered it worthwhile to elucidate the construction and workings of the invention in great detail. Annotated diagrams were also included showing the machine's

Benjamin Beale's Margate 'Machine' with its collapsible hood.

'umbrella' rolled up during transit and unfurled for use in the sea. According to this description the canopy afforded an enclosed bathing area of eight by thirteen feet.

As the mechanics of this apparatus inspired a name by which we now recognise all forms of bathing carriage, it seems appropriate to quote from this explanation at length:

> The Entrance into the Machine is through a Door, at the Back of the Driver, who sits on a moveable Bench, and raises or lets fall the Umbrella by Means of a Line, which runs along the Top of the Machine, and is fastened to a Pin over the Door. This Line is guided by a Piece of Wood of three Feet in Length, which projects pointing a little downward, from the Top of the back Part of the Machine, through which it passes in a sloping Direction. To the End of this Piece is suspended a Cord, for the Bather to take hold of, if he wants Support.
>
> The Umbrella is formed of light Canvas spread on four Hoops. The Height of each is seven Feet, and each is eight Feet at its Axis.

The last Hoop falls to a horizontal Level with its Axis, from whence depends [sic] the Curtain.

The Pieces which support the Hoops are about six Feet in Length; they are fastened to the Bottom of the Machine, but are extended by a small Curve, about one Foot wider than the Body of it on each Side. The Hoops move in Grooves in these Pieces. The Distance of the Axis of the first Hoop is more than two Feet from the Machine; of the rest from each other, something more than one Foot; but no greater Exactness is required in these Proportions, as scarce any two of them are built alike.

Not a great deal of biographical detail has survived regarding Mr Benjamin Beale but his record as an inventor did extend to at least one other transport improvement. His father, Thomas Beale (c.1690–1747), was a glove-maker from Margate and Benjamin, probably born in 1717, appears to have followed the family profession, at least initially. In 1740

Modesty hoods in use during the 1860s.

he married Elizabeth Bindlock of Canterbury. The couple moved to Draper's Farm eleven years later, although by this time it seems likely that Beale was thinking more about the beach than his fields. By 1754 the parish rate books indicate that he was renting stables and a hay-loft from a Mrs Baker, perhaps for the horses that pulled his machines; he later took on additional workshop space at two locations in the town. Mr and Mrs Mount, a couple who visited Margate on Wednesday 16 May 1759, recorded meeting 'One Beale a Quaker the first Inventor of the bathing Machines, and who keeps a Lodging House, [he] was very Civil in walking with Us about the Town'.

Civility was not, however, the order of the day when Beale, driving between Margate and Canterbury in a new light passenger carriage of his own design, was involved in an eighteenth century case of road rage. Bowling along the turnpike road, he met another carriage travelling in the opposite direction. Passing places had, by this time, been provided in adjacent fields but a heated argument occurred over which driver had the right of way and which driver was consequently obliged to back up his carriage. Beale's adversary refused to budge; so did Beale. Events came to a head when the inventor dismounted in order to back his opponent's horses for him. Beale received a blow to the face for his trouble and, sensing the opportunity for some exciting spectatorship, both sets of passengers left their seats to cheer on their respective drivers in the ensuing scuffle. Emerging victorious, Beale, who had had the right of way all along, resumed his journey amidst the triumphal cries of his customers.

Subject to the superior force of the wilful sea, Beale was less fortunate in the outcome of his bathing business. Contemporary trade cards suggest that he went into partnership with J. W. Sayer, Job and Postmaster at the New Inn Livery Stable, Margate. Sayer's business interests – dealing in horses and hiring vehicles of all types from wedding carriages to dog carts – seem to have been well-suited to the additional venture of managing and maintaining bathing machines. The terms of his arrangement with Beale have not survived but Sayer was still operating a bathing establishment in the 1790s. By this time there was considerable competition for customers and nearly forty bathing machines operated during the season, giving the impression of a floating camp in the bay. Indeed, within a decade of Beale's invention first appearing on Margate sands there were three rival bathing rooms running eleven machines between them. Four further bathing establishments had been built near the harbour by the time Beale died in 1775 at the age of fifty-eight. In a rather sad twist of fate, his own machines and bathing rooms had been destroyed in successive storms, leaving him reliant in has last days upon the charity provided by a public subscription.

Had he lived longer perhaps Beale might have been able to re-establish his business. The potent combination of winter weather and stormy seas was, after all, something of an occupational hazard and nearly all the bathing accommodation washed away in the great storms of 1808 was replaced and improved. In 1771 'Philomaris' wrote with considerable hype, in *The Gentleman's Magazine*, about the all-weather perfections of bathing at Margate; 'when the sea, by mere chance, is too rough and boisterous in the bay, the bathing machines find a safe retreat in the harbour; so that the going into the salt water at Margate can never be defeated through the means of bad weather, excepting by violent storms and tempests, which harrow up the ocean in every corner.' Newspaper reports from early in the next century show that not every resort was so fortunate. Sturdy though it was, the bathing machine was not immune to the power of a strong sea breeze. In late September 1801 a horse was killed at Ramsgate when a bathing machine was blown over. Its female occupant escaped shocked but unhurt. The following day a rather more humiliating incident occurred when a second machine was blown down whilst two gentlemen were using it to bathe. *The Morning Chronicle* reported that 'the Machine was totally demolished, and the Gentlemen lost...all their clothes, themselves escaping with difficulty'. Needless to say, this left the poor bathers in rather a delicate position:

In a state of trepidation and perfect nakedness, they trembled up the steps into the bathing room where sat some two dozen Ladies. Each lady held her fan or gown to her eyes; but some, if they lifted their clothes to hide their faces, exposed some other parts, being too fashionably dressed to have petticoats. Such shrieking...and fainting, and scampering and roaring and crying never before occurred in the place.

Not long after the Ramsgate debacle an 'old crazy machine' broke down and overturned at Margate. A newspaper report of the incident considered it lucky the two occupants were male as women bathers in the same situation would almost certainly have drowned! Not that this was much of a consolation to other gentlemen staying in the town. As a result of the late accident they determined 'to go into the water with their *cloaths on*'.

Loss of life was averted in these cases but damage to the machines would have been expensive for their proprietors. Machines on Beale's model represented a huge capital investment but they were absolutely necessary to any town with pretensions to resort-hood. Letters discussing the manufacture of a new bathing machine for shipment abroad in 1785 give the cost at £38.8.11. In 1834 the price was about £60 (approximately £5,000 today). Depending on wear and tear, a machine could be expected to last between thirty and forty years but its value would depreciate rapidly. After two years it could be sold on for forty guineas but after thirty years it might fetch as little as four. Coastal towns eager to capitalise on the fashion for bathing usually started with just one machine; the Kent resorts of Deal, Ramsgate and Broadstairs were quick to follow Margate's example, each having made the necessary purchase in time for the 1754 season. Sometimes this was the result of private enterprise as at Dover where, in June 1768, Cornelius Jones informed the local populace that he had provided a machine 'upon the same Plan as those at MARGATE'. Elsewhere, community spirit was

A bathing machine at Blackpool from an engraving of 1784.

called upon; in May 1796 forty-nine inhabitants of Gravesend each put forward five guineas to purchase a machine from Margate as the first step to setting up a bathing establishment on the Thames.

Further west, Pococke had observed that, as early as 1750, the people of Exeter went to the nearby village of Exmouth ('chiefly inhabited by fishermen and publicans'!) in order to bathe in the sea. By 1759 this resort was boasting of 'a conveniency' for safe and private bathing while Teignmouth, another precocious south Devon resort, had two bathing machines by 1762. More widely known for its early emergence as a bathing centre was Weymouth in Dorset. Indeed, one of the first responses published in *Notes and Queries* regarding the history of bathing machines referred to the apocryphal tale of its invention at Weymouth by Ralph Allen, one of the founding fathers of Georgian Bath who was immortalised as the character Allworthy in Henry Fielding's novel *Tom Jones*. The erroneous date of Allen's first visit to the town in 1763 has been widely quoted since it first appeared in a *Weymouth Guide* of about 1785. A surviving letter dated 15 September 1750 confirms, however, that his habit of spending a month each summer by the sea was already well established by this time. As Postmaster of Bath, Allen had remedied the deficiencies of the national postal system so successfully that he became a wealthy man. His purchase, in 1727, of quarries at Combe Down was followed by such an assiduous promotion of his product that he made Bath stone famously fashionable. Allen sought relief from prolonged headaches beside the seaside where he and his wife regularly drank sea-water and dipped beneath the waves but, however impressive his other claims to fame, he did not invent the bathing machine.

The ritual of bathing was a strangely drawn out process because it could take several hours to prepare for a dip that lasted a matter of minutes. This meant far greater opportunity for affable distraction than might be expected from the medical evidence. It was extremely important that the discomfort of the experience was a shared discomfort and the enthusiastic adoption of the bathing machine was partly responsible for ensuring that patrons, whether following the dictates of physicians or fashion,

Running for a machine at Brighton, from an aquatint after Thomas Rowlandson, 1789.

had a purpose and a place to congregate. In the equation of supply and demand it was most frequently the latter that outstripped the former, so rising early became necessary simply to secure a place in the queue. Arrangements differed widely as can be seen from the examples of pre-eminent eighteenth century resorts Brighton and Margate. According to one diarist staying on the Sussex coast in 1779, the scramble for a bathing machine at Brighton was less than decorous:

> Each man runs to a machine-ladder as it is dragging out of the sea and scuffles who shall first set foot thereon: some send their footmen and contend by proxy; others go in boots, or on horseback to meet the machines:- so that a tolerably modest man, on a busy morning, has generally an hour and a half, perhaps two hours for contemplation on the sands, to the detriment of his shoes, as well as the diminution of his patience.

At Margate, the bathing establishments operated a rather more organised system. Lined up along the sea wall, these buildings provided comfortable waiting rooms equipped with staircases down to the beach from where the bathing machines would pick up dry customers and drop off wet ones. Young women wrote names on a slate applying a strict principle of first come first served, a very proper rule according to one visitor, because 'no distinction is made between the rich and poor, old or young, noble or ignoble'. Despite making it his first task of the day to sign up at the bathing room, the author of *The Margate and Ramsgate Guide in Letters to a Friend* (1797) noted that, even arriving between seven and eight o'clock, there were often twelve or fourteen names ahead of his. At the height of the season the wait could be considerable, especially at low tide when machines had to travel further to reach the sea.

Before breakfast the fashionable bather had, therefore, already encountered a wide circle of acquaintance. Waiting at the bathing rooms

Bathing rooms above the beach at Margate from a drawing of 1810 by T. Smith.

was a perfect excuse for exchanging gossip, comparing improvements in chronic ailments and critiquing the behaviour of fellow bathers. In his 1779 book *Sketches from Nature taken and coloured in a Journey to Margate*, the dilettante George Keate confessed a certain gratification at being recognised from past bathing excursions: 'My lean carcase was complimented on being plumped out since we had last seen each other. I returned as gracious a salute to the bilious gentleman who had the civility to tell me so...A poor crippled figure, with an eye of languor, was commending the improved looks of a lady, whose face wore the colour of an INDIAN pickle...' All this polite banter was accompanied by a dish of tea or coffee, perhaps a little light music on the piano and talk inspired by the London papers provided for visitors. In the evening these bathing rooms welcomed guests again, this time to the delights of dancing or the card table.

Margate's popularity had a great deal to do with the frequent and economical passage available to Londoners on returning corn hoys. At the metropolitan docks these one-masted sloops of 80 to 120 tons exchanged their cargoes of grain for passengers and by 1800 were landing approximately 18,000 visitors during the bathing season. Although this inevitably led to complaints about a decreasing social tone, bathing machines offered a means of constraining seaside behaviour because with payment of a fee, people were buying into conventions established by fashionable society. Other places had less formal arrangements. Labourers from miles inland made an annual trip to Liverpool in order to wash away a year's worth of impurities. But 'being unable to afford a long stay, or to make use of artificial conveniences, they employ two or three days in strolling along the shore, and dabbling in the salt-water for hours at each tide, covering the beach with their promiscuous numbers, and not much embarrassing themselves about appearances'. Noting this custom in his 1795 study of Liverpool life, John Aiken considered that no moral objection could be raised against such simple freedoms if they were conducive to the health and pleasure of the poor.

Modesty came at a price. The bathing machine was invaluable for those who could afford its sheltered protection but the terms of hire were clearly aimed at an elite clientele. Unencumbered by the need to earn a daily crust, these people had formerly spent prolonged periods at spas and were able to shift their patronage at the whim of fashion. In the early days of the seaside using a bathing machine was expensive enough to make it a status symbol. In 1756 it cost four shilling to hire a Margate machine for a week or £1:1s for a fixed period of six weeks. Compare this with the cost of actually travelling to Kent: the stagecoach between London and Canterbury cost eighteen shillings while the passage by hoy cost just two shillings per head. As the century progressed and more visitors came to sample the sea-water cure, the pattern of charging per bathe was established. Prices set in the first decade of the nineteenth century seem to have remained immune to inflation for a long time so at Margate, Ramsgate and Broadstairs a lone woman or child, attended in the bathing machine by a guide, would be charged 1s.3d for a single dip in the sea. Sharing a machine reduced the wait and the cost; ladies would pay one shilling each, while two or more children taking a machine together cost nine pence each. It was assumed that women would not wish to brave

The Marine Parade at Dover with a solitary bathing machine c1830.

the briny without a guide so no such price was offered but gentlemen who lacked the confidence to bathe themselves were penalised for their effeminacy by an extra three pence charge. Further away from London it was possible to get a better bargain. During the 1817 summer season at Dawlish, the cost of a bathe was six pence; between 1 October and 31 May the price rose to one shilling.

It is a measure of their success that Margate bathing machines attracted the attention of the taxman. Following an Act of Parliament in 1799, every machine was subject to duty of half-a-crown payable on 1 September each year, a toll that increased to 7s.6d in 1809. Evidently a useful source of revenue for the harbour company, the duty was raised again three years later. The revenue collectors had apparently considered taxing sea-bathing much earlier and, had a rumour of 1733 proved correct, Scarborough might never have played such a significant role in its promotion. 'The people of this town are at present in great consternation, upon a report that they have heard from London, which, if true, they think will ruin them...They are informed that, considering the vast consumption of these [spa] waters there is a design laid of *excising* them next session; and moreover, that as bathing in the sea is become the general practice of both sexes; and as the Kings of England have always been allowed to be masters of the sea, every person so bathing shall be gauged, and pay so much per foot square as their cubical bulk amounts to.'

Nowadays beach hut owners are frequently required to pay Council Tax but at least access to the sea is free for all. As will become clear, this was a hard won right. We can paddle, swim and surf without paying a fee. Thankfully, we are also no longer obliged to submit to being ritually dunked below the waves by a 'dipper'.

Chapter Three
Seaton Carew to Skegness

'NAZ DROWIE!' said the lighthouse keeper. 'It's the only Polish word I know. Naz-drov-eyay. It means Cheers!'

I had been standing on Whitby pier, focusing my camera along the line of multicoloured beach huts when I felt myself being watched. Behind me sat a weathered old man, stationed by the lighthouse door taking coins from tourists who wanted to climb to the top. His mop of white hair was squashed under a navy blue flat cap and the lines on his face mapped a life at sea. Trade was obviously slow so I put my camera away and went to ask him about the huts on West Beach.

He looked around furtively: 'I'll tell you a story that I only found out last year. Not a lot of people know about this.'

He told me about the Polish Signals Regiment stationed at Whitby during the Second World War.

'You see that building on the top of the cliff?' He pointed up at the Royal Hotel. 'That was their barracks and they used to signal from there to the end of this pier. They sometimes used the beach huts for signal practice too.'

The lighthouse keeper knew this because the previous summer he'd met a group of returning ex-signalmen, now in their eighties. He remembered how smartly they were dressed, walking along the pier in blazers with medals proudly pinned to their chests.

'I recognised their language you see. Polski! I said to them. Naz drowie!'

The greeting came back from the veterans, who all reached inside their breast pockets for little silver flasks with which to salute their new friend. As the cherry vodka was passed around the story of the beach huts emerged. After that came the buffalo vodka:

'Imagine vodka mixed with Marmite and four times proof,' he instructed. 'Well, I went home and my wife said I looked a bit tired. Yes! And four parts pissed, I told her!' The lighthouse keeper chuckled at the memory. 'The beach huts must've seen plenty of vodka when those boys were about!'

I wondered what the young soldiers had thought of Whitby with its picturesque ruined abbey and brightly coloured seaside huts; but so few of them ever returned home to share their experiences, let alone made it back to Yorkshire. The story had a desperately sad end. From Whitby the Poles had been posted to Monte Cassino, an Italian monastery where the Germans were holding prisoners of war. Of their 2000-strong regiment only about a hundred men survived.

The huts themselves, however, were emphatically cheerful. Red, yellow, blue and green, 115 of them lined up along the promenade. Over the winter the huts were sent into hibernation, hidden away in the cavernous tunnel housing the cliff-lift, where men from the Council could paint and repair them away from the feisty North Sea. Their annual return to the seafront was a sign to locals that summer was on its way.

I met the Beach Inspector who offered to give me a guided tour. As we walked along the row he pointed out the oldest huts, the ones that had been there, year in year out, since the 1920s. Their identifying features included a slightly steeper pitch of roof and a gap under the eaves where the wind still whistled through. These huts also used to have windows with real glass but the openings had been boarded up and newer huts didn't even bother because of the constant vandalism. It was clear that maintenance could be a real headache.

We stopped in front of a red hut or, to be correct according to Council parlance, a red *chalet*. I hoped that my trip would provide a definitive explanation of the difference between a hut and a chalet but the Whitby examples were supremely unhelpful in this respect; they looked like the sort of shed-type structure usually known as a beach 'hut', with four wooden walls under a gabled roof. It seemed there was a good chance that the choice of name had more to do with setting the social tone than describing the building style.

Chalet thirty-one belonged to Joyce, who could be seen most days sitting outside in the gap designed as a firebreak, wrapped up in well-practised layers of clothing, knitting in her deckchair. She was a chalet regular and had been for thirty-seven years. Although the chalet was closed up the Beach Inspector was adamant she'd be back. 'Joyce'll live for ever,' he assured me. Other regulars included the ex-Beach Inspector who still kept a chalet so that he could come down every day to check all was well in his old domain. Then there were the people who, though they came less frequently, were no less loyal. Working down his booking list the Beach Inspector's finger paused as he recognised the names of people from Australia and Canada, emigrants who chose to come back to Whitby for a week's hut hire, having quit their Yorkshire homeland on a ten pound ticket in the 1950s.

I was disappointed to miss all these characters but it was early July and the season had yet to really begin. As the late-afternoon breeze was chilling its way off the sea into my bone marrow, I had to concede that it was unsurprising only a very few chalets were occupied. I climbed up the grassy slope behind them, looking back from my higher vantage point across a distinctly English view. At the horizon grey sky met greenish-grey sea. The lacy white froth of receding waves lightened the middle distance and running along the foot of the cliff were the bright huts, strung out like a joyful ribbon between land and sea. All of a sudden I felt more positive about the prospects for my coastal trip.

Things had not started well. I'd tried to find the country's most northerly huts before setting out and, after several telephone calls to Tourist Information centres, had decided to begin my beach hut tour at Seaton Carew in County Durham. I was travelling by public transport and, after a few delayed trains, finally made it to a stop on the branch line; it couldn't really be called a station because there was nothing there, not even any hint of a place name. I was the only person to get off.

An old lady walking her dog directed me towards the seafront. The bleak, flat landscape was more impressive than I had expected but there was no obvious sign of the huts I'd come to see. A broad sandy beach stretched into the distance with the silhouettes of heavy industry bearing down on the edges of my view. To the left was Hartlepool; to the right, beyond grass-topped dunes, were the tall smoking chimneys of Middlesborough. Against this backdrop, with a camouflage coat of sandy-coloured paint, the four rows of wooden chalets seemed to blur into insignificance. Built as blocks rather than individual huts, they were capped by a low-pitched roof, cut away at the front to give each door its own little porch. A faded sign advertised day hire for the competitive rate of just five pounds.

'Are you going to pull them down?' a voice called behind me.

Across the concrete strip, which marked a break in the row, a man was kicking a ball about with his grandson.

'Are you going to pull them down?' he asked again.

Having seen the notebook in my hand this local resident had assumed I was making some sort of official survey and was dismayed to learn that I had no power to promote demolition of the forlorn-looking huts. In his view they had ceased to be attractive to anyone but vandals and arsonists – hence the gaping hole where numbers seven to thirteen used to be. Better to get rid of them, he thought, and put up some benches instead. My instinct was to disagree, even though it seemed unlikely the Council would spend the necessary money on repairs. People might pay thousands of pounds for a beach hut in the south but in Seaton Carew they couldn't give them away.

Deflated by this realisation, I took a train to Middlesborough, then another one to Saltburn-by-the-Sea. A few paces from the station I was welcomed into a Bed and Breakfast with a plate of chocolate digestives and a huge pot of tea.

'Do you want any washing done?' asked Pat, my landlady. Her other guests were in the middle of walking the Cleveland Way and she had just loaded several pairs of their thick socks into her machine.

'No thanks, I'm all right. This is the first day of my trip.' As I disclosed the purpose of my journey, Pat's husband Frank came into the room.

'Oh yes,' he said with perfect understanding, 'we have a young man like you come to stay sometimes. He goes up and down the place looking at diesel engines.'

That comparison shut me up; however much I wanted to, it was impossible to refute my status as a beach hut anorak. There was nothing for it but to head back out to the seafront.

To the south, evening sunlight bathed the russet headland while above me the sky was battleship grey. In marked contrast to Seaton Carew, the land here fell away in dramatic cliffs. I took advantage of the Victorian cliff lift before it closed for the night and wandered along the pier, my elongated shadow stalking me on the moist sand below. Until 1860 Saltburn had been a hamlet where most inhabitants made their living from fishing, seal-catching and smuggling. Then Mr Henry Pease of the Stockton and Darlington Railway Company came along, picturing in his mind's eye the trains that would run along his extended line, carrying wealthy holidaymakers to well-equipped hotels and bathing machines.

The beach huts I spotted from the pier were built later but they had a unique claim to fame. They were Grade II listed, the only examples in the country to be included in the English Heritage list of buildings of special national importance. The two tiers of ten chalets, stepped into the cliff where the winding road from town flattened out into a car park, were permanent brick structures with cream painted render and red double doors. They were built in the 1920s, and notwithstanding the slightly mock-Tudor gables at each end of the low roofs, they made me think of California more than Cleveland. Each row had a central block with unusual Art Deco, Spanish Hacienda-style features. Still a little crestfallen from my afternoon in Seaton Carew, I climbed up to the second level and unlatched the red picket gate to the secluded area in front of the chalets. I wanted to know more about their history but there was no one around to ask.

Back at the B&B, Frank had warmed to my subject. He'd been thinking about the Saltburn of his childhood, those formative years he'd spent on the beach to escape from summer hay fever.

'What time are you planning on leaving in the morning?' he asked me.

Books on local history had been pulled from the shelves and he now proposed to give me a tour of all the places where there used to be beach huts.

After breakfast we set out in Frank's purple car. We began at the Beck, the stream that emptied onto a pebbly beach near the Ship Inn, where there had been a miniature railway and six wooden chalets. Frank was once First Mate at the boating lake next door.

'It was my first job,' he remembered. 'Must've been about the time I fell in love with one of the five Welsh Babes performing at Payne's Theatre.'

Below the red headland there had been more chalets, bigger ones that people lived in after the War. Frank's friend Joe had one until the storms of 1951–2.

'We were all drinking at the Ship Inn. It was a pretty rough night. Joe went home; found water coming in the front door and his wife escaping out the back! They went back the next morning and there was nothing left.'

In another ravine, east of the pier, we hunted for archaeological evidence. The wooden huts, which, according to Frank, used to leak in the rain, were long gone but hidden in the grass were the concrete steps that once connected the two rows.

I waved goodbye to Frank and took the train from Saltburn via Middlesborough to Whitby. The picturesque coastal line to Scarborough closed a long time ago so I travelled the next part of my journey by bus. Apparently, this route also offered fine views but I saw nothing since the driving rain outside had made the windows fog up. There's a local saying that it only rains twice a year in Scarborough – once for six months and then again for three months! As I stepped out of the bus into a large puddle, I wondered where the British sense of humour would be without such changeable weather.

By the time I reached the end of St Vincent's Pier the downpour had stopped. Marjorie arrived at the same time and, finding a dry seat, offered to share. Her white curls were protected underneath a clear plastic headscarf but so far, she was not enjoying her day trip.

'I liked Southport better,' she confided.

She extracted a meat pie from her bag and as she sat eating and swinging her short legs over the bench, Marjorie told me how, since becoming a widow, she'd decided to take advantage of the outings laid on for people of the 'third age.' Yesterday she'd walked the length of Southport pier.

'The lady I sat next to on the bus wouldn't come with me because of her arthritis. It hurt my legs after a bit but I did it.'

Marjorie went off to find a teashop where she could wait until it was time to rejoin the coach and I set off for the South Bay chalets. The walk took me through Scarborough's old harbour, past amusement arcades, fish stalls and rock-makers; below the massive Victorian Grand Hotel and past the Spa Pavilion. I'd seen the Edwardian bathing bungalows from the pier but they were better close-up. With clay-tiled roofs and ornamental wooden verandas, these blocks had an air of gentility, more like summerhouses than sheds. One block could even boast bay windows, though the original glazing pattern of small square panes had been removed in favour of vandal-proof boarding painted in the same Council colours as at Whitby.

The South Bay Superintendent let me into his chalet-cum-office. It was surprisingly roomy, with clean white walls and a fitted corner cupboard. He told me that most of the chalets were hired by the season and were equipped with a table, four chairs and a kettle.

'Until about three years ago you also got a two-hob electric cooker and grill but the Council was getting huge bills because people were using them to heat the chalets on cold days. The electricity's been cut off now so I recommend people bring extra blankets with them instead.'

'Are there anymore chalets along here?' I enquired.

'If you go along to the old swimming pool there are still a few but a block of about fifteen was demolished yesterday. There'd been three fires in nine days so the Council had to do something.'

All these tales of arson were getting a bit depressing but when I got to the demolition site it was easy to see why vandals thought it was fair game. The old lido felt remote, neglected; not to say completely unloved. A bright red warning sign announced 'Pool closed KEEP OUT', a message reiterated by the tall, mean metal fence. The open-air swimming bath still had water in it but the diving boards were gone and the fountains were covered in black mould. Although the changing rooms and terraces were bricked up, I could see from a brief glimpse of interior tiles and architectural detail that a lot of money had once been spent on this facility. The only sign of more recent investment was a row of ugly breezeblock chalets built on a concrete balcony in the Sixties, hardly a sufficient antidote as far as vandals were concerned. I noticed two young men sneaking through the wire fence and decided it was time to leave.

The trek over to North Bay was a long one but in the nineteenth century it was social hierarchy, as well as distance, that separated these two stretches of sand. Fashionable ladies who appeared in a new outfit each time they visited the Spa would not think of setting foot in the allegedly colder, less refined North Bay. And yet it was here that the innovative bathing bungalows first appeared in 1910, less florid but of a similar design to those in the South Bay. Later blocks had been added, some with pitched roofs, others flat and featureless, but all with consecutively red, blue, yellow and green doors. There were still a few people around: chalet residents enjoying some sunshine at the end of an otherwise dreary day, dog walkers doing the same, and one highly visible security guard, dressed in a fluorescent yellow jacket, beginning a seafront patrol that would not end until four o'clock the next morning.

With a portion of freshly fried fish and chips, I wandered into Peasholm Park where strings of coloured lights encircled the boating lake and white swan-boats bobbed next to the island. Charming Chinese lanterns hung from posts decorated with dragons' heads. In fact, despite the rain and the derelict poolside chalets, Scarborough was charming. I read the brass memorial plaques fixed onto benches throughout the park. The one dedicated to Mavis Brailsford remembered 'many happy hours spent in Scarborough'. I sat there.

Next morning I took a train to the smaller resort of Filey. Walking from the station I followed a man picking litter. On his feet he wore brown socks and polished leather shoes. Above knee-level his outfit was rather less conventional. First there was a dress, patterned with delicate flowers and with a lace collar; then, on his head, attached under the chin by a length of white elastic, was a straw bonnet. People involved in setting up cake stalls and tombolas along Union Street had also dressed up, although the other men were mostly in trousers. I had arrived during the town's twenty-second Edwardian Festival, a celebration of that period when the nineteenth century resort and the older fishing village were joined together. Other entertainments planned for later in the day included a somewhat un-Edwardian bucking bronco and a display of line dancing.

Resisting these temptations I made my way towards the grassy cliffs and seafront hotels. Ahead was another wide expanse of sand, sheltered to the northeast by the veiny red outcrop of Filey Brigg and southwards by chalky Flamborough Head. There were huts in both directions. Along Royal Parade utilitarian rows from the 1960s were interrupted by a new block built the previous year. Here each varnished wooden door had its own porch with a pitched roof and, up above, clerestory windows let in light beyond the vandals' reach.

In the opposite direction Baker's Beach Chalets were prettier. Stacked one tier on top of the other, they had turquoise veranda posts and gates in front of each chalet that were painted the colour of butterscotch. Watched by inquisitive tenants, I climbed the central stair and interrupted a couple drinking tea with their adult daughter.

'I hope you don't mind me asking, but what is it that you like about Filey?'

The man looked nonplussed.

'I used to come here when I was a girl,' said his wife. 'My husband's German. We live in Hamburg but we've brought the children back lots of times over the past thirty years.'

'Has it changed much?' I asked.

'No, not really.' She thought about it: 'When I was little the beach used to be packed with rows of green canvas changing tents. And I suppose there are a few more amusements now. We like that it hasn't changed.'

The chalets were built above the slipway, giving residents a good view of the to-ings and fro-ings of the twin-keeled fishing boats, known locally as Cobles. If holidaymakers were attracted by the continuity of the seafront then this was something else again; Filey fishermen had been launching Cobles direct from the beach since the Middle Ages.

Bridlington, on the other hand, hadn't looked back since the railway brought massive numbers of Victorian excursionists and it earned the long-winded nickname of 'Leeds-plus-Hull-cum-Sheffield-Super-Mare.' Their numbers may have shrunk but the city trippers were still loudly in evidence when I arrived that Saturday afternoon. And it looked like their town planners had also taken a busman's holiday here in the Eighties. I walked along the ugly stretch of Victoria Parade to the dull, flat-roofed chalets of North Beach. The sand itself was strewn with debris which, on closer inspection, turned out to be chalky pebbles; broken off and worn down bits of Flamborough Head. I walked past a young girl in pigtails and pink wellies who was staggering to transport a large lump of this useful material to her sand castle building site. With her hands cradling the boulder, her face was a picture of dogged determination.

The other side of the harbour, past the crumbling Spa theatre, the Council had invested in major improvement works to Princess Mary Promenade. A nautical mile of seafront had been upgraded by

Bauman Lyons Architects and, in the year 2000, their contemporary chalets were up against the Millennium Dome for a Royal Institute of British Architects award. It would be facetious to suggest that these chalets were probably more popular than the blighted Dome but what a coup for the humble beach hut! The new chalet block confirmed the continuing importance of beach huts while proving that this traditional seaside feature could move with the times. The design was neither ultra-modern nor overly nostalgic; it was a sort of middle way. Above each set of timber doors a large window peaked under the protection of an individual off-centre gable and these gables rose and fell in lilting waves along the roofline. In between the brown posts and the brown doors, each of the thirty chalets had its own brown bench, bracketed onto the post and attached to the cream wall. Water and electricity were supplied as standard and outside every chalet was a small strip of lawn, separated from the promenade by a bright blue water channel that fed into the new paddling pool.

There were older freestanding huts along the south Belvedere Promenade and where the concrete walkway petered out another set of the architect-designed chalets had been erected. Opposite these was an orange metal platform to which were attached metal girders and zigzag metal tubes. On the fence surrounding it a notice had been put up by East Riding Council, stating in a rather pompous tone that 'This structure is a piece of public art not a playground'. I felt chastised for my ignorance; how could I have failed to recognise the bathetic cultural statement being made behind the fence? As a member of the public I clearly should have been thrilled to see modern art being created in my name. Well, call me a philistine but that regeneration money would have been better spent on a playground that didn't need a notice to tell people what it was.

I wondered how the hen party staying at my B&B would have reacted to the display of modern art: hopefully with a few well-chosen expletives. I'd first seen them in the bar when I went downstairs to find out why there was no towel in my room. The landlord went to fetch one but confessed that towels had a habit of disappearing so he'd stopped putting them out. Next morning all the girls, except Jackie who was always late, were noisily finishing breakfast when I sat down at my table-for-one. I ordered a pot of tea with my fry-up and felt everyone in the room turn their eyes in my direction. Never have I felt such a Southerner as I did in that moment.

From Bridlington, I rattled out of Yorkshire on a train bound for Kingston-upon-Hull. I was heading for Lincolnshire but the lack of a rail bridge over the mighty River Humber meant transferring onto the reduced Sunday bus service. The brief rush of being suspended over the estuary on the majestic Humber Bridge was soon replaced by humdrum domesticity at the little station of Barton-on-Humber. I got off the bus and back on the train. While the driver took unhurried leave of his girlfriend's lips, a less sentimental couple boarded at my end of the single carriage vehicle.

'I'm going to fucking Cleethorpes and if you want a Sunday dinner you can go the pub.' She spat the words at her partner, who sat down to continue the argument about washing and football and cooking and loafing.

'We've left!' she cried in disbelief. 'The train's only bloody left with you on it. Wha'you coming to Cleethorpes for? I'm going on my own to get away from you!'

It was impossible not to eavesdrop. I didn't want to but some ridiculous English reserve kept me glued to my seat; moving would just have been too obvious. At the end of the line, Cleethorpes took on a whole new attraction for me too.

The station was right next to the beach and I could hear the throng of weekend visitors enjoying themselves on the sand. I left them to it and walked in the opposite direction, away from Cleethorpes. As I walked the fine pale sand gave way to a lumpier variety, thick with twisted worm casts until it all but disappeared under Marram-covered hillocks. Still there was no evidence of any beach huts. Just as I was about to give up, a brick building that looked like a bus shelter came into view. It was the first of a small crescent of similar structures with brightly painted doors and overhanging hipped roofs propped up with brick pillars. The pillars looked wrong somehow; too heavy and ungainly, they made the huts look stodgy. In all I counted sixty huts, arranged by the dozen into cosy semi-circles. Further along this curvy row the original metal veranda posts had survived. Tubular supports soared between ground and roof on a steep diagonal, connected to the sidewalls by short sections of railing with an equally steep compressed 'V' pattern. The jaunty metalwork suggested 1950s Modernity and the difference was remarkable; these huts looked playful rather than dour. They were more colourful too, with metal painted to match doors.

Most of the huts were locked but outside one I spoke to a lady up a stepladder who was applying mint green paint from a tin.

'We've had it about six years,' she told me from her elevated position. 'We were just visiting for the day from Sheffield and there was a For Sale sign so we bought it.'

'Do you remember how much it cost?'

'£400, I think.' She stepped off the ladder. 'Would you like to come in for a cup of tea? My husband Brian will be able to tell you. I'm Catherine.' She teased open the wet door, 'Mind the paint.'

Brian was inside reading the paper. His wife introduced me: 'This young lady wants to know about the chalet. It was £400 we paid, wasn't it, love?'

'And another hundred for the solicitor. Mind you, the Council told us they've got a waiting list now; asked us if we wanted to sell. We don't though.'

While Brian talked, his wife put the kettle on. There was a double gas hob and cold running water from a small Belfast sink. Front and back, hidden behind the wooden shutters, were glazed double doors. The boarded exteriors gave no hint of this relative comfort.

'Do you come for the beach?' I'd lost sight of the sand some time ago and was curious to know the attraction of this out-of-the-way place.

'Maybe some people do,' replied Catherine, 'we come for the quiet and it makes a change from home. The beach is just the other side of the dunes. We're next to the Cleethorpes Coast Local Nature Reserve; it's a nice place for a walk.'

The huts were certainly in a quiet, restful spot but Cleethorpes itself was pretty empty by the time I'd walked back. The old-fashioned wooden swing-boats were static in the evening sunshine and a faint smell of manure was all that was left of the donkey rides. There were no idle passers-by to be tempted into amusement arcades playing loud pop songs on repeat. Going home time had been and gone.

After another full English breakfast I bid farewell to the B&B owner who'd insisted on showing me photos of his daughter's wedding as I munched my way through sausage and egg. I was going to Mablethorpe by bus – via Grimsby and the inland market town of Louth. Not a direct route but the only one available without a car.

On arrival, I climbed the Pullover. This wasn't a Mablethorpe rite of initiation involving knitted clothing but the name given to that spot along the high seawall where locals would traditionally 'pull over' provisions and imported goods which arrived on shore. It offered a great vantage point to the flat landscape on either side. And ahead of me was another spectacular Lincolnshire beach. The golden sand just went on and on, stretching as if into infinity.

The flat-roofed rows of brick chalets along North Promenade were all closed up but things were more animated in the other direction. Outside a cream wooden block a lady sat knitting next to a red front door.

'Oh yes, I've been coming here for the past forty years. No place like it. Came with my mother before that and we always have a chalet.' She was from Leicester, about ninety miles away. She wore a blue cardigan and sat in the shade. In the sunshine by the beach her granddaughter was holding a tiny baby. 'That's my great-granddaughter,' she told me proudly.

Further along the row, a man invited me to keep him company while his wife was at the bingo. His ample vested form filled the stripy deckchair. A transistor radio chattered away in the background as we sat on the prom, periodically shooing away tiny sand flies.

'It's a good place to relax this. The wife and I've just had our knees done.'

They lived just outside Barnsley. 'You've heard of the Miners' Strike? Well, it started in our village. We were lucky, our cottage had about an acre of land. I used to grow vegetables. When I worked down the pit I took my greens there to sell. All the takings went in a big jar. It paid for the family to come here.'

They'd been holidaying in Mablethorpe for the past thirty-two years.

'We still stay in the same boarding house. They don't do evening meals like they used to but that's ok. We just have a salad or something in the chalet at lunchtime and get fish and chips for supper.'

He looked at me seriously. 'Do you know about computers?' he asked. 'You've got to know about computers these days. My boys, they're like me, good at lifting things, not clever, but my daughter, she knows about computers.' He was proud that his children could afford to have holidays abroad even though he didn't want to join them.

'I like it here and it's not changed much. I've got these friends. Their son's a millionaire, made his money in Cash and Carries. He bought his parents a chalet at Sandilands. It's posher there; there are doctors and accountants and solicitors with chalets there, next to the golf course.'

The tide was gradually encroaching on the sand in front of us.

'Don't get me wrong; they've got a lovely chalet, very plush. The Council were selling some off along there and we thought about it but £43 for a week's hire isn't bad, is it? I know Mablethorpe's a poor man's resort but it suits me.'

I got up to leave. His wife would be back from bingo soon.

'I'll tell her I've been chatting to a young lady while she's been away.' There was a cheeky glimmer in his eye.

I smiled; we said goodbye. 'Just make sure you know about computers,' he advised, 'then you'll be alright.'

There were more chalets as I left Mablethorpe. I liked the row of individual square examples in colour-coded groups of four because they were unashamedly garish: bright blue ones next to scarlet then jade green. But they weren't my favourites.

Around a bend in the promenade another line began, a particularly unusual line with a distinct air of nautical exoticism. These huts were made of concrete with corrugated asbestos roofs. On that bland description they shouldn't have been attractive – but they were. The walls were hung with concrete tiles, chamfered at the corners, while the concave roofs rose gracefully into pinched peaks creating a silhouette more reminiscent of Chinese pagodas than Lincolnshire beach huts. It's slightly embarrassing to confess the excitement these tiny structures engendered in me. It would probably be too psychologically disturbing to work out the why but anyone who has, or has ever had, a collection, no matter the subject, should understand. It was like getting the last card in a set or the rare treasure that, even as an expert, you'd never seen before. I was on a high as I walked those couple of miles along the seawall to Sutton-on-Sea.

There were plenty more huts as I got closer to the village. Most were of the more traditional gabled type but one caught my eye. On its grey felt roof were the words 'Chalet Booking and Information Office'. It was closed but I'd already made up my mind to return the next day and hire one.

Tuesday morning proved to be very wet and a bit cold. A less conducive day for hut hire would have been difficult to imagine. At least there was no one queuing in the booking office. Aside from the lady who took my twelve pounds and handed me the key to chalet number ten, there was no one around at all. Before stepping back out into the rain I asked the booking officer if she could explain why I was hiring a chalet rather than a hut. She didn't really see the distinction and perhaps I was being pedantic but I was beginning to think the choice of name might be a regional thing – for some reason Northern resorts definitely seemed to favour chalets.

My chalet was painted pillar box red. It was the same as the colourful detached type I'd seen at Mablethorpe with windows and a white veranda at front and rear. I unlocked the door, drew the flowery curtains and surveyed my home for the day. The sidewalls were horizontally panelled with a warmly varnished timber that went up and over the pyramidal roof space. There was a sink and an electric kettle sat on the draining board. The kitchen units held a few essential items of cutlery and crockery. It was really quite cosy. After some wrangling I opened one of my four blue and white striped deckchairs and sat down.

It was just me and I wasn't really sure, now that I'd got it, what I was going to do with my hut. Relax, watch the world go by; that was the idea. But the world had seen the torrential rain and decided to stay at home. A fishing boat bobbed across the grey horizon for about ten minutes. That was a little bit of excitement. Then a man in head-to-toe yellow waterproofs walked past, his head down against the slanting precipitation. Nothing else happened all morning.

My double veranda was wasted. By using one leg of my deckchair I just about managed to prop the front door ajar so that I could hear the waves without getting too rained on. I couldn't *see* the waves because they were the other side of a thick concrete barrier. These coastal defences were necessary because the land behind my chalet was below sea level and rather too flat for its own good. Despite this well known fact and the threat from melting polar ice caps, bungalow building was continuing apace. Most of the new residents were pensioners who perhaps felt that the flooding risk was not something that need be a worry in their own lifetimes. Maybe they were right but if the seawall was ever breached again, like it was in the storm surge of 1953, it wouldn't just be the beach huts that felt it.

On Saturday 31 January 1953, low and high pressure areas came together to create abnormally strong winds, blowing off the Arctic circle across the North Sea to England's east coast. At the same time, the Spring tide rose about eight feet above predicted levels, making it some ten feet above the low-lying Lincolnshire marsh land. The surge hit in the evening as the falling tide was pushed back in twenty-foot waves against the shore. Meteorologists were observing the situation as it moved down from Scotland but there was no warning system to alert people living along the coast. They just carried on with their daily business. At about 5.30pm a stretch of timber piles and sand dunes between Sutton and Sandilands was breached. By 7 o'clock there were gaping holes in the Seawall. The water pierced Bohemia Promenade, breaking through into Trusthorpe Road, washing some 900,000 tons of sand and water into and beyond the streets of this small holiday resort.

Thousands of people had to be evacuated from around the Lincolnshire coastline as the clean-up continued and police dug bodies from the sand drifts. Among the Sutton losses were a whole family from Leicester who were visiting for a weekend-break. A local man saw what he thought was a bundle of cloth caught up in a hedge; it turned out to be the body of a small child. The death toll for the area was forty-three. Countrywide the figure exceeded 300 and even higher numbers perished in the Netherlands.

The line of chalets, which included my temporary residence, had been built on top of a colonnade to get around the change of levels between the banked up seawall and the low-lying village behind. From a distance the little huts looked like train carriages hurtling along a viaduct. My stretch of the viaduct lacked the smart Doric columns of the original because it had been replaced after the '53 floods. It was sobering to think that there I was, lounging in my deckchair, at the point where the huge waves crashed through the seawall on that fateful night. With five long years of war only too vivid in people's memories, a spirit of resilience prevailed. Money was sent from Canada to rebuild and strengthen the seawall, a gesture that helped to explain why the paddling pool below my chalet was shaped like a maple leaf. Six months later, the holidaymakers were back.

The clinking of teaspoons recalled me to the present. I had neighbours! I went to knock on the door of chalet number nine.

'It's Eddy's birthday.' His wife invited me in from the rain and motioned for me to sit in one of their deckchairs.

'Happy Birthday,' I said. 'Shame about the weather.'

'I thought it would be a nice celebratory treat,' said Eddy. 'It's been years since we had a beach hut so we thought we'd hire one at Sutton.'

'It *is* July,' interjected his wife. The three of us let out a collective sigh. 'We decided to come anyway,' she went on. 'I've bought my book and we'll just make the best of it.'

They were good company but when the rain gave up its symphonic pattering on the roof I set out, with obsessive resolve, to see every single hut along the promenade. There were hundreds of them in single file along each separately named strip of the concrete seawall. From the beach, with the land falling away behind them, the higgledy-piggledy little roofs created a unique and diminutive skyline. There was the square council type; the traditional gabled variety with names like 'Driftwood' and 'Restmore'; and yet others side-on to the sea with large picture windows and raised verandas. Among this jumble there were also a couple of concrete chalet blocks and a few with my favourite pagoda roofs.

Golf Course Promenade threw up some even more unusual specimens including the only Arabic hut name of my whole trip – رامادا 'Ramada' – and a one-off 'Barrett home'-style chalet. This mini slice of suburbia was built entirely of pale brick with UPVC double glazed windows. I couldn't help thinking its owners were missing the point but then this was Sandilands, otherwise known as the 'posh' end. Prices here ranged between £4,000 – £5,000 for a hut measuring eight feet by eleven. For eight foot square at Sutton it was a considerably cheaper £1,500 – £2,000. Whatever the benefits of its more secluded location, when the rumbles of thunder came and the sky turned a deep, purple-tinged grey, Sandilands was a long way from my lodgings with the Watson family in Sutton.

Lenny Watson was home from university helping out in his dad's hardware shop. Before I'd begun my madcap beach hut adventures, that was how I used to spend my summers too. Lenny's dad knew my dad from hardware conventions and, although we'd never met, he very kindly agreed to put me up for a few nights. He'd even given Lenny the day off to take me to Skegness.

We drove via Chapel St. Leonards, passing the curiously named 'Beach Nourishment' site at Anerby on the way. I liked the idea of 'nourishing' the coastline; it had a hint of tenderness that masked the essential desperation involved in battling natural forces of erosion. On the horizon we could just make out the huge dredgers busy farming sand from the seabed to feed the fragile shore. Some of this dredged material had already made its way onto the beach at Chapel Point where the white row of wooden beach huts had the added protection of chunky granite boulders designed to dissipate the power of waves hitting the seawall.

Chapel St. Leonards was one of those coastal villages that only became a seaside place with the advent of popular motoring. Now the green was ringed with souvenir shops, stocked with plastic novelties ready for the school holidays. Although it was hard to get to without a car, a few pioneering visitors had used the beach as a place to pitch their tents. From the 1930s more permanent timber chalets began to appear along the dune embankment. They didn't have metal shutters then; perhaps they didn't need them. It was a sad indictment of early twenty-first century life that the only hut we found open that morning was unwillingly so. A hole had been kicked through the door, revealing fluffy white clouds chasing each other across pale blue *trompe l'oeil* walls.

A couple of miles down the coast we passed the vast acreage of Butlins Ingoldmells, the first Butlins holiday camp to open in 1936, catering for 500 people who slept in chalets the size of beach huts. Above and beyond the accommodation, Butlins offered a whole world of family orientated, on-site entertainment and a welcome degree of independence from the old-fashioned and often strictly regulated seaside boarding houses. The site expanded rapidly and now had capacity for 8,500 happy campers.

I was staggered that the Lincolnshire coast still attracted so many people but on top of this number there were all the static caravans. Boasting some 24,000 of these immobile mobile homes, Lincolnshire had the highest density in the country which, when seen from the air, gave whole swathes of countryside the look of an immense domino display.

Caravan fields surrounded Skegness, otherwise known as Lincolnshire's Blackpool. The town had made a virtue of its windy location and certainly lived up to it as we walked along the prom. When the sun came out Lenny and I stripped off layers, tying jackets and sweaters around our waists. Then the sun vanished behind fast-moving clouds and goose pimpley arms had to be quickly re-covered. As if we hadn't noticed, the Jolly Fisherman popped up everywhere to remind us that 'Skegness is *so* Bracing'.

The character and the catchphrase were put together by the Great Northern Railway in 1908 when artist John Hassall's poster was first used to promote a special three-shilling excursion from Kings Cross. Smog-guzzling Londoners were supposed to be attracted by the prospect of a sea breeze around their nether regions that could make even the portliest Jack Tar skip along the sands. Since then the Jolly Fisherman had probably become the most famous holiday advertisement ever drawn and, as the town's mascot, adorned everything from key rings and sticks of rock to seafront banners. His advanced years also seemed to reflect the Skegness clientele on that July day. I had to step out into the road to avoid two mobility scooters parallel parked on the high street while their male drivers had a chat and at lunchtime we were forced into the corner of a little café, surrounded by white perms and zimmer frames. There would probably be more young people about in a few weeks time but it was hardly surprising to find that the chalets were all peopled by pensioners.

The brick block was part of a man-made landscape dating from the 1930s. Behind the chalets a network of miniature canals called The Waterway provided an alternative route along Grand Parade, though I only saw one boat and a few crisp packets float under the bridges.

The vibrant blue paddling pool was a similar colour to half of the chalet doors, the others painted a darker navy tone. Like at Mablethorpe there were doors at front and back to catch the sun as it moved throughout the day.

'We've got ants' said one lady when I asked about what was included in the chalet hire. 'The Council sends a man with a spray but it's a bit of a nuisance when they get in your sandwiches.'

Her husband, who had been beachcombing, was returning with an old tennis ball in his hand. There may have been an exciting tale behind the discovery of this mundane object but I decided not to wait and find out. It was time to leave Skegness and start the next leg of my journey.

Chapter Four
The redoubtable 'dipper'

Among the current rash of 'celebrities' deified and despised in equal measure by glossy magazines, whose names will be remembered after the passing of 200 years? Rich footballers and their wives, pop stars, soap stars? Or the people who serve them – the celebrity hairdressers, fashion designers, personal trainers? There is no sure fire route to an everlasting reputation. History is as fickle as fame. Yet there are those who leave an indelible mark in spite of relatively humble lives. Take Martha Gunn, for example. Her name will forever be synonymous with the long redundant profession of 'dipping'. She ducked the heads of royalty below the Brighton waves and when the town was overflowing with aristocrats in the late eighteenth century, anyone who was anyone had been dipped by Martha Gunn.

Born in 1726, Martha spent her working life standing in the sea. This apparently did her no harm as she lived to be eighty-eight. Her impressive longevity was certainly a factor in her celebrity and Mrs Gunn's tombstone in St. Nicholas' Churchyard, Brighton, proudly records that she was 'particularly distinguished as a bather in this town for nearly seventy years'. The men and women who worked among the bathing machines at resorts up and down the country were often characters of local repute but Martha Gunn's fame transcended Brighton's boundaries. A folk song called her the Queen of the dippers and *The Morning Herald* dubbed her 'The Venerable Priestess of the Bath.' Martha was so famous she appeared in satirical cartoons alongside the Prince of Wales and Mrs Fitzherbert. Her image was

'Martha Gunn and the Prince of Wales', oil painting
by John Russell (1745-1806).

spread throughout the English-speaking world in the form of a Toby jug, an apparently popular souvenir judging by the fact that several different manufacturers produced their own versions. In all of them Martha is seated with a jug of sea-water in her hand and a distinctive shell-like bonnet perched atop a mob cap on her head. In 2004 one of these Toby jugs, made in around 1790, was sold at auction for £2400. Not bad for a woman whose chief claim to fame was her ability to withstand hours of wet feet and wet skirts whilst helping ladies of a more delicate constitution in and out of bathing machines. Among the internationally renowned works of art in the Royal Collection there hangs a pastel portrait of Martha Gunn; she even had a pub named after her.

And on top of all that Martha Gunn inspired a stereotype. Her ample form, clothed in layers of thick serge, was adopted as the standard representation of her profession. Dippers were usually caricatured as stout old women with warty faces and an unnatural predisposition for subjecting their clients to a near-drowning experience. Their physical presence was depicted as yet another unpleasant aspect of the salt water cure. The painter John Constable felt such distaste for the coarsely spoken Brighton bathing-women, whose daily task it was to present unwilling patients to the waves, that he referred to them as 'those hideous amphibious animals'. This impression of aged and weather-beaten fishwives waiting outside every bathing machine pervades seaside histories but it deserves some qualification.

First, and most obviously, Martha Gunn cannot have been an old woman for all seventy years of her career. She began ministering to the ill and terminally fashionable in her twenties but the most frequently quoted anecdotal sources date from her old age when, though she had given up bathing, Martha was still to be found at six o'clock every morning primed and ready with her pitcher superintending on the beach. 'While I've life and health, I must be bustling among my old friends and benefactors; I think I ought to be proud, for I've had as many bows from man, woman and child as the Prince hisself; aye, and I do believe the very dogs in the town know me.' Undoubtedly they did. And so did the writers of a guide to Margate and Ramsgate who, in 1797, used Martha's age as a means of discrediting their competitor resort. The female bathing attendants in Kent were emphasised as 'well behaved *young* women, very different from the clumsy old women guides at Brighthelmstone'. However, as a service job that could generate handsome tips, the position of dipper was probably filled by women of all ages.

Like many of the early seaside institutions, dippers owed their existence to the precedents set by inland spas. As early as 1667, when the local lord of the manor enclosed his spring at Tunbridge Wells, female estate workers were employed to immerse visiting patrons. Each patient paid two shillings and sixpence at the start of treatment. Known as the dipper's welcome penny, this served as a sort of insurance against over-zealous handling. A further sum of ten shillings and sixpence was paid upon leaving, doubtless often with true gratitude for the prospect of escape.

If first time bathers had reservations about getting up close and personal with the sea, these cannot have been aided by confinement in the gloomy horse-drawn box of a bathing machine. Windows, if there were any, were small and high up in order to guard against peeping Toms. The floor was wet from the dripping customers who had already

Brighton 'dippers' in action. Aquatint from *Harry and Lucy's Trip to Brighton* by Whittemore, c1829.

taken their turn and the smell of the mouldy canopy clung to the walls. As the wheels crunched across the sand, a jostling mixture of emotions filled the sensitive mind: apprehension, fear, anxiety, excitement, even hope. Such sublime sensations were encouraged but when the machine became stationary, when the only motion was the water outside – what then? Facing the turbulent waves was tantamount to an act of initiation, a test of will; humans against nature. Yet, like a child jumping in the artificial surf of a modern swimming pool, every effort was made to ensure that this first exposure was as safe as possible. The season, the time and the number of dips was proscribed by medical authority; the bathing machine with its hood ensured privacy and the additional services of an expert attendant all removed the physical elements of risk to non-swimmers.

The cautious bather was taken literally and firmly in hand. Waiting in the water, the dipper might begin with kind cajoling words but would not be deterred by any lack of success. Once her charge was in the water, be they man, woman or child, she would grip the waist or shoulders and, as the next oncoming wave was about to break, would plunge the patient headfirst into the rushing swell. Eyes, nose and ears were assaulted by the icy water but still the bathing woman held fast. Struggling for breath the patient's heart rate soared and the survival instinct escalated into panic. Then, suddenly, it was over. Coughing, spluttering and crying, the bedraggled victim was released from this torture to be given a vigorous rub-down by the dipper. As colour began to return to the bluest extremities the next round began; a new wave, a new struggle. Repeated several times more according to the doctor's advice, this ritual was peculiarly embraced by the British.

And people soon got used to the experience. Even the shy and shivering young misses who were principal fodder for the cartoonists. Looking on from the shore, a diarist at Brighton in the 1770s considered that bathing must be humiliating to fine ladies: 'They appear more deplorable than so many corpses in shrouds, and put me in mind of the old dialogue between Death and the Lady.' Nonetheless, the practice continued to attract more and more devotees and at least the mode for the dishevelled wet-look made no distinction between ranks. In September 1791 *The Times* carried a spoof letter from 'Miss Peggy Dripping at Margate to Miss Polly Teacaddy in Aldersgate Street'. As a comment upon the increasing popularity of bathing among lower-born Londoners, Miss Dripping expressed her joy at finding herself in such a genteel watering place. She followed the fashion of bathing every morning; 'but its [sic] not so delightful to be soused over the head and ears in brine. I tastes the water in my mouth all day, and feel it go jog jog in my ears for hours after my dip. Ma' stuffs her ears with cotton, and I believes I shall do so with mine.'

Higher up the social scale, Fanny Burney took her first dip at the small Devon fishing village of Teignmouth. It was August 1773 and she had been recommended to bathe as a means of hardening herself against the recent affliction of a dreadful cold. In her diary, she noted the obscurity of the place and the poverty of the women who wheeled the bathing machine into the sea themselves, having never apparently heard of this task being delegated to horses.

> I was terribly frightened, & really thought I should never have recovered from the Plunge – I had not breath enough to speak for a minute or two, the shock was beyond expression great – but after I got back to the machine, I presently felt myself in a Glow that was delightful – it is the finest feeling in the World, – & will induce me to Bathe as often as will be safe.

A fine advertisement for the benefits of bathing for health *and* pleasure.

Whereas women were expected to approach the sea in terror, their husbands and brothers negotiated a fine line between displaying their mettle and hiding their fears. Writing about Great Yarmouth in

The stereotypical dipper made even the bravest man quake.

1777, James Rymer painted a particularly unattractive picture of the emasculated man who submitted to the new, and as he saw it, luxurious manner of cold water bathing: 'Is it not a shame,' asked Rymer, 'to see a great, fat and hairy fellow enter a bathing house, and approach the reservoir in tremor, and be treated therein as if he was a fine, timorous and delicate miss?' Perhaps such a specimen deserved the ridicule of the Norfolk inhabitants who were more used to the agility of herring and mackerel, upon whose oily bodies the town's prosperity was founded. Many male bathers did, however, employ the services of a bathing attendant, often of the same sex but not always. John Baker didn't record whether he was fat and hairy but the accounts he left of a visit to Margate in 1777 suggest he was fairly timorous. In between moans to his diary about the wretched suffering of his life, Baker recorded being dipped by Mr Mitchener, proprietor of one of the town's bathing rooms. A tall and stout man of fifty-five, Mitchener obviously provided the hobbling Baker with a vision of everything he was not. The invalid's insecurity revolved around the fact that he was four months short of his sixty-sixth birthday. Had Baker been alive today he probably would have blamed his weakening condition upon his genes; his father had died twenty-two days short of reaching *his* sixty-sixth birthday and this was clearly a precedent Baker felt doomed to follow. After nine excursions into the sea, and many more complaints against the salt and the air, he went home to await his fate.

The author Tobias Smollett, on the other hand, was a noted advocate of swimming and sent one of his characters in *The Expedition of Humphry Clinker* to sample the joys of Scarborough. Smollett himself made extended stays on the Italian and French coasts, being one of the first Englishmen to appreciate the potential of the Côte d'Azur. His fictional Mr Melford praised the efficiency of bathing machines but expressed a love for swimming 'without the formality of an apparatus... You cannot conceive what a flow of spirits it gives, and how it braces every sinew of the human frame'. As might be expected, the range of watery experiences was huge and for every aquatic connoisseur there were probably just as many who, like Peggy Dripping's father, swore off the whole idea after the first attempt.

> Poor Pa', he'd like to be drown'd yesterday. He would bathe after dinner, and being a little bosky or so, got out of his depth and sunk; but he was soon hauled up – but so frighten'd, he'll ne'er dip any more. He says, when he sunk he could no more breathe than if he was suffocated, and he heard the water pouring into his ears for all the world as it rolls through London Bridge. Poor man, he was so fatigued, that he got drunk again when he came to our lodgings, and soon after went to bed.

A rather ignoble encounter but not nearly so nasty as the Exeter man who had to be rescued with a mussel dredger in 1871. Gamely sporting a belt guaranteed to keep an elephant afloat, this non-swimmer lived to rue his faith in gimmick publicity. Raised from a watery grave by the good sense of a boatman and his fiercely pronged instrument, our poor friend was left with several permanent reminders of his folly in a manner not dissimilar to that of a tortured heretic!

Learning to swim isn't necessarily an enjoyable experience at whatever age you start. Many beach hut fans are dedicated to the ritual of a daily swim that ownership of a hut permits. Everyone on Plymouth Hoe, for instance, knows Muriel who, now in her eighties, still swims in the sea every day come rain or shine. She is as much a fixture of the place as the hut in which she changes for her dip. I wish my own love of beach huts were founded upon such healthy and sensible reasons but I am still carrying around the psychological scars of a particularly memorable swimming lesson at the age of seven. I was doing quite well in the shallow end of the council pool, so much so that my teacher obviously thought it was time for me to progress into deeper water. My opinion on this move was not consulted, perhaps it was considered irrelevant, but I definitely did not feel ready to give up the comforting knowledge that my feet could touch the bottom whenever required. Clutching the rail at the side of the pool, I found the volume of water below me in the deep end most disconcerting and quickly climbed out on the premise of needing the toilet. I went into the changing rooms and locked myself into a cubicle. There I sat, tears streaming down my cheeks, until it was time for my mum to take me home. I can swim, don't get me wrong; I conquered my distaste sufficiently to master the basics but I will never enjoy it. It's stupid and I know it's stupid but there you have it. Hence my sympathy for the historical accounts of young children being subjected to the uncomprehending insistence of burly dippers.

In his autobiography Ernest H. Shepard, famous as the illustrator of *Winnie the Pooh*, recalled his introduction to sea-bathing at Eastbourne under one arm of a not-so-tender bathing woman, his brother Cyril tucked under the other. The boys fought against the red, brawny arms that looked as though they were covered in barnacles but they were no match for their torturer. In a voice whose soothing qualities had been eradicated by years of dealing with protesting young boys, she repeated the words 'Dippy go under, dear!' with each immersion. Ernest must have squirmed with particular ferocity because on handing him back to his parents the dipper exclaimed, 'Well, that's the last I want to see of 'im!'

Julian Hawthorne, the son of American writer Nathanial, had a similarly harrowing experience at Whitby which caused him to claim that 'nothing else is so terrible in the world...to a small, naked, shivering boy as the British bathing-woman'. Hawthorne's description of an ogress, with hands stretched out like the tentacles of an octopus to seize her victim, may exaggerate all the stereotypes but these women clearly held a sort of bogey-man status in the minds of infants. 'If the hair of a boy of ten could turn white in a single morning,' warned Hawthorne, 'there would be many a hoary-headed youngster in British watering-places.' This rather disturbing image of white-haired boys in sailor suits is matched at the other end of the scale by the portrayal of

Bathing Woman. "Master Franky wouldn't cry! No! Not he!—He'll come to his Martha, and bathe like a man!"

The battle between child and dipper as depicted by *Punch* in 1850.

the Herculean bathing women at Clontarf, outside Dublin, who had apparently been known to 'whip up a stout and elderly gentleman, and carry him, *nolens volens*, far out into the sea, dip him three times, and bring him back helpless as a child!'

Yet, like the rule of nanny in the Great House, these aquatic nursemaids also inspired grudging affection. Much of the embroidered resentment against dippers may have been the result of their unusually powerful and dominant position. Like the formidable seaside landlady who became the butt of mid-twentieth century end-of-pier-show jokes, the dipper's status as a matriarch and businesswoman made her an object of alarm and often ridicule. No matter what a person's rank on land, it was the robust bathing woman who held sway in the water. Some operated on the beach with their husbands but others acted independently. At Scarborough the machines were owned by three rival widows: the Widow Field, the Widow Hunter and the Widow Laycock, who openly advertised their freedom from male authority. Like them, the women who employed brute strength to manoeuvre Fanny Burney's bathing machine at Teignmouth were accustomed to hard labour; from the sixteenth to the nineteenth centuries their men folk had traditionally earned a living in the fishing grounds off Newfoundland where they spent the months of March to October every year. It is hardly surprising then that, witnessing the annual rowing match between the women of Teignmouth and neighbouring Shaldon, Miss Burney credited her Devon sisters with 'a strength and hardiness which I never saw equal before in *our Race*'.

Behind the caricature of a barnacled battleaxe were women concerned with the economic realities of business. Coach passengers from London who alighted in Brighton's Castle Square were met by a delegation of dippers who assembled every evening to distribute their trade cards. Mindful of their considerable profits, the established 'Old Bathers' took swift action when, in the spring of 1780, rival bathing

PATRONIZED BY THE LATE DR. HUNTER.
—o—
BRIGHTHELMSTON SEA BATHING,
The Old experienced Bathers for the last Forty Years.

This is to acquaint the Nobility and Gentry, resorting to Brighton, that the under-mentioned Bathers,

MARTHA GUN,	SUSANNAH PATCHING,
ABIGAIL MILES,	HANNAH HOWELL,
(*Smoaker's Wife,*)	ANN TAYLOR,
MARY GUILDFORD,	KEZIA SHORT.
SUSANNAH BEATY,	BARBARY ALLEN,
MARY MOORE,	(*Smoaker's Daughter.*

Continue to Bathe the Ladies as usual, with careful Men and good Horses to conduct the Machines in and out of the Sea, at the East and West ends of the Town.—Attendance given every Morning.

☞ *Orders received at MARY GUILFORD's, near the Bath.*

FORBES, PRINTER, BRIGHTON.

Early nineteenth century trade card advertising the services of Brighton's 'Old experienced Bathers'.

machines appeared on the beach. Martha Gunn and her colleagues Mary Howell, Mary Corby, Abigail Miles, Susannah Patching, Ann Langley, Ann Smith and Martha Johnson placed a notice in the *Lewes Journal* proclaiming the continuation of their superior service. Members of the nobility and gentry were reminded that these ladies had a thirty-year record of satisfied customers since the days of Dr Russell himself. These were not women to be walked over.

Three years later, twenty-one year old George, Prince of Wales, made his first trip to Brighton to visit his dissolute uncle the Duke of Cumberland. His delighted reaction to the town ultimately led to that marvellously hyperbolic concoction of domes and pinnacles that is the Royal Pavilion. The exotic forms that were mixed and melded together there had a huge impact upon defining playful frivolity as a hallmark of seaside architecture. If only the Prince had employed his favourite architect, John Nash, to create a matching bathing machine; would there have been bright Chinese papers on the wooden walls or a parade of onion domes along the machine's roof? However effervescent the decoration, it's unlikely that the Prince's swimming instructor, John 'Smoaker' Miles, would have permitted on *his* watch the sort of rowdy, rakish behaviour for which the Pavilion became a byword. Another Brighton celebrity, Smoaker was devoted to his royal patron but was not above pulling the heir to the throne out of the sea by his ear when occasion demanded. There was one occasion when, despite cries of 'Mr. Prince, Mr. Prince, come back!' the royal swimmer had gone out further with the fishes than his mentor thought safe. Once securely ashore, a rather miffed and soggy Prince was told in no uncertain terms by Smoaker that 'I ar'nt agoen' to let the King hang me for letten' the Prince of Wales drown hisself; not I, to please nobody, I can tell 'e.' When Smoaker became too old to save either the Prince or his own neck, he was awarded a royal pension in acknowledgement of his faithful service.

It was not at Brighton, however, but at Weymouth that sea-bathing gained the official seal of royal approval. As a sort of early physiotherapy

King George III's first dip at Weymouth performed to musical accompaniment in 1789.

following his first attack of madness, George III was recommended
to take a course of dips on the Dorset coast. Wherever the King went
diarists and reporters were wont to follow. Every detail of the royal
family's daily routine was recorded for public consumption so the
inhabitants of Weymouth were rightly concerned to promote the image
of their up-and-coming town. Unlike his eldest son, the recuperating
King did not live excessively whilst at Weymouth and there were some
very slow news days indeed. *The Gentleman's Magazine* had this to say
for Friday 31 July 1789: 'Nothing material. The Royal family in perfect
health. Weather rainy'. All the more reason to create a publicity stir
when His Majesty first took to the waves.

According to Fanny Burney, by now Keeper of the Queen's Robes
and a member of the roving court, the town had gone into patriotic
overdrive. In an impressive display of blanket coverage the motto 'God
Save the King' could be seen above every shop door, on children's caps
and labourers' hats, all over the bathing machines and in bandeau on
the bonnets of the royal dippers. The same words were also stitched
in large letters around the ample waists of these women as they
went to encounter the waves: 'Flannel dresses, tucked up, and no
shoes nor stockings, with bandeaus and girdles, have a most singular

appearance; and when first I surveyed these loyal nymphs it was with some difficulty I kept my features in order.' Poor King George! Already naked for his immersion, any chance of a dignified dip was shattered in superbly comic fashion by the band of musicians who, concealed in a neighbouring bathing machine, struck up a chorus of 'God save great George our King' as soon as the royal brow touched the water. We may like to believe we live in a more media savvy age but just two days later Londoners could buy their own souvenir print of this scene complete with musicians standing in the water serenading their rather nonplussed ruler.

The bathing women of Weymouth produced no personalities to vie with the likes of Martha Gunn; we don't even know the names of those lucky ladies who got to dip the King. Perhaps Princess Mary would have preferred a slice of her brother's racy life for she wrote of Weymouth in 1798 that 'this place is more dull and stupid than I can find words to express'. The greatest diversion for Mary and her sisters seems to have been sewing and gossiping with the Queen in an eight-seater bathing machine pushed as far out to sea as possible. Whatever the royals felt about the resorts they patronised, their presence was an economic boon ensuring a rush of visitors, albeit temporarily. In 1801 the royal physicians sent Princess Charlotte, the five-year old daughter of the Prince of Wales, to Southend where she was dipped by Mrs Glasscock, a woman who knew the business benefits of such a client and advertised accordingly. It wasn't much of an endorsement, however, that at the age of fifteen, when the Princess was old enough to make her own choice, she chose Bognor.

The royals were undoubtedly leaders of fashion but it was still too early for there to have been much discernible style in the costumes people wore for bathing. Men generally divested themselves of all apparel, including their powdered periwigs, while women were most likely to don the sort of shapeless sack that had long been *de rigeur* at inland spas. At the end of the seventeenth century Celia Fiennes described the garments worn at Bath as 'made from fine yellow canvas, with great sleeves like a parson's gown, the water fills it up...so that your shape is not seen and it does not cling as close as other lining'. There doesn't seem to have been much advance on this egalitarian shape over the next century. It was often part of the dipper's job to undress and dress her customers but as this whole procedure took place inside the bathing machine, the potential audience for designer bathing gear was strictly limited and there was little impetus for change until a beach culture began to develop. By the early 1790s an entrepreneurial hotelier in Blackpool was advertising bathing caps and dresses for sale but distinctive individual costumes were still sufficiently unusual in 1814 to stimulate the following report in the *Kentish Press*:

> The wife of a respectable citizen has excited a good deal of curiosity at Margate. She bathes in a green dress, without a cap; and attached to the shoulders of the dress is something resembling fins. She swims remarkably well, and the peculiarity of her paraphernalia, together with her long black hair, have occasioned many to believe, who saw her bathe, that she was a mermaid, and they have actually written to their friends, assuring them of the fact.

The Margate mermaid's loose hair was almost more *risqué* than had she been spotted bathing naked, against which there was no prohibition. Hair was usually plaited and rolled around the head, or wrapped up in a scarf with combs and pins. More prudish bathers, or those who feared the sun's rays, sought protection from a waterproof oil-cloth bonnet or cap, always in white. This was a particularly popular option on the Continent where the stronger sun inspired some to favour broad-brimmed straw hats in the water. It was a great gesture of freedom for a woman to let down her hair as she emerged from the water and doubtless the casual (or professional) voyeurs along the shore anticipated such moments excitedly. Young gentlemen also often wore their hair long in a pigtail but when this ceased to be fashionable, dippers grumbled of the inconvenience caused to members of their profession: 'The bathers at Brighton complain bitterly of the trouble they have in pulling the young gentlemen out of the sea since they have cut off their queues [pigtails]. Till one of these docked fashionables is drowned from this circumstance, the rage of cropping will not wear out.' Who would have thought a hairstyle could present such a risk to health and safety? In the mid-nineteenth century it was the fashion for chignons that caused *Punch* to publish 'The Margate Bathing-Woman's Lament'. Apparently there had been a downturn in trade and blame was attributed to the difficulty of women re-arranging their coiffure post-bathe. In order to safeguard the dippers' livelihood, *Punch* joked that 'The Parliament should pass a law, Which there's sufficient reason; That folks as wear the Sheenions should Bathe reg'lar in the season.'

If the baroque bodies of Thomas Rowlandson's cartoon bathers are anything to go by, cellulite certainly wasn't an issue for late eighteenth and nineteenth century women. We don't know what proportion of women chose to bathe naked but contemporary illustrations, although

Naked bathing at Margate as imagined by satirist Thomas Rowlandson 1798.

they make comic fodder of the habit, are certainly common enough to suggest that independence from stays and corsets was an attractive element of the sea-water cure. Perhaps altered standards of beauty have changed our attitudes too much for these images to remain titivating but sex has always been a strong presence at the seaside. Throwing off inhibitions was not as easy as throwing off one's clothes but the seaside did provide a recognised marriage mart with the possible bonus of legitimately sizing up the talent (quite literally, if a woman was prepared for an immodest peek at the naked men sporting in the waves!) that could not be found in any other socially acceptable context.

Female dippers are known to have attended male bathers but if these women were really as ugly and weathered as their stereotype would have us believe, then there was little danger of illicit liaisons. In 1778, at the Dutch resort of Scheveningen, near The Hague, a visitor noted that young women held the clothes of nude males whilst they bathed. They then gave the men a rub-down as they came out of the water and helped them to get dressed. Moralists dubious about this practice were assured that the nauseating stench of the fishermen's daughters made their social inferiority so obvious and their persons so unappealing that these girls escaped any attempts at seduction.

However pungent their aroma it was only rarely permissible for men to assist female bathers. Given the town's reputation for ribaldry it was perhaps unsurprising that the exception was to be found at Brighton. In 1841 Dr Augustus Bozzi Granville, self-appointed roving reporter, published his three-volume treatise on the state of the nation's spas. He was only just persuaded of the necessity for women at Kemptown to be transported to the ready-positioned bathing machines in the 'brawny arms of stout broad-shouldered fellows employed for that purpose'. Were the shore not so dangerous such a practice would be highly objectionable. As it was, Dr Granville couldn't help remarking on the almost indecent fashion in which 'these modern naiads cling to their lusty neptunes while the latter hurry through the waves with their fair cargoes, until they deposit them in the floating bath-room, where a female attendant is at hand to help and guide them in and out of the water' – and perhaps still their beating hearts.

Part of the problem was that bathing near the Brighton shore had long meant dipping in a foul-looking mix of seaweed and sewage. At most resorts drains emptied onto the beach so without the assistance of a machine to facilitate transport into deeper, hopefully cleaner water the supposed health benefits of sea-bathing were, at best, negligible. West of the Brighton fish market there was the added pollution caused by coal-brigs discharging their cargoes inconveniently close to the red and blue bathing machines. The rapid pace of Brighton's growth required ever increasing quantities of black gold and many a fine lady found herself obliged to take an extra dip in order to wash off all the coal dust accumulated while bathing. The innocent days of coastal purity were more short-lived than we imagine. James Gillray, the famous caricaturist, forgot to pack his rose-tinted spectacles on a visit to Margate in 1807:

> Scene ye Machines in Muddy water, dead dogs, Fish Guts, Greens and filth swimming about – naked men among ye machines – Bathing women entering from one machine to ye other, young Ladies looking thro' Telescopes at ye Naked Figures in ye Water. High Wind. John Bull & Family waiting on ye Stairs of Bathing House.

So perhaps the sea wasn't as clean, the women weren't as modest, the dippers weren't as old and scary as we might have been led to expect. And if that was the case, perhaps there was also more to the bathing machine than we might always have assumed.

Chapter Five
Heacham to Southwold

The next leg of my journey would take me into East Anglia. I was aiming for the Norfolk coast but The Wash got in the way. At Skegness I boarded a train that carried me miles inland across a patchwork of fenland fields, via Peterborough and Ely to Kings Lynn, on the right side of the vast estuary at last. From Kings Lynn I caught a bus to Heacham. As a signpost came into view welcoming me to the village, I picked up my backpack and swayed towards the front of the vehicle. The sea was nowhere to be seen but the bus driver pointed me towards the incongruously named Palm Beach Holiday Park. Tropical it was not. 'Closed' signs hung in the doors of the bingo hall and the frying shop, and in the car park a man sat in a booth waiting for the influx. He looked up and smiled as I walked past, then went back to his crossword.

With the serried ranks of static caravans behind me I walked over the dusty ridge that led to the beach. The tide was out, The Wash was empty, though in its haste to retreat the sea had left a silvery wet film which made the sand glitter in the shifting sunlight. Despite having so little in it, the landscape felt vast, immense, inspiring. It was the seaside equivalent of the flat fens, dominated by the sky's rapidly changing moods. In front of me a boy was learning how to fly his kite next to the zigzag groins where his mother had spread a tartan blanket. To my right was a line of white beach huts. The first one I walked past was numbered ninety-eight though I only counted sixty-three in the row.

This inconsistency was explained by gaps where once huts had been, gaps that were now bound to remain because of modern planning restrictions.

Following the concrete seawall towards Hunstanton I was welcomed to the town by more white beach huts arranged into two rows, front and back. Mechanical noise hissed from number thirty-two. Its entire contents were neatly arrayed outside the door; two tables, numerous chairs, windbreak, gas cylinder, mugs and a big red-handled saw. A young man with blond hair was inside, kneeling in jeans to sand the floor. The noise stopped as he came outside.

'Is it yours?' I asked while he was rubbing dust off his hands.

'No, no. I just work on the beach huts; it's my job, maintenance and stuff. We build new ones too but we're running out of plots. These were put up here to make a quick buck,' he confessed. 'Actually this one's quite big but the ones at Old Hunstanton, they're this size and bigger. I work on those too.'

On my first visit to Hunstanton the town had been full of leather-clad bikers eating ice-creams with chocolate flakes. This time the sandy beach was crowded with children in school uniform, each wearing a coloured sticker for identification purposes. Craig was in the red group and had been caught throwing sand. His teacher's admonishing words carried on the breeze as I walked along the promenade. Past the amusements there were two blocks of 1960s concrete huts. Above them a vivid green lawn sloped up to the Golden Lion Hotel, a landmark of the socially selective resort of 'New' Hunstanton, laid out from 1845 by local landowners, the Le Strange family. Over the years it had become less exclusive, passing that mantle back to Old Hunstanton where the only development was a hamlet of grey-roofed huts nestling in the dunes.

Although the sky was a blissful blue it was late afternoon when I descended the cliff to Old Hunstanton and chirruping crickets rather than hut residents kept me company as I wandered among the sandy hillocks. In the most densely packed area, nearest the Le Strange Arms

Hotel, the huts were three deep, raised up on stilts for a sea view over the dunes. On summer weekends incoming roads were snarled up with people clamouring to find a peaceful spot. Not today: the children were still at school and their parents at work. I met just one family enjoying the pre-season calm. Under the gable of hut number 196 the Housemartins were settled in. The downy chicks, seeking food and attention from their proud parents, hid shyly when Graham Last took me along to make the introductions. From the mud and straw nest, six pairs of eyes looked down on us.

'Funny really,' said Graham, 'there's a waiting list of about fifty people for huts along here but these fellows have managed to skip the queue.'

At this end of the dunes, where the single line of huts backed onto the eighteenth fairway of Hunstanton golf course, Graham was coming to the end of a day's painting.

'I'm doing inside,' he told me. 'I did outside last October.'

Large double doors were propped open onto the veranda showing off the spacious interior, a deluxe model at eleven by fifteen feet. The still-wet woodwork was pristine white.

'Would you like something to drink? I was just finishing up but there should be a couple of cans of Coke left in the cool box.'

I accepted gladly as he removed the lid of the blue box and handed me a can.

'Our hut was built in the 1930s. You see the bungalows on the other side of the golf course? Well, the huts along here originally belonged to them.'

Graham invited me in for a tour. At the back were two doors, leading to a little changing cubicle on the left and a similar sized kitchen complete with gas cooker on the right. The hut even had its original gaslights.

'They still work,' he proudly assured me. 'You can hook them up to a gas bottle and they're fine. It's all very well arranged in here. This is the crockery cupboard,' he said, opening a door cut out of the back wall, 'but you can get access to it from the kitchen too.'

The author as a child on the beach at Cromer, Norfolk

The sun sets over beach huts converted from bathing machines at Southwold, Suffolk

The photo that started my passion for beach huts taken at Herne Bay, November 1998.

Edwardian bathing bungalows in Scarborough's South Bay

Architect-designed beach huts at Bridlington, Yorkshire

The unique post-war pagoda huts at Mablethorpe, Lincolnshire

Graham Last's beach hut at Hunstanton, Norfolk

A buried hut in the dunes at Brancaster, Norfolk

Huts on stilts at Wells-next-the-Sea, Norfolk

While we'd been chatting the sea had crept back in and entirely coated the beach. As the sun gradually sank in the sky it shot its lustrous rays through a patch of cloud turning the water below into a pool of rippling mercury. For a brief moment everything around me was coated with an iridescent glow and I understood why the huts here were in such demand.

Next morning I climbed on board the 'Coast Hopper', sole passenger on the bus as it sped out of Hunstanton past ladies in white uniforms out early for a game of bowls on the cliff top. It wasn't far to Brancaster but the beach was a mile and a quarter walk from the bus stop. Thankfully traffic on the beach road was intermittent, mostly dog walkers and golf-players. The huts were hidden in the dunes, high up above an expanse of sandy shore; they were smaller than at Old Hunstanton, with a more marked resemblance to garden sheds. They also suffered more from the vulnerability of their location because, far from protecting the huts, the shifting Brancaster dunes were actually engulfing these little dwellings. Where the steps led up from the beach a white hut had been left to its fate. Side-on to the sea its walls were half buried, so consumed by its environment that its owners could no longer get through the space where the door used to be. Others among the grey and brown huts were slowly succumbing; behind one open door a child's bucket lay forgotten with two floral cushions on a carpet of pale sand, contributing to the effect of tranquil abandonment.

The huts were owned by the Royal West Norfolk Golf Club and leased to members. I passed three of them on my way to see the Club Secretary; middle aged women dressed in expensive-looking golf gear whose expressions made it obvious they weren't used to seeing backpackers in their clubhouse. Feeling uncomfortably humble I knocked on the Secretary's door and was shown into a first-floor room with superb panoramic views. The Secretary handed me a chart marked with the locations of all fifty-five beach huts. Of these five would soon to be buried, sixteen were partly buried and two had been completely overcome. Three more were recorded as 'non-existent, demolished and burnt to the ground'.

'We're not supposed to move them because this is an Area of Outstanding Natural Beauty and we're not allowed to put up new ones for the people whose huts get buried. They just have to wait until a hut is surrendered and they will be given first refusal.' I got the impression that administering the huts was the Secretary's least favourite job. If the shifting sands weren't enough there was also increased vandalism to contend with.

'It's a family beach but we also get people coming for raves; they come for the weekend and there's a strong temptation to use the huts for sleeping in or for firewood.'

The Club was founded in 1892 and had owned the dunes since then. It seemed golf widows were not a new phenomenon because the hut colony was established for their benefit around the same time. Some, including the local council, considered the surviving huts a shabby nuisance yet the Club Secretary admitted there was a waiting list. Clearly there were other people like me who saw their picturesque qualities.

I hopped along the coast again, on to Wells-next-the-Sea. I'd dreamt about the huts there before seeing them so even on my first visit there had been an uncanny feeling of *déjà vu*. I was excited to be back. The beach was a decent walk from the town and even at the end of the road it remained invisible, hidden by a forest of pine first planted in the late nineteenth century to fix the dunes and protect the reclaimed agricultural land behind. Only after crossing the slipway was the loveliness of the beach revealed. To my left a curving line of huts trooped along the sand below the dark green trees. There was no limit on the colours used here and all the bright buildings were perched on stilts. I made my way along the arc of elevated huts, past 'Wellsangelz' and 'Dun Shrimpin'.

At number forty-five I met Mrs Olive Pigney. Approaching her eightieth year she was a lifelong devotee of Wells' beach huts. She owned the next-door hut too and her nearest neighbours were her younger sisters.

'My grandchildren are the fifth generation down here,' she told me.

Inside the navy blue hut a saucepan of long-life milk began to bubble on the little gas stove. Olive made coffee, which we drank sitting on the white wooden box seat. The hut was simple inside but it had everything necessary for a day at the beach: deckchairs and a table, pots and pans, even a sink with a soak away for water fetched from the nearby standpipe. I asked how long she'd had her hut.

'Well now,' Olive began, 'there have been lots of huts. My grandfather had canvas bell tents before the beach huts started, they were yellow and white striped. I've got photographs of Granny Marsh with all her best china up in the dunes. Grandad used to take it all up in the boat.'

After the war ended in 1918, Olive's grandfather dismantled the gunnery hut that had been erected for soldiers practice-firing out to sea from the East Hills.

'He halved it and carried it in pieces on one of his four boats, half of it to his backyard and the other half he re-assembled on the beach. And it was mahogany; varnished mahogany inside, with three layers of wood and on the outside it was corrugated iron.'

This was the hut, number fifty-five, that Olive remembered from her childhood.

'It was higher than an ordinary beach hut, it was taller, and inside was a bench with a locker underneath; we used to sit there for our meals. There was a cupboard on the west wall with a door that could drop down to make a table.'

She was picturing it in her mind's eye as she spoke.

'Now often Grandad would sit, perhaps when we had to go into the beach hut when it rained or something like that, or it was particularly cold, and he would sit and sing "When we get older, we get the cold shoulder, that's what they do when you're old!" And we used to sing it too. Enid remembers it and I remember it.'

The hut was sturdy and received coats of red lead, a waterproof paint used on ships, whenever Olive's father could bring some back from his trips as a merchant seaman. It was still no match for the 1953 floods. The hut was smashed by the intense power of the waves and the saltwater killed the pine forest behind.

We took a walk along the beach together, Olive telling me all the while about the hut owners, past and present. The oldest huts were concentrated in the middle section because the storms of '53 and '78 had taken those on either side.

'I'm amazed,' she said, 'how many of the old huts have gone in the last two years that were part of my childhood. They always used to be built by Dalliston's the undertakers. They did repairs too. You could always rely on Dalliston's.'

There were new huts going up along the line, narrow ones with attractive detailing on the veranda gables, commissioned by the Holkham Estate who owned the beach. I'd noticed an advert in the Estate Agent's office offering one of these for £12,000. The lease was for ten years but annual rent was an extra £80 plus VAT and then rates were £70. Olive stopped me in front of a similar one. She knew the owners; they were given it as a wedding present and had just fitted a gas fridge to cool their wine.

Walking towards us was the Beach Supervisor, binoculars hanging around his neck and a faded flat-cap on his round, bearded face. Olive was already waving at the man.

'Oh, you must meet Peter Emerson. I bought number forty-five from him. His father Herbert Emerson used to have it. It was Herbert's aunt and uncle that built it originally, in about 1924, I think. It's called 'Prongs' because that's the name of the lighthouse off Bombay where his uncle used to be lighthouse keeper.'

Like Olive, Peter had grown up on the beach.

'There was a tribe down here in the summertime. You either biked down or took the bus.'

Olive remembered Able's rickety old bus too, 'but when *I* came down it was only a penny.'

'My mother had the telescope pointed straight down the beach road,' continued Peter, 'she could see us coming back and knew when to put the potatoes on.'

He was sad that his own children weren't interested in the beach. He'd sold the family hut to Olive but lots of the people who wanted them now were outsiders.

'As for me,' said Olive, 'when they bury me, they'll have to knock the sand out of my ears!'

I left Wells and made use of the 'Coast Hopper' one last time to get to Sheringham. The route meandered through more pretty villages built of brick and flint, making an un-timetabled stop at Salthouse so the bus driver could pick up a portion of fish and chips. A couple of my fellow passengers also disembarked to buy bags of samphire from a roadside stall. After that the driver sped up, aware that his tea was getting cold.

On the East Promenade at Sheringham there were short rows of wooden huts, stained in primary colours. Teenagers threw Frisbees across the path next to an ugly shelter called The Tank, presumably named because its bulk resembled that armoured vehicle but perhaps also because of its potential for harm. On one wall, a sign warned of 'Electricity – Danger of Death'. A police patrol car drove slowly past. At the west end of the beach two retired gentlemen sat outside a brown hut.

'No doubt about it, this is the best spot,' said one.

'Yes, indeed,' said the other, 'more vandalism down the other end.'

'Are the huts here all year?' I asked.

'Oh no, love,' answered the first. 'Between October and May Bank Holiday this hut's in my garden. Use it as a garden shed over the winter but it's nice to have it here in the summer. Friends usually come down about 3 o'clock because they know there'll be a brew. Oh yes,' he chuckled, 'I've got lots of friends.'

Along the prom one of these friends turned around to shout at the pair: 'Hope you're going to stick around,' he yelled, 'we've got some ladies coming down about nine.'

'We'll take anything,' the hut owner called back with a twinkle in his eye. 'We're not proud!'

Above the promenade there were interwar hut blocks, one of which, with its red doors and rounded central gable, reminded me of the

1920s chalets at Saltburn. More unusually, there were also shelters on the beach itself. On closer inspection these turned out to be wooden-framed changing tents of the sort that used to be common around the coast. There were only five left here though, frankly, that was five more than I'd expected to find. I thought they'd all disappeared. The old canvas had been replaced by a plastic-coated tarpaulin material in patriotic shades of red, white and blue, covering the low-hipped roofs as well as the sides and doors. One tent even had a window. They were remnants of a past era but their padlocked exteriors gave no clue to their real vintage. Preoccupied with the tents, I would have failed to register the beach surface had it not squeaked beneath my feet. For the first time in days I was standing on pebbles, grey flint pebbles that made a brittle noise as they rubbed against each other. The contrast with sandy Brancaster and Wells just reinforced what a variety of coastal geography I had already seen. With that thought in mind I set off towards a Youth Hostel full of students and a microwavable curry-for-one.

Next morning I took the 08.28 train to Cromer. Smells of freshly baked bread wafted across to the station from the adjacent supermarket and a road sign welcomed me to the 'Gem of the Norfolk Coast'. Souvenir shops in the town's old streets were marketing the famous Cromer crabs in their window displays: fluffy crabs, flying china crabs for the wall and yet more crustaceans crawling across printed aprons and tea-cosies. From in front of the Victorian *Hotel de Paris* I stared out to sea; beneath me the spindly legs of the pier were half submerged under the high blue tide. A tractor was pulling a fishing boat, the 'Joanne Elizabeth', onto the east beach and other in-coming boats were unloading their catch near the lifeboat station. I walked past two blocks of post-war brick huts, my progress reflected in their large picture windows, before reaching a cosy triumvirate of wooden huts at the end of the concrete promenade. Nestled under the cliff, the middle one was painted bright daffodil yellow. Beyond them, the path turned to sand so I retraced my steps.

West of the pier George Charles Bone's 'Cromer Shellfish Stall Est. 1851' was opening up for business and a grey-haired lady was getting settled next to a green door at the end of another chalet block. It didn't take her long to realise I was a captive audience for her grievance against the two old dears who'd tried to create a garden next to her chalet.

'Look what they've done! They've collected pebbles from the beach and planted geraniums in the border!' I was clearly supposed to be as aghast as she was. 'You're not supposed to remove anything off the beach. They've denuded that bank and what for? Those poor plants aren't hardy enough to survive the salty winds.'

Apparently, the ladies responsible could not understand why she was upset. 'Well,' she tutted in conclusion, 'I'm sorely tempted to return those pebbles to their rightful place.'

I was still carrying my backpack and, her spleen vented, it suddenly occurred to her to ask why I wanted to know about her hut. I told her about my trip.

'And what does your mother think,' she wanted to know, 'about you travelling around on your own?'

Excusing myself with reassuring words on my mother's behalf, I continued along the promenade, past colourful sheds of the Sheringham variety, to a double-decker hut block built in the 1930s. Then it would have been called a 'bathing station', complete with a central café and toilet facilities, and designed with flat roofs and curved upper ends in the Modern style. Behind the block, matching concrete shelters sat in the zigzags of a meandering cliff path, their round forms roofed with flat discs like squashed Modernist mushrooms.

After zigzagging up the cliff, I found myself in busier streets that were now adorned with blackboards showing today's crab prices. It was still too early for lunch so I wandered through the open door of an antique shop instead. On the glass counter was a box of old postcards.

'Can I help?' asked a lady with dangly earrings. 'Are you looking for anything in particular?'

'Pictures of beach huts,' I replied, explaining the purpose of my search.

'We used to have one on the west beach.' It turned out that she and her husband had spent many happy hours in the upper middle chalet of the 1930s block I'd just been admiring. 'Vandals got in somehow and filled it with flammable material. It all melted down into the café; pyromaniacs they were. The police never caught them and we've never had another hut, it was just too sad.'

She paused then had another thought. 'Have you been to Southwold? They're very expensive there, aren't they? Pretty place though. We went a couple of years back.'

I nodded as my fingers flicked through a bundle of cards. 'I'm working my way round.'

'What about Mundesley, just along the coast?'

It was going to be my next stop.

'There are Mundesley huts all over the place now.' She made it sound like there was a plague of them. 'The operating contract went to a farmer but about eight years ago he sold them off. There's some down on the allotment here and the one we bought is by a lake in France. Mayenne region. I bet I've got a picture somewhere.' The owner disappeared out the back.

'Here, you can have this.' She handed me a slightly fuzzy photo of a white wooden hut with a flat sloping roof. It was sitting on grass next to a green-looking pond. I stowed the photo at the back of my notebook.

'Last I heard, Richard, the farmer I mentioned, had some left. How are you getting to Mundesley?' She gave me directions from the bus stop. 'You'll see a sign for eggs and other things. Turn in there and if you're lucky you'll find the old beach huts in his barn.'

I was distinctly tempted by this incongruous detour and was prepared to chance my imprecisely noted directions. Only, when I got to the bus station, there was no sign of the Mundesley bus. The one that connected with the service to Great Yarmouth had already left and without it I would have to go via Norwich, which would add at least another two and a half hours to my journey. As I stood fulminating on the inadequacies of the Saturday timetable, a direct service to Yarmouth pulled in. The doors opened. I got on and asked the driver if he was going via Mundesley. He wasn't. I got off and he went for a cigarette.

He came back and I got on again; the Mundesley beach hut barn would have to wait. We chatted the whole way to Great Yarmouth because no one else got on. Not another person the entire journey. After a full run-down of his time as a soldier in Belfast ('exciting; great people, the Irish') and a litany of complaints about Norfolk where his elderly parents had chosen to retire ('expensive and dull; I'm thinking of buying a place in Belfast'), he dropped me next to the shopping centre in Yarmouth.

'The sea's that way, love. Have fun.'

'Thanks,' I said, still rather regretting the Mundesley business.

The sun was out and the town was busy with holidaymakers. An avenue of souvenir shops selling rock and ribald T-shirts funnelled people towards the beach and Marine Parade. Not expecting much of Great Yarmouth, I allowed myself to be swept along with the crowd, arriving opposite a bizarre cartoon playground and the entrance to Britannia Pier. Looking for beach huts along the 'Golden Mile' proved fruitless. My tourist map showed chalets next to the Wellington Pier but those had been boarded up with corrugated iron and sprayed with graffiti. It was sad but the state of the pier was sadder still. Designed in fantastic Art Nouveau style by the Borough Surveyor J. W. Cockrill, Wellington pier pavilion was erected in 1903, taking just twelve weeks from start to finish. Its twin entrance towers were capped by little green mob-cap domes, charming but now shamefully neglected. Britannia Pier still offered the old brand of seaside entertainment but the resort could no longer sustain two such venues. The Wellington's future looked uncertain at best.

As part of his seafront development Mr Cockrill also purchased a Victorian Winter Garden from Torquay in Devon. The iron and glass building was taken to pieces, put on a barge and arrived at Great Yarmouth without a single breakage. It was now the unique survival of a once common building type. Then there was the Windmill, one of the country's earliest purpose-built cinemas, the Empire, and the Hippodrome, which still used original Edwardian technology to fill the circus ring with water for twice-daily performances. In short, and much to my surprise, I found that Great Yarmouth could boast one of the best preserved collections of seaside entertainment buildings in Britain. And with them it seemed to have retained an infectious sense of seaside fun. I'd been infected, for sure. Despite having found no beach huts I could feel myself developing a decided affection for Great Yarmouth.

When I finally did find a few huts beyond the Venetian Waterways, that just about sealed the deal. It didn't matter that the huts were quite ordinary or that they pointed towards an offshore oil-rig. They'd been around for the last seventy years so they were as much a part of the place as the piers. It was true that the boarded up Victorian hotels near where I stayed had a slightly unsavoury air but as the setting sun bathed them in a pink glow, my view was literally rose-tinted. Even the clouds had turned into candy floss.

Next morning I walked to Gorleston, Great Yarmouth's posh sister. It was going to be a hot day and a few keen families were already staking out their beach territory with windbreaks. Behind the pale strip of sand a row of chalets defined the border between sea and shore. I counted twenty-one, split between three flat-roofed blocks. On the beach side they wore brown protective shutters but along the prom it was a different story. A couple of years ago the huts had been picked to appear in an advert for Vauxhall cars. The ad people turned up with pots of bright paint to create a bold contrast as the car sped past for their commercial. They'd only painted a few but the man in charge of the chalets, a short Glaswegian without much hair, liked the effect and finished the job. A mint green wall was paired with a bright orange door, bright yellow and pale pink were put together; the colours should have clashed but instead they made these plain 1950s blocks look very contemporary.

England's most easterly resort was next on my itinerary but by the time my bus arrived in Lowestoft the sun, which rises here before anywhere else in the kingdom, was almost mid-way through its daily cycle. There were plenty of people around; strolling along the promenade, sunbathing on the sand and spilling out of beach huts. Yet even on such a pleasant summer Sunday more of the huts were closed than open and whole stretches of the beach remained empty of human clutter. Bob and Vera Owen assured me that the sand would be littered with bodies come August.

'There are parasols up all over the beach and it looks very Continental,' said Bob as we sat outside the hut they'd been renting for the past three seasons.

'And you should see it when the Airshow's on. Every hut is open and there are thousands of people covering the promenade and the seafront – and it's all free. They finish with a Hurricane flypast.'

Lowestoft's huts were a mixture of old and new. Below South Cliff there were interwar concrete chalet blocks, painted cream with doors and shutters of alternate red, blue, yellow and green. The former Victoria Bathing Station was built over two storeys, originally offering small changing cabins that had since been knocked two-into-one for bigger beach huts. The Owens' hut was in a single-storey block of the same period. It had a yellow door with matching wooden board where the window had been.

'We've always had one up this end,' Vera told me, 'because it's a bit quieter and there's more room in front of the huts. The promenade's wider here too.'

There were blocks of 1990s huts near Claremont Pier, each designed as a row of continuous gables above the breezeblock and brick shell. The stable doors were painted in the same bright colour scheme but as the new huts opened directly onto the prom their outside space was limited.

Having offered me a cup of coffee, Bob had been rummaging around inside the hut looking for the gas cylinder to heat up some water. He reappeared to take my order so I assumed he'd found the requisite fuel source.

'White, no sugar please.'

'OK. Well, I can't find the cylinder so if you just wait there I'll pop to the café and get you a cup.'

I wasn't expecting such attentiveness. 'I'm fine really, don't worry about it.'

But Bob would not be dissuaded and returned five minutes later with a polystyrene cup full of steaming liquid. I sipped my coffee and took instructions on how to get to Pakefield, just a short walk south beyond the last seasonal wooden huts along the beach. I hadn't got very far when Bob caught me up.

'Just wanted to let you know that I've found it! The gas cylinder was there all the time. Isn't that just typical?!'

Pakefield was greener and more rural than its resort neighbour. Small fishing boats rested on its shingle beach, several of them wrapped up in tarpaulins criss-crossed with the sort of knots that only mariners and boy scouts know how to tie. Along the grassy shore there was a higgledy-piggeldy row of dark wooden huts, functional and weathered, for the use of fishermen rather than the day-trippers who chose Lowestoft. Above them were fourteen more huts, this time arranged around a well-mowed lawn. Several had the verandas and glazed doors of recreational huts but their paintwork was flaking and bits were falling off. The side of hut number three bore the name W. A. Thacker, along with the prices of mullet and local smoked haddock; wooden fish trays were piled up high against the entrance. But for a little sparrow, perched atop a faded notice that read 'PRIVATE Hut Owners Only', there was no one around.

Pakefield was over-grown and laid-back but I would have to buck up my ideas for the smarter sights of Southwold, known throughout the land as a beach hut Mecca. With only one road into the town, Southwold was not a place you passed through. Time seemed to elapse more slowly in this corner of Suffolk and when the town guide promised 'old world charm' and 'Instant Nostalgia', it meant it. Even before reaching the seafront I noticed huts on the horizon; a diminutive line of coloured gables was visible from the road across a lush green meadow of grazing cattle. The town's tallest buildings were a lighthouse and a medieval church tower. On top of that the whole place was wrapped in a comforting odour of maltiness emanating from Adnams Brewery. Urban hankerings for a simple life could readily be satisfied amid the pretty streets and uncommercialised seafront. That was why people wanted to buy holiday homes here and why they were prepared to pay over the odds to own a pastel-coloured, wooden hut-shaped slice of the dream.

Prices had been rising for more than a decade. With each new high, journalists tramped over to Southwold to enliven the property pages of national newspapers with a story that had become so popular the local Beach Hut Owners' Association actually had a dedicated Media Officer. In 1995 huts in the Gun Hill area could be had for about £12,000, a figure that was already considered expensive. Five years later they had more than doubled in value and with a price tag nearer £30,000, a Southwold beach hut could cost more than a two-bedroom terraced house in Lowestoft. Despite the lack of facilities and the very obvious risk from stormy seas, the booming market created demand from investors who would rarely – if ever – use their seaside bolthole but helped push prices towards the heady reaches of £45,000. Had people gone mad?

Well, maybe a little. Except, when you hear, time and again, how much owners love their huts, how much they treasure the memories of the generations who've enjoyed this little room with a view and how unwilling they would be to part with it, whatever the price, you realise why, when one of the 245 huts finally does come on the market, there will be a queue of people ready and willing to pay for the same privilege.

It may be the buoyant twenty-first century economy that makes this possible but the appeal of the humble hut is largely backward looking. Gingham curtains at the window and china teacups on the shelves portray an imagined post-war Golden Age when we were satisfied with less because the abundant 'more' of modern life had yet to be made freely available. Make-Do-And-Mend was a necessity rather than a lifestyle choice and, when computer games were the stuff of science fiction, well-behaved children spent happy hours playing with a bucket, a spade and some sand. The part of us that remembers the 'good old days', whether we lived through them or not, is the part that is attracted to beach huts. At least, I know that's the case for me. And it must be the case for the grandparents who buy a hut to offer their children's children a glimpse of the life they grew up with or the thirty-something couples who take their offspring to the seaside resorts they visited with their own parents.

The question of whether or not all this nostalgia was healthy seemed rather irrelevant when the most consistent and therefore important thing to emerge from all the beach hut stories I'd heard was the strong sense of family and community. Among the varied and witty names given to Southwold huts, many were chosen in remembrance of people, pets or places. No. 157 was known as 'Bambi', nickname of the owner's mother who bought it new in 1953; 'Floyd's Place' was named after the owner's skate-boarding dog. 'Albert Road' had been in the Fuller family since it was built fifty-odd years ago and paid homage to the present occupant's great grandfather, William George Fuller, who built the real Albert Road in east London in 1898. Looking even further into the past, 'Cove' remembered the whaling ship of the same name that sailed from Newcastle to the Arctic between 1812 and 1833 under the command of owner Penelope Bray's great, great grandfather, George Palmer.

This habit of naming huts was more personalised in Southwold than anywhere else around the coast so a stroll along the promenade threw up many enigmatic offerings for the idle passer-by. People were beginning to pack up by the time I arrived but the two ladies in number 158 looked contentedly ensconced so I stopped to ask about the origin of their hut's name, 'Tynewold'.

'Are you with the BBC?' asked Ann Thornton, clearly wary of yet more media attention.

'Er...no, I'm just here on my own,' I stumbled, not used to being taken for a reporter.

'Well, the first part comes from a happy holiday my parents spent on the Tyne. They teamed it with Wold, as in South-wold, and that's what they called their house.'

In 1958 Ann's father, Barrett Jenkins, a town councillor, was asked to design a beach hut for the Centre Cliff area where a new promenade had been created as part of the post-war sea defences.

'He made two designs but this was the first one to be built. The concrete prom's thinner here so the huts are wider across. Some have four-hinged doors, which means the whole front can be opened onto the veranda but ours has three sections. The middle one stays put; that's where the table was, so you couldn't be seen eating your lunch.'

The story had a rather romantic twist.

'One evening, not long after the hut had been erected, my father took my mother for a walk along the prom. He told her he'd got the keys with him so they could have a look inside. Mother was very impressed and said how lucky the owners would be. She was cross though, because they'd used the name of her house above the door. The penny didn't drop and she kept looking back as they walked away, asking who owned it and worrying about the name. It was a complete surprise when my father handed her the keys to keep.'

The way Ann described her parents using the hut made it sound idyllic.

'Mother used to do her shopping in the morning then go down to the hut to cook the food she'd bought. Father would close the shop for lunch and come down. After he went back to work mother would stay till about 5 o'clock then close up and go home.'

Although Ann and her brother still had keys, the hut now belonged to Sarah, whose husband, in a gesture that would have delighted Barrett Jenkins, also surprised her as they walked past one day. Inside, on the back gable wall, Sarah had painted the famous Southwold seafront with its beach huts overlooked by the white lighthouse. The numbers on the huts looked random but were in fact a clever way of remembering family birthdays. Sarah and Ann told me about the huge party on Millennium Eve when most of the huts were opened up, lit by lanterns, while everyone waited to see the sun emerge through the clouds ready to toast the new century with shared champagne. On their recommendation, I set out for the new pier, the first to be constructed in Britain for more than forty-five years.

From being a grotty, emasculated and finally unsafe structure, Southwold pier had been reborn. At 623 feet long, it offered refreshments and mechanical amusements with an irreverent edge, like the Bathyscope, which took me to Southwold under the Sea – the lost city of beach huts! – where executive fish go to retire. From my vantage point above the waves there were huts stretching out either side of the pier. To the north were the cheaper ones, relatively speaking, which had to be lifted off the promenade each autumn to hibernate in the car park away from strong seas. To the south, near the pier entrance, was a short row of white huts, which, unusually for Southwold, all looked the same, with white gables and blue doors. These huts-for-hire had long retained the little iron wheels used for rolling them on to the sand but progressive rustiness caused them to be declared a health and safety hazard and the wheels were removed. Even more exciting as historical remnants were the regally named huts beyond the concrete prom; the few beach huts actually sitting directly upon the beach. 'Edward ii' and its anonymous neighbour Hut 243 were recycled bathing machines; double ones with doors front and back, just like those shown in old sepia photographs. By the time I'd walked back to them these huts had become silhouettes against the setting sun's sky-blue pink lightshow. I had succumbed to the famous Southwold charm – but perhaps *that* had always been a foregone conclusion.

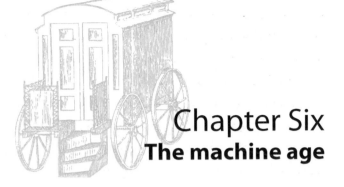

Chapter Six
The machine age

odern seaside histories enjoy poking fun at the bathing machine. Extinction of this beach dinosaur is portrayed as a jolly good thing and any occasional sentimentality tends to be tinged by a humorous dig at outdated moral values. I don't propose to champion its resurrection on our shores but I would like to point out that really, when you think about it, the bathing machine wasn't such a stupid idea. Combining somewhere to change with a well-established mode of transport does have a certain logic. It must have done, or why else would the principle have endured for two centuries?

An early twentieth century publicity-cum-souvenir brochure for 'Pettman's Unrivalled Sea Bathing' at Cliftonville, near Margate, drew attention to the 'very wide divergence between the primitive bathing machines of a century ago' and those now in use that had been 'so improved upon during these long years that they would appear to have little affinity with their ancient predecessors'. Cultural expectations of what a visit to the seaside meant had been transformed over the previous century and it would be unfair to suppose that the standard of facilities provided in 1800 would still be acceptable a hundred years later. Despite increasing criticism, the bathing machine had proved itself to be an indispensable item of beach equipment. The form of Benjamin Beale's invention was determined by function and the flatteringly rapid plagiarism of his machine at neighbouring resorts demonstrates just how well the hooded carriage fulfilled its purpose. But times were changing. More and more people were travelling to the seaside for pleasure rather than health and, in an age defined by industrial and technological advance, new inventors were labouring to achieve the ultimate, updated bathing machine.

Instances of design modification during the bathing machine's first century were seldom noted in contemporary literature even though local variation doubtless occurred. Not everywhere followed the Margate example; at Brighton it was probably a point of competitive honour to resist adding hoods to their wheeled wooden boxes, described in the 1790s as 'about double the size of those of the sentries in St. James's Park'. The consequent lack of modesty was derided by guidebook writers in Kent but the risk of bathers exposing themselves did not seem to unduly harm business in the Sussex resort. Other places took Beale's design and modified it. The first machine at Lowestoft was advertised in 1769 by Mr Scrivenor Capon, landlord of the Crown Inn. Soon the queues of local gentry were long enough to justify the presence of five further machines. Though these were based upon the Kentish model Capon appears to have dispensed with the need for horses by using a rope attached to a windlass at the landward end of the carriage. Other resorts with shingle, steeply sloping or excessively sandy shores followed a similar practice. More unusual was the fenced bathing area depicted in a late eighteenth century drawing. Underneath the modesty hood,

— A BATHING MACHINE. —

The unique Lowestoft machine complete with cage.

bathers were penned in by a low lattice screen attached somehow to the main body of the vehicle. Neither very comfortable nor practical looking, this bathing cage was unique to Lowestoft.

By the early nineteenth century, resort expansion was being driven by escalating demand from the middle classes. As seaside historian John K. Walton has pointed out, the elite vogue for sea-bathing peaked just as commercial and industrial prosperity was beginning to spread. In 1781, a man named John Crossier recorded the sensation of bathing from a Margate machine as 'one of the greatest luxuries I ever experienced'. His words were more than mere hyperbole. At that date sea-bathing was an expensive and exclusive pleasure; in short, it was a luxury pastime. But as rapid industrialisation led to the creation of new wealth, industrialists who aspired to a place among the leisured classes increasingly saw the seaside holiday, with everything it entailed, as a necessary social ritual. And if the modern equivalent of taking two foreign trips a year has been immeasurably assisted by the proliferation of no-frills airlines, then transport improvements in the 1830s and 1840s helped make seaside resorts significantly more accessible to those who had status envy but limited time and money.

Little provision seems to have been made for the less financially flush visitor but in Ramsgate it was possible to hire what was known as a 'skeleton machine'. If an illustration, dated August 1828, in the quaintly titled 'Family Album for the Use of Hawkins Francis James Esq. open to the contributions of all charitably-disposed persons among his Family and Friends' is reliable, then this machine consisted of little more than a gabled wooden frame on four small wheels. According to this sketch, given as a comparison to the 'very commodious and clean' machines that were available with awnings, the 'skeleton' variety was aptly named; through the open sides of the machine a seated, apparently naked, figure can be seen inside. For the price of a penny 'you are not quite so *private as some people would wish to be*'. If such accommodation was supposed to fill the bathing machine's usual role as a dressing room, then this was something of an understatement.

Sketches in the holiday diary of Hawkins Francis James Esq. of a hooded bathing machine (No.1) and a 'skeleton' bathing machine (No. 2) at Ramsgate, 1828.

A description written in 1793 by Zechariah Cozens, sometime employee of the Royal Sea Bathing Hospital at Margate, suggests a possible explanation for this bargain service. It has always been assumed that the early bathing vehicles were entirely wooden but according to Cozens' report this was not the case; rather 'the sides and top are framed, and covered with painted canvass [sic]'. He went on to claim that 'in the course of more than 30 years' experience, hardly any improvement has been made upon them'. If no further changes were made in the next thirty years then the 'skeleton' machines seen in 1828 could feasibly have been examples of this type of construction stripped of their cloth overlay. Whatever the explanation and however inexpensive they were, I can't help thinking the idea of see-through bathing machines rather defeats the object of their existence; perhaps they were a short-lived attempt at re-using old stock to squeeze money from gullible city patrons. Travelling across the sand, these open equipages certainly must have kept spectators entertained. Machines of 'humbler appearance and at reduced charges, belonging severally to Messrs Lucas, Pearce, and Marshall', were advertised at Ramsgate in 1842 but these were not remarked as being so humble that they lacked any substantial form of walls or roof.

With people flocking to the seaside in greater numbers during every year of Queen Victoria's reign, operating a fleet of bathing machines could prove to be a nice little earner. Proprietors tended to have other full-time occupations, often as boatmen, fishermen, boarding-house

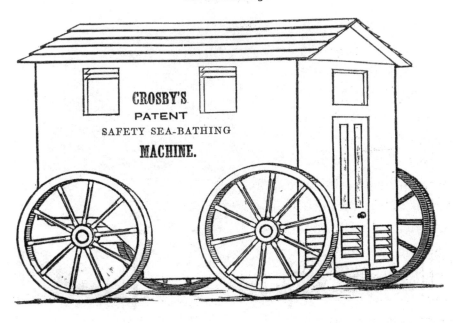

Illustrations of T. W. Crosby's patent machine from *Crosby's Scarborough Guide'* of the 1860s.

keepers, publicans or
shopkeepers, using their
seasonal bathing busi-
ness to provide supple-
mentary income. Their
machines were often re-
gionally distinctive but
few people who actually
worked in the business
went to the trouble of
patenting their designs.
Nonetheless, the popu-
larity of bathing inspired
several outsiders to come

Hugo Westman's patented bathing machine design
was used at Brighton.

up with more or less successful schemes for improving on the existing
model. At Scarborough an innovative 'Patent Safety Sea-Bathing Machine' appeared on the South Sands in about 1853, the brainchild of local joiner and undertaker Mr T. W. Crosby. Apparently on the drawing
board since early 1847, this ingenious contraption, which was described
as larger but not quite so heavy as those already in use, received its all-
important patent on 30 July 1852. Aimed at totally eliminating the need
for contact with the open sea, Crosby's machine featured a raised dressing room at the landward end from which, by means of four internal
steps, the carefree naked bather could descend into a pool of salt-water
let in through low-level louvres in the door and floor. As ropes were
provided for the bather to cling onto during the process of immersion,
attendants were superfluous and 'the cumbrous bathing gowns are entirely dispensed with'. A good idea in theory, there is no indication that
it took off in practice. Eventually Crosby probably went back to the considerably more reliable employment of making coffins.

  We don't know what Hugo Westman did for a living but the fact that
he came from the inland city of Birmingham might explain why the 'improvements' he patented in 1882 were a trifle less ambitious than those

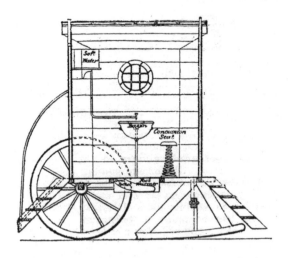

A section through Henry Maples' design for a bathing machine made of corrugated iron.

of Mr Crosby. His objective was 'to render bathing machines more useful and convenient and to shield the occupants from the view of spectators'. To do this Westman proposed waist-high screens outside the sliding doors of his machine. A modest little platform was thereby enclosed and the bather could descend a miniature spiral staircase into the sea. The interior featured a dressing table between two built-in seats on one side and on the other, a seat or couch 'sufficiently long and wide enough to lay down upon'. Having provided space for exhausted bathers to recline, Westman was mindful of their comfort and therefore proposed to 'prevent the sudden jerk now occasioned by the pull of the horse when the machine is to be moved in or out' by connecting 'the traces to a hook or hooks with India rubber buffer or other spring'.

Just by scouring the patent records it is impossible to know which among the many useful or bizarre inventions actually enjoyed any success. However, Westman's design had quite a distinctive roof shape and it seems that his bathing cars were in fact adopted at Brighton. In 1871, a critic styling himself 'Piscator' heaped scorn upon the Sussex resort's existing machines, calling them 'old, rickety, ill-conditioned, and ill-smelling concerns, only fit for the rougher class of bathers'. Their design had changed little since the mid-eighteenth century and still resembled 'an over-grown dog kennel'. Edwardian postcards show a different type, which, though they lack Westman's patent screened stairs, do have the low, softly arched roof designed to afford 'the required height while limiting the area exposed to the wind'. As his drawings show, the sides of the raised middle part could be fitted with ventilating louvre boards. At Brighton these roofs were painted yellow above two-tone green panelled sides and a brown undercarriage.

In the 1880s two rival companies were established to exploit another patent, this one granted to Henry Maples for innovative, double-skinned bathing machines made of corrugated iron. Port-hole windows gave his design an appropriately nautical feel but the interior fittings were decidedly more sophisticated than those set out by Westman. 'In the floor is a well for hot water, in which is a receptacle to receive the towels to warm them preparatory to use. A receptacle is also placed in the floor for the soiled towels &c., and a wash basin with supply tank of fresh water is fitted on one side.' Next to the sink Maples also illustrated an ingenious 'Concussion Seat', though whether this name referred to a hoped-for reduction in head injuries occasioned by the normally bumpy ride or actually indicated the state bathers could expect to find themselves in after falling off this conical spring during transit is a moot point.

Notwithstanding this possible design flaw, Maples' invention was evidently considered to have real commercial potential because both the 'Hygienic Sea-Bathing Machine Company' and the 'Patent Improved Sea Bathing Machine Company' set out to secure the rights to manufacture and licence it. Both speculations were established in London by predominantly London-based shareholders and though they proposed to 'carry on the business of proprietors of bathing machines and bathing establishments, and to establish baths and bathing establishments in the United Kingdom or abroad', none of these men appear to have had any prior experience in this line of work. Even with the active participation of the engineer-inventor himself, the former enterprise seems to have had little success and by August 1892 both companies had been liquidated.

One of the few patented designs that *does* seem to have enjoyed a genuinely favourable reception was Walter D. Fagg's bathing carriage, erected and operated in his home town of Folkestone. This vehicle provided a row of changing rooms that stretched out to sea instead of

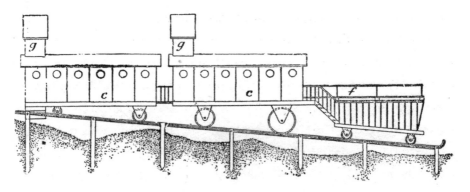

Walter Fagg's patent bathing carriage ran on tramlines and could supply the same accommodation as fifteen traditional machines.

cluttering the water's edge, as was habitually the case with traditional machines. According to the inventor's own description,

> Fagg's Patent Bathing Carriage comprises a number of cabins on an iron frame fitted with wheels, running on a tram line. The floor is horizontal and remains so at all states of the tide. The carriage is drawn up and down by a wire rope, and can be worked by hand, gas or other power. The cabins open on either side into a corridor. At the sea end is a safety crate in which non-swimmers can bathe in safety. Diving boards are arranged at the sides and end of the crate from which a 'header' can be taken into the deep water, a thing unsafe from an ordinary machine. An attendant is in waiting to supply towels etc. He also has charge of the key of the cabin, thus security is insured of the property of bathers.

As manager of the Folkestone Bathing Establishment Company and a local councillor, Walter Fagg was far better placed to bring his novel ideas to fruition than the white-collar city workers backing Maples' invention. Yet local influence could not guarantee that the resort's select clientele would favour his carriage with their custom if the product did not fill a need. It evidently did. More than 22,000 people passed through the twenty-nine cabins of Fagg's bathing carriage during its first two seasons in 1889 and 1890.

Three years later Fagg approached the Board of Trade for permission to widen the existing rails from fourteen to twenty-five feet in order to run a second carriage alongside that already in operation. Despite objections voiced by the Folkestone Municipal Reform League regarding the potential danger of these tramways to boatmen, the Board were obviously convinced by the inventor's argument that provision of the same accommodation would necessitate fifteen old-type bathing machines 'each with Chains and Crabs crossing the beach which is of more inconvenience'. Fagg also had popular support on his side. Several hundred testimonials were collected from satisfied customers, a selection of which featured in a promotional brochure. The advantage of safe clothes storage was appreciated by Mr Fred Keer while others, including H.V. Sayer from Dulwich, praised the enclosed bathing cage as a capital facility for non-swimmers. F.R. Bishop from Paddington liked it better every time he tried it and a bather from New York stated the belief that it surpassed 'all Yankee ideas'. One of many London visitors, G. Marshall, enthusiastically wrote that the carriage 'licks creation. The best bathing place in the kingdom'. Up against some extremely fierce

A late nineteenth century albumen photograph of Fagg's carriage in use at Folkestone.

competition, it was nevertheless considered by D.A. Wallett as the 'finest invention of the Victorian era'. The last word, however, goes to R. Robinson of London, who wittily stated that he 'should like to see a *Fagg-simile* of it at every bathing place'.

This was not to be. There are no recorded instances of Fagg's bathing carriage being used at other resorts although it did survive at Folkestone into the Edwardian period. At Weymouth a similar idea was pursued but the separate ladies' and gentlemen's bathing 'saloons' appear simply to have been elongated versions of the traditional wheeled machine featuring eight cabins on each side. At Southsea, canvas changing tunnels were mounted on high wheeled platforms to offer group facilities.

Both locally and nationally, bathing machines exhibited an endearing degree of quirkiness that has since been reflected in the design of their modern successors. Patented models never achieved widespread success and regional differences reflected the fact that the operators were often also the architects and builders of their own fleet. In some areas there was an established model, as in Kent, where Benjamin Beale's design of a high set cabin overhanging the wheels was adapted and enlarged in the later nineteenth century to provide double accommodation from semi-detached cubicles. At Cliftonville in the 1890s there were 'fully one hundred most comfortable and thoroughly ventilated bathing machines, all constructed on Mr. Pettman's premises and designed according to the latest modern principles'. Modesty hoods had been replaced at the seaward end by fixed triangular screens and the new machines, also supplied to nearby resorts, no longer ferried bathers to and from the shore. It was probably Charlotte Pettman (1835–1918), daughter-in-law of the original owner, who instituted a more efficient and profitable system that saw patrons travelling out in groups to a line of static machines, ranged in the water like small sea-borne terraces echoing the grand cliff-top houses. There were still waiting rooms, just as there had been in the eighteenth century, but engineering advances meant that at Newgate Gap, the Pettmans built theirs on iron stilts so it could be dismantled out of season to avoid expensive storm damage.

Machines built by the Pettman family of Cliftonville replaced modesty hoods with triangular screens.

Elsewhere there were different precedents. Along the East Anglian coast, from Felixstowe to Clacton, would-be bathers had to walk the plank to reach machines lined up in the sea. The shore slipped away quickly into deep water so there was no real need for horses to pull the machines. Instead, each changing box was fitted with a convenient if rather precarious looking gangplank that trailed behind on a pair of small skid wheels. As far as design was concerned, horizontal timber planks were strengthened on the outside by an exposed frame that appeared as decorative arcading. A similar method of construction was used for wooden threshing machines, suggesting an overlap of techniques and probably also labour from the agricultural hinterland. Local variation was determined by the neighbourhood skills base and nowhere was this more apparent than in Northumberland, where the machines at Tynemouth and Whitley Bay had a unique maritime quality. The clinker-built vans were fashioned like boats, their horizontal planking bent into shape between the arched door openings at either end. In postcard views each of these curvaceous machines seems to be a slightly different shape from the next. Captured *en masse*, their effect is quite remarkable, resembling a bizarre synthesis of upturned fishing boats and Romany caravans.

Designed for new recreational uses, Victorian seaside architecture revelled in the exotic. Buildings were allowed to be more playful by the sea, making reference to faraway and fantastical places. Arguably one of the most outstanding symbols of nineteenth century engineering, pleasure piers were regularly topped by wedding cake confections, all ornamental ironwork and onion domes. Yet very little of this flamboyant escapism made its way into the design of bathing machines. Probably the most exotic-looking examples were to be found in southwest England, at Weston-super-Mare, and then from the 1870s at Paignton. With their distinctive roofs pinched smoothly into finial-topped points, these panelled bathing boxes had the oriental air of a mobile Turkish kiosk.

The arcaded construction of Essex machines seen here at Walton on the Naze.

Diversity in bathing machine design was matched around the coast by a rainbow display of colour ways. The limitations of early photography may give the impression that the Victorian beach was a dull and dour place but the bright hues of modern beach huts are, in fact, a characteristic inherited from their wheeled forbears. There was no rule that bathing machines had to be painted white. Scrapings taken from an Eastbourne machine, restored to its former glory following years of masquerading as an allotment shed, showed that it had originally trundled across the sands in vertical stripes of bright red and yellow. The same shape machine, derived from the Brighton sentry box type, was used all along the Sussex coast. At Bognor Regis, Frederick W. Jenkins, a builder who had moved from Eastbourne in 1891, decked

Due to the slope of the shore Eastbourne machines had huge wheels.

out his fleet of machines in blue and white. He seems to have chosen a popular colour combination; at the quiet Devon resort of Budleigh Salterton, the unusual hexagonal machines were made of oak with panelled sides painted the dual colours of a summer sky.

The cumulative effect of these colourful vehicles must have been very attractive but there were also practical and commercial considerations. Mr W.J. Flint of Bexhill advertised the fact that his machines were painted blue and white because, quite apart from aesthetic considerations, a distinctive strip helped to identify rival companies on beaches where there was more than one operator. In 1871 Brighton could boast 254 licensed public bathing machines under the management of twenty different proprietors and their assistants. With so many to choose from it was important that customers could easily tell them apart, both in order to decide who should get their sixpence and to save time in the game of locating their chariot once the bathing ritual was completed. In 1856 Messrs. Darling and Font operated their plain white machines at Ramsgate alongside a competitor with more artistic inclinations: 'Pearce – the poet Pearce – owns gorgeous, decorated machines, some striped yellow and red, like the Arab's garb, others painted green as an opening bud, others blue as the eyes of Ondine. The bard Pearce is not ashamed of what he is, but has painted over his machines in bold yellow letters, "P.H. Pearce, poet".'

No blank wall was beyond the reach of Victorian capitalism. Mr Pearce demonstrated an imaginative spirit of self-promotion that was matched and quickly overtaken by heavyweight brand names. Before long, bathing machines had become mobile advertising hoardings proclaiming the benefits of, among other products, Beecham's Pills, Pears' Soap and Singer sewing machines. As one American visitor noted in the mid 1890s:

> Each little house is generally girdled with the patent-medicine sign of some enterprising Briton, and the bather is advised to try all sorts of doubtful compounds for his

various ailments. There was a society founded in London to discourage advertisements in public places, by pledging its members to refuse to buy anything advertised in a railway station or other conspicuous spot. Apparently, to judge by the frequency of signs everywhere, this society is not in a very flourishing condition.

Today we expect our countryside and our coastline to be free of such rapacious commercialism; no such qualms about polluting natural beauty spots were entertained by Victorian businessmen. In 1865 the Pears' Soap Company raised its yearly advertising expenditure to £126,000. The brothers Thomas and Joseph Beecham increased their outlay from £22,000 in 1884 to £120,000 in 1891. Such firms dominated in fiercely competitive markets and the seaside offered them access to a huge number of potential purchasers. The pharmaceutical giant Beecham's even promoted its product on the ocean waves, supplying boat owners at popular resorts with free sails that were painted with

In the nineteenth century bathing machines were turned into mobile advertising hoardings.

details of its powders and pills. Their savvy sponsorship was more than repaid when the company was able to piggy-back on the heroic rescue of two drowning holidaymakers at Southsea by a skipper sailing under the Beecham's name.

At the opposite extreme from these collective facilities, wealthy seaside connoisseurs may well have commissioned their own personalised bathing machines. Members of the royal family certainly enjoyed the privilege of distinctive appliances. That reputedly made for George III was still in regular service at Weymouth until the summer of 1914. Its unusual octagonal shape spawned imitations but only one bore the royal coat of arms beneath its pyramidal roof. At Mudeford, further west on the Dorset coast, there were *three* machines that could claim to have accommodated the mad King, though only temporarily so. Following a visit to a local notable, the monarch was due to continue on to Weymouth by sea. In order to save his feet from getting wet *en route* to the royal barge that would convey him to the royal yacht, the entire supply of Mudeford bathing machines were set end to end in the water to form a discreet bridge. More dignified than wading through the shallows, His Majesty was nevertheless subjected to a three-gun salute from the Loyal Christchurch Volunteer Artillery as he hopped between the machines. Even the cannon on the Isle of Wight were called upon to thunder a salute across the water. Given such a noisy record of acquaintance with bathing machines, it is remarkable that the King ever set foot in another – who could predict when a band of musicians or soldiers might appear to interrupt the sound of lapping waves?

In September 1845 Queen Victoria also had cause to travel between sea and shore in a bathing machine. Neptune, it seemed, was no respecter of rank and refused to alter the tides at the French resort of Tréport in recognition of a royal visit.

> Though the KING OF THE FRENCH was up early to receive
> the QUEEN, the sea would not rise before its usual hour,
> and there was consequently not water enough to allow of

THE QUEEN'S LANDING.

A *Punch* cartoon of 1845 depicts Queen Victoria being ferried to the French shore inside a bathing machine while Prince Albert rides on the roof.

HER MAJESTY'S landing in the customary manner. LOUIS-PHILIPPE, however, was not to be baffled, and he thought at once of a bathing machine. The *heureuse idée* was acted upon, and the QUEEN was driven in triumph to the shore in a machine, for which CRICKETT or FLOAT of Margate would give any money, since it has been immortalised by a royal progress.

In characteristic fashion, *Punch* provided an illustration in which Louis Philippe rode the bathing horse, Queen Victoria waved a royal handkerchief from the machine's window and Prince Albert rode astride the roof! The periodical noted that 'this is certainly the age of machinery; but the bathing machine is not the one whose triumphs we expected to be called upon to record in the middle of the nineteenth century'.

The Queen had her own bathing machine in the grounds of Osborne House on the Isle of Wight, where a restored version can still be seen today. She did not share George IV's passion for Brighton; she hated the architecture of her uncle's Pavilion and described the people there as 'very indiscreet and troublesome'. Royal attempts at sea-bathing were too widely observed to be comfortable so the growing family retreated to spend summer holidays at Osborne. On 30 July 1847 the Queen drove to the beach with her maids and took her first ever dip in the sea from a sparkling new bathing machine. The rectangular cabin was handcrafted at a Portsmouth coach builder's yard and measured twelve feet by seven feet with a pitched roof. Inside there were 'three apartments with room and dressing room with a flight of steps leading from it to the sea with a canopy over it and a rail round it and silken net to prevent the Royal children from getting into the sea'. Controlled by a hand-powered winch, the machine's wheels were eased in and out of the water along granite channels in a specially constructed slipway. It was in the detail, however, that this machine showed its regal qualifications: 'The handles of the doors and windows were silver and it was painted a cream colour, white, gold, and a light blue, and [had] golden beading inside...'

Royal patronage was extremely important for holiday resorts, a fact that explains the continued presence of George III's bathing machine at Weymouth. After the Spanish queen regent, Maria Christina, decided to build a summer residence at San Sebastian, the local authorities couldn't believe their luck. The provincial government were so keen to express their gratitude that they presented her with a royal bathing machine, complete with Moorish turrets. Like Queen Victoria's specimen it ran on rails but was powered by a stationary steam engine below the cliff. Whether or not it was this present that secured Maria Christina's loyalty, she continued to visit San Sebastian every year between 1887 and her death in 1929.

Even before the nineteenth century dawned the bathing machine had begun to go global. Inhabitants, or ex-pats at least, in both the East and West Indies were apparently able to enjoy the 'renovating waters of the ocean' thanks to machines manufactured in Margate. As early as 1785, a group of English families living in Ostend commissioned a machine to be constructed for their private use and then shipped across the North Sea. The Margate firm of Francis Cobb and Son handled the order, but their suggestion for a cost-saving second-hand equipage was dismissed due to the different coastal conditions at Ostend. The purchasers desired 'proper shafts for use with either one or two horses' and higher, broader wheels than normal to compensate for the muddy local sands. A century later this Belgian beach would be packed with hundreds of colourful bathing machines but the merchants who took delivery of the hooded example in September 1785 confessed themselves to be incompetent judges of its suitability, although 'we dare say it will meet our friends' approbation'. Development of seaside resorts was slower on the Continent and it was the English precedent that set standards. The bathing establishment at Travemünde on the Baltic coast, for example, was founded at the turn of the century and by 1822 had a plentiful supply of machines with collapsible Margate-type hoods.

Further afield, efforts were made to introduce bathing machines on the eastern seaboard of America. An English clothier, Henry Wansey, visited Long Island in the summer of 1794 and noted in his journal that 'a Mr. Bailey, of New York, has just built a very handsome tea-drinking pleasure house' at Gravesend; 'he intends also to have bathing machines, and several species of entertainment'. A few years later a hotel proprietor at Nahant advertised 'a machine of peculiar construction for bathing in the open sea.' It was also an hotelier who, in 1847, provided bathing machines free of charge to all parties staying at the Brighton Hotel near Melbourne, Australia. Resorts down under frequently adopted names from England's most famous seaside towns and, in defiance of the obvious physical differences, set out to imitate the facilities available around the much cooler coast of the Old Country.

Yet no one embraced the bathing machine quite as wholeheartedly as the English. Today this may seem to be a rather amusing historical eccentricity but when moralists and evangelicals started getting on their soap boxes during the mid-nineteenth century, it was the bathing machine that was charged with the very difficult task of maintaining modesty on the Victorian beach.

Chapter Seven
Sizewell to Southend

Public transport options along the Suffolk coast demanded so much procrastination that I'd persuaded my long-suffering boyfriend (a beach hut anorak by default) to come out with his car. I'd promised him a relaxing day in a beach hut at Felixstowe but there were two stops we had to make on the way. First was Walberswick, next to Southwold, where the cluster of black huts relied on a belt of weed-covered dunes to keep summer trippers at arms-length. Peace reigned in the village on a Monday morning but it was different on warm weekends when cars circled the streets looking for space to park. At the far end of a wiggly row one old hut incorporated a curvaceous vintage caravan, tar blackened and with a spindly chimney poking out of the roof. A curtain of pearly-pink beads hung at the open door of number nine but there was no sign of the owner. Unadulterated blue filled the sky and every colour in the flat landscape was clearly defined. But for the huts, which sat in tranquil collaboration with the nettles and dunes, there was little sign of human life. Except, that is, for the looming white ball of Sizewell nuclear power station on the tip of the southern headland, our next destination.

Sizewell was quiet too but I had expected that. Frothy waves rushed over the shingly sand and a few fishing boats were pulled up above the high ater mark. I counted a grand total of five people on the beach – and that was apparently a crowd by Sizewell standards! Near the modern hulk of the power station was a short terrace of nineteenth century fishermen's cottages, horizontally weather-boarded with black stained timber. The same colour wood covered the two blocks of beach huts, which, if they were not entirely camouflaged among the surrounding bracken and gorse bushes, were certainly very unobtrusive. More than anything they looked like elongated bird-watching hides. Yet at closer quarters, the one pair of doors flung open to the morning sunshine revealed full glazing and bright blue paintwork behind the shutters. A retired couple were sat outside on spongy sun loungers, a windbreak at their backs and individual parasols entirely obscuring their heads.

I approached Mary and Jackie who were sitting in deck chairs outside another hut, eager to find out why they'd chosen this unlikely spot.

'It's quiet,' replied Jackie, 'and everyone knows everyone down here.'

'You should have been here yesterday,' Mary chipped in, 'we had cream teas yesterday. Everyone brings things and we share them around. Walter's got a big vegetable garden and David brings fresh figs from his tree.'

That side of things sounded idyllic enough but we weren't really getting to the nub of the matter.

'What about the reactor?' Such an obvious question seemed absurd, almost insulting. They clearly wouldn't be here if they were at all worried. Still, I had to ask.

'It keeps the water nice and warm for year-round swimming. The outfall probably raises the temperature by about six or seven degrees.'

Jackie had had her daily dip already. 'It's about seventy-two degrees although the downside is that there's a lot of jellyfish around at the moment. Dorothy at Number five; she must be over eighty by now. It hasn't done her any harm. If people are put off by the reactor that's fine with us.'

Mary agreed. They were happy to have the place to themselves.

By this point we were running late to pick up the key for our Felixstowe hut, a tardiness made worse by my adamant misinterpretation of the directions. After some aimless crawling through terraced streets near the docks, we finally met Barry and Julia who mercifully decided to forgive us. Their hut was, in fact, in the opposite direction away from the docks, towards the golf course and Brackenbury Fort. Having shown us around and taken us through the finer points of operating the gas stove, they left us to it.

The gabled hut was white inside and out. Built-in corner cupboards provided storage space up to the roof and along the walls bench seats padded with blue and white check fabric hid more usable space. It was functional, if a little musty through lack of use. We pushed open the double front doors then put up two folding chairs in the entrance and just sat for a bit. Blue sky, a delicious lunch from my newly acquired vintage picnic set, washed down with champagne in plastic glasses; this was the beach hut vision I aspired to – and yet I'd got so used to running around that this respite proved frustratingly hard to deal with. Surrounded by so many huts I was simply unable to sit still.

Our hut was in the second tier above the sea wall but further along there were third and fourth levels atop the low cliff. Thanks to my itchy feet I ended up, not in my own hut but on Carpenters' Row, in someone else's.

'This one used to belong to Stella who I worked with at Marks & Spencer,' said the lady in number 592. 'Her husband was a master builder and I reckon he must've built the hut about forty-five years ago.'

It was the same for most of the other huts in this tier, built in back gardens by their owners and transported down to the coast a section at a time – hence the name Carpenters' Row.

The hut's interior was a cosy shade of pale yellow with plentiful cupboards and a full-size gas cooker. On the long day-bed along the right hand wall the lady's husband was snoozing after a full cooked lunch. The hut had a very snug feel and was obviously well used by its retired owners.

'Over the past sixteen years we've made friends with all the dog-walkers. They go past everyday and keep an eye on the hut for us. We get Christmas cards from some of them and they'll always write "Hut OK".'

As a girl, her once yearly visit to Felixstowe with Sunday school had been a real treat. Now retired, with a well-equipped hut and the shipping times to identify the massive vessels enlivening her sea view, she was still clearly enamoured of the place.

Of all the places I'd been to around the English coast, Felixstowe was one of my favourites. From near Landguard Fort where people sat in their parked cars to watch the action at one of the country's busiest container ports, along the seafront and by the Spa Pavilion, through the area where our adopted hut sat amidst its siblings, to the dozen or so by the Martello Tower at Felixstowe Ferry; the town had a very satisfying concentration of huts. Dependant on the whim of each individual owner, there was no regularity to the pastel colour palette stipulated by Suffolk Coastal District Council and the overall effect was the better for it.

With my eye now rigorously trained to spot small gabled roofs at one hundred paces, I noticed more hut profiles down a side street behind the seafront amusements and went to investigate. Facing inwards around three sides of a square lawn, they were the complete antithesis of those at Pakefield. The grass here was the well-manicured green of the Suffolk and Felixstowe Bowling Club. Perhaps my liberal definition of a 'beach' hut was being unreasonably stretched to include these fifty-three huts but they were certainly very close relatives and bearing in mind that a huge swathe of hut clearance had taken place just four streets away, where hundreds more examples from the same era had once stood in ordered rows behind the beach, it seemed worth finding out more.

Although Club rules dictated cream painted huts there was still a surprising range of tonal gradations. Some of the bargeboards were picked out in dark green but with or without this detail the huts' appearance was far from uniform. As Mrs Robinson explained to me while she cooked lunch, they were all homemade.

'You have to be a member of the club for two years before you're eligible for a hut but there's a waiting list. This one was built by my Dad in 1934 and we've had it in the family since then.'

In the early days Mrs Robinson and her parents had travelled down by train from Ipswich to Felixstowe's long-gone beach station. During the War they switched to bikes but they came all the same, so that her father could play bowls. She remembered some of the characters who'd been a part of the hut scene, like Lenny who owned 'Spare Moments' at number forty-six. He had a hairdressers shop in Ipswich and used to cut hair in his hut at the weekends.

She turned down the hob under a boiling pan of cabbage. 'We've got electricity here now, which is nice; means we can have a microwave and a fridge as well as the cooker.'

The electricity was switched on in April when the bowling season began and switched off again when it ended in October.

'To see it at its best you should really come back in the last week of July when the big tournament's on.' She painted a picture of all the open huts and the competitors dressed in white moving across the green turf on Finals Day. 'We get here for seven thirty and cook breakfast before the doubles and triples start playing at nine o'clock.'

I'd never felt remotely attracted to bowls before but I ended up wanting to come back and left with a promise to try and re-arrange my schedule. I couldn't as it turned out because with only two months to see all England's beach huts, there just wasn't time to go backwards. My chauffeur was about to return to work, so I pushed on towards Harwich.

Despite being visible across the estuary from Felixstowe, getting to Harwich relied on a suitable bridging place, which meant another big detour inland. The unexpected location of the Tourist Information office in a supermarket car park also increased our mileage; we drove around Harwich and next-door Dovercourt not realising that the first port of call for most visitors was the ferry terminal near Safeways. A polite uniformed woman found me a Bed and Breakfast room in a bungalow and got out her orange highlighter pen to mark beach hut locations on a map.

As I found next morning, the three main concentrations of huts along the seawall were pretty self evident. A run of huts kept the Low Lighthouse company though neither they nor the wooden lantern, built

in 1818 and now a Maritime Museum, made as much impact on the
skyline as the line of tall cranes opposite at Felixstowe Docks. The size
and frequency of the incoming traffic compelled attention. Whilst I
was walking along the promenade one of the biggest ships in the world
reversed into the dock. The Sovereign Maersk dwarfed everything; at
374 metres long – that's equivalent to three football pitches – it could
transport 6400 containers at once.

Whereas the ports had been transformed into vast international
depots, their successful modernisation had not been matched by
the former seaside resorts on their doorstep. This was hardly unique
but at Harwich and Dovercourt local residents had fought hard for
improvements to their stretch of shore. I met Betty Holloway and her
daughter Mandy outside the swimming pool behind the long row of
West End huts. These indomitable ladies had led the campaign.

'For the last two years we've had no major trouble because of the
CCTV. The Council invested £45,000 to get a European Blue Flag for the
beach and this is the second year we've had it.'

Given that we were standing metres away from such a busy shipping
lane Betty's boast was an impressive one. The fact that over the same
period there'd been ninety new beach huts put up was a clear reflection
of this improved environment.

'It was awful before,' Mandy told me. 'We picked syringes off the
beach and sometimes you'd see illegal immigrants coming ashore. The
place was a dump and the Council didn't care.'

Mandy came down here to walk her dogs and one day got so angry
about the state of the seafront that she sent a letter to the local paper.
There was huge support for the issues she'd raised and a public
meeting was held which the women described as being 'like World
War Three!'

They set up the Harwich Beach Hut and Seafront Users' Association
ten years ago to deter vandalism and generally make the area a nicer
place to be. Betty was Secretary. Most of the hut owners were members
and the majority of them lived nearby. Ground rent had been set at

half price for locals to encourage more regular use of the huts, for the simple reason that vandalism was less likely when there were people around. Members of the Association paid a yearly charge of £15 to fund a professional patrolman with an Alsatian but volunteers also took turns as night watchmen. In the early days Mandy's kids loved patrolling with their mum at midnight.

'One of our best, Don, died recently and he's very much missed. We used to call him the Chocolate Box Man because he dressed all in black and wore a utility belt. It's funny what people get up to; one time, Don disturbed a couple of lovers on the beach. He shone his torch and a girl ran one way and a man the other!'

Another volunteer, Basil, found his cap and high visibility jacket were very useful for scaring off potential troublemakers. Betty and Mandy had lots of tales to tell.

'One boy broke into twenty-two huts. He's just come out of prison. There he was, with black bin-liners full of stuff,' said Betty. 'Eileen chased him and caught him – he got fifteen months.'

The first twenty-one Dovercourt huts were erected in 1912 and the number steadily rose until they were all washed away in the 1953 floods; the whole of Harwich was under water following the storm surge and people had to row to work. Recently they'd started becoming desirable again. Prices were hardly in the Southwold league but a hut that might have sold for £50 a decade ago could now fetch £900, an eighteen-fold increase compared to the four-fold rise in Suffolk. I asked Betty if she had a beach hut.

'No and I can't swim either, but I still fought to keep the pool. Twenty years ago the Council were deciding how to prioritise their spending and they went for the Crematorium over the pool. We went over there with banners that said "Life before Death" and we won.'

Truth be told, neither Betty nor Mandy really got the fascination with beach huts. And yet they'd still helped raise money to keep one fully equipped for community use; the previous year there'd been a three-day tabletop sale and quiz night to pay the rates. There was no doubt the Harwich and Dovercourt huts were very lucky to have such dedicated advocates.

My next destination was Walton on the Naze. The grey waters of high tide were crashing against the seawall so I walked along the country's third longest pier for a panoramic view of the shore. Directly south of the pier five rows of huts were stacked up behind each other; the cliff itself had almost disappeared under their dense display of coloured gables. In fact the whole of the visible coastline seemed defined by the rise and fall of hut contours, slotted in wherever the slope down to the sea allowed. I tried to imagine this view seventy years earlier, the huts open and overflowing with members of the Walton August Visitors' Association. City holidaymakers arrived *en masse* with their friends and neighbours, having pre-booked hundreds of these seafront dwellings. It must have been a lively and profitable time for the town.

This part of the Essex coast could boast one of the country's highest hut concentrations so I got up early next morning to continue my survey. From Walton the huts just kept going to Frinton-on-Sea, then Holland-on-Sea and Clacton-on-Sea, nearly two and a half thousand of them. They began at Hipkins Beach near Walton's eponymous Naze, a small, wildlife-rich peninsula that marked the county's easternmost point. The rumour amongst Council tenants was that one of the private huts at Hipkins Beach was equipped with a shower. In the beach café I met Mr Hipkin, whose family had bought the beach and the refreshment kiosk that went with it ninety years ago. I limbered up with a few questions about the price of huts (between £1,200 and £2,500), the number available for daily and weekly hire (ten) and the size of the waiting list (a staggering fifteen years!). Mr Hipkin made me a mug of super strong tea and I broached the subject of showers.

'Well I must say I haven't heard that!' He seemed amused but unconvinced by the gossip. 'There's no running water you see and no electricity so the only way it could be done would be with a solar panel and a plastic bag. The water would have to be poured through a plastic bag – but I haven't seen anything like that round here.'

I wandered among the huts and had to agree with Mr Hipkin. One hut had a spectacularly large picture window, installed to maximise the sea view from the double bed taking up most of the inside space; it didn't have a solar panel though and nor did any of its colleagues. Despite this lack of green energy there was plenty of greenery: hedges, rockeries and rose bushes, weeds admittedly, but also hydrangeas and hollyhocks; the huts could have been ornamental features in an English country garden.

I walked back along the prom to Walton, past the pier and the hundreds of huts along south cliff, towards Frinton. After a dog-leg bend in the seawall the little cabins – lots of them raised on stilts – seemed to get a bit more subdued in appearance, as if to denote the changing social tone between popular Walton and exclusive Frinton. White and creosote-brown were predominant, the same limited colour range that characterised the Whalings. Where the name came from I don't know but the sense of scale it imparted to the most desirable row of huts in Essex was entirely appropriate. These were on stilts too; proper tree-trunk stilts of a good girth, tall and cross-braced. As the clouds gathered above me I stood on the sand dwarfed by the continuous platform carrying the dark, low-gabled structures. Without direct access to the beach they presented a long line of blank faces. They brooded, these huts. Beside them the pretty Southwold variety were effeminate and insubstantial. And where the Southwold huts gave onto and became part of the life of the promenade, at the Whalings everything was private.

Nowhere else in the country was the hutter's domain so clearly defined. Facing the golf course, each beach hut had waist-high timber screens enclosing an individual deck free from the stares of casual passers-by. This side of the hut had no windows, only air vents and doors. I tried to talk my way into one of these little sanctuaries and after a slightly wary chat over her gate a lady invited me in to the hut she'd had for thirty years.

'It's great for the grandchildren and my great nieces because there's a lock on the front gate and you can keep them in. My friend asks if I'm going down to my shed but I don't think people down here like that description.'

I kept quiet about the title of my book.

'Not that that stops her visiting. Oh, but you become very popular when you've got a beach hut!'

Inside it was dark but quite cosy with three large windows facing the waves.

'I love the plash, plash of the water under the hut,' she told me, 'and you can see the London barges passing and the Harwich container ships on the horizon.'

The whole hut was about that view; a view of the sea from on top of the sea. I felt like it was sucking me in.

I liked the solidity and functional, unpretentious, design of the Whalings but couldn't quite figure out what it said about Frinton as a place. The town had been cultivating its own exclusivity since the end of the nineteenth century and was still clinging on against any perceived expansion of the 'Kiss-me-Quick' trade from neighbouring Walton and Clacton. Recent battles over the sale of refreshments on the beach, or fish and chips on Connaught Avenue, had been reported in the national papers as examples of parochial snobbery ripe for mocking by the metropolitan press. On that basis I was expecting Frinton to be all straight laced and anti-seaside, which it wasn't. The trader who'd attempted to get around the prohibition of seafront kiosks by selling flags for a pound in order to give away 'free' ice creams may have lost his case but you could still get ice cream from a shop in the town and the not-very-exclusive Stock Clearance Centre sold lilos and buckets and spades. There was a pub-cum-wine bar and plenty of independent shops, an increasing rarity these days. The business zone came to an end where the Greensward, a large swathe of grass formerly grazed into perpetual neatness by local sheep, began. Beyond that it was just the beach huts and the sea. Except for the insensitive insertion of a lumpen block of concrete flats it was all perfectly nice.

The town clearly had its foibles but I was interested to hear what a group of three Islington Yummy Mummies, sitting outside a rented beach hut, thought. They'd come because they wanted their children to have a taste of the old-fashioned seaside and their main spokeswoman confessed to being an *habitué* of the resort.

'My parents used to bring me here when I was a child so I suppose I've been coming for about thirty years. People of my parents' generation, they probably remember Frinton in the 1930s. They used to stay in large Edwardian villas with their nannies.'

The lack of amusements and comparative isolation within easy reach of London made the little resort popular with the nannied classes.

'I've been told that in the twenties there used to be signs along the sand that said "No Amputees on the Beach". It was after the First World War and they thought the ex-soldiers would offend the delicate sensibilities of visitors.'

'So have things changed since you've been coming here?' I asked.

'I keep coming back because the beach is great, it's clean and safe. I don't know; for all this fuss about the pub and the fish and chip shop, nothing's really changed. The place attracts lots of retired people and you do notice it when you take the children into town. There don't seem to be many other kids around and especially not teenagers. There's sort of a missing generation.'

While we'd been talking the women's collective offspring, aged between about seven and twelve, had come off the beach to request jumpers, leaving their sculpted sand aeroplane to the mercy of the incoming tide. It wouldn't last long and neither would Frinton if these children didn't also choose to bring their own children back in the future.

Next morning I set out for Holland-on-Sea, in between Frinton and Clacton. Under a clear blue sky, bronzed pensioners were setting out chairs and sun-loungers along the seawall. They all looked extremely healthy, not least the couple I got chatting to who were sat outside their hut dressed in cycling shorts. Two bikes were propped up against the side wall. Both the husband and wife had hut history.

'My mum had a hut at Walton called Shalimar,' the wife told me. 'That's going back about fifty years when the huts meant income for locals. She always saved it for us for two weeks a year though, for when aunty came down in August. We needed the money then and I remember you used to see signs in people's front windows: "Hut to Let". You got about £3.10s and it was tax free. Mum had a B&B in Walton, she used to do half-board and people liked to have the hut for during the day.'

Her husband was local too. His father had had a hut at Frinton.

'Growing up next to the sea we all just used to swim as second nature, and we'd get changed in the huts. When it was wet we'd just sit in there and play cards.'

But they weren't allowed near the beach as young children because of the war.

'My grandfather, Mr Kerridge,' continued the man, 'he was a council worker. They thought they'd cleared all the mines but he trod on one. He was blown to smitherines; they had to put stones in his coffin because they couldn't find enough of the body on Walton beach.'

Now it was their turn to be grandparents. The beach hut was a favourite place for their five grandchildren, a treat that also held the promise of a trip on the road-train to the Clacton amusements. I wasn't much interested in the arcades but when they told me it was two miles back to Clacton pier the little wheeled train took on a new appeal. I paid my fare and hopped on.

I got off near the pier and found an attractive block of bathing bungalows with mock-Tudor gables and wooden verandas in the Scarborough style. They'd recently had a new coat of vivid sky-blue paint; the coat of graffiti was more recent still. I headed south towards Jaywick to see what was left of the interwar plotland. Martello Bay came first, named for the two round towers at either end. Behind the seawall were modern houses and flats, then the dwellings got smaller after the pink and white striped beach bar where the Jaywick bungalows took over.

In 1928, a property speculator called Frank Stedman bought several hundred acres of reclaimed marshland at Jaywick to build a holiday estate. After the first six houses went up construction was halted because of drainage problems. In an attempt to circumvent council regulations on sewerage, Stedman applied for permission to erect beach huts instead. His real intentions were pretty clear because the so-called huts had up to six rooms. In response the council directed that they could not be used for sleeping in, though of course they were. In August 1929 *The Daily Chronicle* reported that 'for £50 you can acquire the freehold of 1000 square feet with a hut upon it, coloured so gaudily that you would feel as if you were living in a revue'. The estate continued to expand and holidaymakers from London crowded into the Jaywick Club for dances and amateur entertainments, creating happy memories that would attract them back later in life. By 1970 there was little of the original Jaywick spirit left, just two original streets, Brooklands and Grasslands, that hung on amid newer suburban sprawl. The council had proposed wholesale demolition several times but the unmade roads with their bungalows – some well-cared for, others so flimsy as to be miraculous survivals – were still there, protected and separated from the pale sandy beach by a hulking concrete seawall. Picturesque they were not. And yet there was something in their defiance, in the hard-won right to self-determination represented by those little buildings that made them strangely attractive.

As I stopped to look at some of these seafront buildings I overheard three elderly ladies in conversation. Each had a perm and a small dog on a lead. Although they were living the post-war retirement dream of a little place by the sea all three had lost their husbands. One, with an unbelievably full head of dark hair, confessed that she didn't know what to do with herself. It was heartbreaking to hear her companions agree. I wondered how many of the bungalows with cheery names like 'Happy Returns' or 'Why Worry' were now home to lonely widows.

There had been a plotland development at my next destination too. In its early days Point Clear was advertised as 'the farm by the sea' complete with a long line of beach huts at St Osyth Stone. After enquiries at the Post Office and fruitless detours down a series of cul-de-sacs I was forced to conclude that these had long since disappeared. The fact that most of the images I'd seen showed flooded or storm-damaged huts probably should have given me a clue. I walked past the static caravans of Orchards Holiday Park, around another Martello tower and finally found some huts. There was one small problem: the bright huts of Brightlingsea were the other side of a wide tidal creek.

I'd been led to believe that there'd be a ferryman ready to take my pieces of silver in exchange for safe passage across the water. Though my faith in this possibility faltered as the minutes passed by, I still waited on the muddy sand hoping that one of the many weekend boats would come my way. The beach was empty but a solitary litter picker appeared, a man who, it turned out, was a hut owner at Holland-on-Sea. He confirmed my worst fears; the ferryman had retired. This was bad because if I couldn't cross the creek it would take a good couple of hours to do the journey by bus. I would have to ride all the way inland to Colchester then back out again, a *really* long way to get to a place I could see in front of me.

While I was weighing up my seemingly limited options, a four-wheel drive crossed the sand and reversed up to the water's edge. Two men and several children in life vests clambered out then set about unhooking a small speed boat from the back. Despite knowing that this was my best chance I felt unaccountably shy about asking for a ride. By the time I'd finally decided to go for it the boat was already in the water. I removed my shoes and socks, rolled up my dry-clean-only trousers and waded towards the boat. I can't thank those nice men enough for giving me a lift but I'm glad the crossing was quick; I sat at stern, with the weight of my rucksack threatening to topple me overboard, trying to make polite conversation with a couple of disinterested ten-year-old girls.

Back on dry land, I walked the damp off my feet, happily heading along the jetty towards the huts. The absentee sun had even decided to return. At hut 218 I gratefully accepted the offer of a cup of tea, de-bagging myself before sinking into a folding chair.

'How long have you been here?' I asked the lady who handed me a steaming mug.

'Today, we got here quite early. It was high tide at 9.30 so we went in for a swim then.' She was still wearing her costume.

'We've had the hut since 1972,' her husband told me.

They spoke of the changes they'd seen: the loss of the railway that once ran behind the huts and the recreational waterway in front that used to be busy with cargo vessels heading upriver to their hometown of Colchester. Their most glamorous revelation concerned Joan Collins, who had apparently lived on a boat at Brightlingsea during the Fifties. The beach huts couldn't compete with that level of celebrity and despite having a local MP among the owners, prices were still relatively cheap at about the £2,500 mark.

I continued my walk along the front past Bateman's Tower, a two-storey octagonal structure built in 1883 as a recuperative folly for the consumptive daughter of John Bateman, seven times mayor of Brightlingsea. With its roof lopped off, it now served the less romantic function of administrative centre for sailing races on the Colne estuary. Beyond it the shore wiggled inward accompanied by more huts. Here the receding tide had exposed a shingle beach and seaweed covered sea defences. Two teenage boys were riding their bikes over the bladderwrack, making it pop like bubble wrap.

From Brightlingsea I took a bus into Colchester where I found a B&B on the route to my next destination, Mersea Island. In the morning I was ready with time to spare but the bus failed to appear. A phone call to the public transport information line revealed that it went a different way on Sundays and the next service would not depart from the central bus station for another two hours! Not for the first time I felt the lack of a car. Thankfully my wait was enlivened by the company of a nice white-haired lady who, after I'd explained my mission, told me about her own beach hut experiences. Her family used to take holidays in a caravan in Mundesley ('Have you been to Mundesley?' 'No, because I had bus problems – arghhhh!'). She described the lovely bright coloured huts and how two or three families would club together to pay the four pounds a week hire charge. Her bus pulled out of the station first and she waved at me from her window seat. I waved back, still amazed at how random strangers always seemed to have a beach hut story, no matter where I met them.

On my bus, the driver proceeded to take a frustratingly indirect route, turning the other way at every Mersea signpost to the point where I actually sighed out loud when we crossed the causeway onto the island. At West Mersea I counted 364 huts overlooking the Blackwater Estuary. Colchester Borough Council set no rules about paint colour but there was a general consensus in favour of green, brown and white, either alone or in combination. The private huts at Seaview Holiday Park, leftover camping chalets from the 1950s, had stuck to similar shades. Contrary to expectations, their view was of each other rather than the sea, set vertically as they were in a line away from the beach. The rest of the site had been filled with static caravans, a fate that hut owners in East Mersea were trying very hard to resist on their own patch; since 1990 the number of Coopers Beach chalets had been reduced from 300 to twenty-five.

The island's eastern side had traditionally been quieter and more agricultural than the west where most of the 7,000 or so inhabitants lived. To compensate for this, in the early 1930s members of the East Mersea Golf Company built their wives beach huts on farmland near their course. The wooden huts were large enough to sleep a good-sized family with verandas at the front and cook houses at the back. Milk and water were delivered daily by horse and trap; the postman included the huts on his round and twice a week the butcher would stop by. Having been commandeered in World War II the huts were then sold to Mr Cooper with 500 acres of land. They'd been upgraded to 'chalets' at that point and things had ticked over nicely until Mr Cooper's death. Then a large leisure company took over with plans for a caravan park and the battle began. The Coopers Beach Chalet Society was set up to mobilise support, an application for statutory listing was submitted and, when that failed, residents went to the European Court of Human Rights to try and defend their hut community. Joy Puritz told me why the hut built by her grandmother was worth fighting for: 'The first holiday of my life was in that hut. I was three and a half and I can remember how exciting it was.' No other building was as important to Joy's family as that little hut where they'd spent their holidays for over seventy years. The hut's future looked regrettably bleak but it was hard to imagine the replacement mobile homes would ever be so cherished.

Next day I was on the Thames estuary, making my last stops in Essex before going through London and out the other side into Kent. I stopped briefly at Chalkwell where there was a weird row of changing cubicles. Tall and rectangular, built of beige fibreglass, they resembled alien landing pods as much as any beach hut I'd ever seen. On the train passing through Southend-on-Sea I tried to spot the world's longest pier, stretching a whopping 2158 metres or 1.341 miles over the estuarine mud flats – so long in fact that it had its own railway to carry people to the end. The reason for its impressive length was abundantly clear when the tide went out. Without it the boats that sailed up the Victorian Thames would have got stuck in the mud, unable to disgorge their cargo of happy East End trippers. Nowadays they all came from London by car, up the A127. And they did still come, I'd seen them. Not today but on a sunny Sunday in May when hundreds of lobster-red bodies milled around a prom strewn with litter. It was like Torremolinos-on-Thames. And just to ensure I got the full-on experience, evening traffic back into the city ground to a halt when two cars stopped so the drivers could have a fight on the carriageway! Small wonder the beach huts stuck to the calmer edges of rough-and-ready Southend.

I stayed on my shiny new train to the end of the line at Shoeburyness. From the station packed with resting commuter trains I found my way to the end of another line, hut number 566 at Shoebury Common Beach. Number one was somewhere in the hazy distance towards the office blocks of Southend. On the opposite shore loomed the industrial silhouette of Sheerness power station. Yesterday my view from West Mersea had been dominated by Bradwell nuclear reactor. These vast facilities were not man's prettiest addition to the coastal landscape but you couldn't really ignore them.

The first huts I walked past were of the standard gabled type, opening onto the concrete promenade. After number 395 a thicker strip of shingle allowed the row to decamp onto the beach, albeit on stilts. The tide was too high for me to walk in front of them but even from the rear I noticed the change to fancier verandas and brighter colours on the beach. My great aunty Sylvia went through a few huts along this shore in the 60s and 70s. She told me how the council would place an ad in the local paper and how they'd turn up on the allotted day to queue from nine o'clock in the morning to put their name down for a hut. The trick was to take the whole family; father went in first followed by his brother, uncle and any other available relation, each booking the same hut for a different week through the season and ending up with a nice monopoly. After the council huts, Sylvia hired from a private owner for a couple of years before actually buying a stilted hut further along the prom at Thorpe Bay. When they moved to Cornwall in 1980 they sold it to a hairdresser and were soon re-investing in a Cornish hut.

As I wandered on, the smell of barbequing meat assailed my hungry nostrils. Three middle-aged women were sat outside their hut, heaped plates of salad resting on their laps, waiting for kebabs to cook on a disposable charcoal grill. All along the hut row, people were getting on with the job of relaxing in the sunshine. Just past number 140 I climbed the front stairs to meet a man reclining on his veranda, little knowing that I'd stumbled across another star of the small screen. Like at Gorleston, this hut and its two neighbours had been filmed for a TV advert, providing the backdrop for the promotion of orange squash.

'I can tell you exactly when it was,' the retired owner assured me as he got up from his chair, 'because I've kept all the tide-tables since

1987.' He'd added marginalia to these slender booklets as a reminder of interesting events.

'It was only a few years ago that the location scouts came round,' he said, flicking through the pages. Much to his surprise he found the day's filming noted down next to 10 June 1994.

'Well, I didn't think it was that long ago! I remember they came with the cameras about six in the morning and gave us all breakfast and lunch. My hut was re-painted pale yellow and there were two pretty girls on my veranda all day throwing a big orange ball. One of them had to throw it into the next hut where a man on a sun-lounger caught it. He threw it to the camera and in the advert it turned into a slice of orange. It took a whole day to make an advert that lasted for a couple of minutes – amazing!'

Photos of the film crew were pinned to a noticeboard next to a card that read 'Happy 80th Bert'. My eye was caught by a lovely watercolour showing a group of people in front of the huts.

'Do you like it?' Bert asked.

'It really captures the atmosphere. Who's it by?'

'I belong to a painting group and it seemed like a nice subject. It's another thing I took up after retiring.'

When he began drawing his pension it was the prospect of owning a beach hut that made Bert move from London to Southend. During the war he had been stationed at Calshot Spit, a seaplane base on Southampton Water. He told me there were beach huts there too so I promised to try and find them as I carried on around the coast. The tide-tables were still lying in a pile on his little table.

'What's the date?' he asked. 'I'll put you in.'

Chapter Eight
Sea, sex and segregation

Crowds of spectators lined the promenade, three or four deep, to watch the floats pass by in the Blackpool carnival of 1930. Miss F. Locke, Britain's Cotton Queen, had already smiled and waved her way along at the head of the procession. As people looked on, they tapped their feet to the sounds of one brass band after another; children pointed at the miniature model of the Blackpool Tower, decorated with flowers, as a team of horses pulled it in the direction of its majestic parent. The next float featured a bathing machine, number thirty-seven, taken off the beach to form part of the pageant and surrounded by a group of young women wearing bathing costumes and date placards illustrating the evolution of attitudes to female flesh. Bikinis had yet to be thought of, but Miss 1895 was baring considerably more arm and leg than Miss 1880, who wore long gathered bloomers under a knee-length, elbow-covering dress. At the back of the float was Mrs Grundy, the personification of prudery, like Mary Whitehouse in a corset, shaking her umbrella in protest at the disgraceful decline in moral standards.

Symbols of a past age, Mrs Grundy and the bathing machine have become linked in our image of Victorian values, just like swooning women and piano legs. But the Mrs Grundys of this world (many of whom were actually *Mr* Grundys) should have had little cause for complaint if the bathing machine was fulfilling its designated role as mobile bastion of female virtue. This it could not do without the compliance of its clientele and if the rules for modest deportment had to be continually restated it was because they were not being obeyed. Just because the nineteenth century witnessed an excess of proscriptive manuals, published by ardent moralists, it does not mean that we should presuppose either a captive or a willing audience. Voices raised in disgust against the indecency of English bathing practices speak loudly from the pages of history but this may simply be because, until mid-century, people weren't listening. More striking than the volume of complaints are the vibrant and lively scenes they describe.

From its earliest days the seaside has been associated with an undertone of sexual freedom. The very act of undressing to enter the water gave a piquancy to scenes of social interaction that could be found nowhere else. In the words of a late Victorian music-hall song, 'You can do all sorts of things at the seaside that you cannot do at home.' That sentiment has been amplified over time and many Brits are attracted to the sun soaked beaches of Faliraki or Ibiza because of this extended sexual licence. But whatever happens in the clubs and bars, on the beach men usually keep their trunks on. Public nudity is a minority pastime. We still generally accept that something should be worn to keep private parts private. It may, therefore, come as something of a surprise to learn that during the period of our history we most associate with inhibited sexuality, with the bathing machine and with wives who were told to 'lie back and think of England', naked male bathing was commonplace. Even more of a jolt to received wisdom is the fact that women openly watched. A letter to the Editor of *The Times* on 5 October 1841 complained that at Scarborough women were '"not...single spies, but in battalions," promenading, or standing on the shore, and at the distance of only 20 or 30 feet, [from] some 50 or 60 men bathing and disporting in the sea, "naked and not ashamed!"' Admittedly this was early in Victoria's reign but a good twenty years later, men were still declining to wear drawers though they were often deposited from their bathing machines in water that was barely knee-deep.

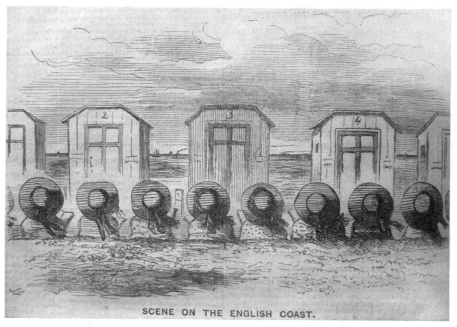

SCENE ON THE ENGLISH COAST.

This *Punch* cartoon of 1855 suggests that Victorian women were not shy about observing the action at bathing time.

The wooden changing room on wheels was surely supposed to prevent not encourage such impropriety? Without this facility, so we have been led to believe, the beach would have been a dangerous place for the angel of the hearth. Delicate feminine sensibilities imposed by a patriarchal society would have been thrown into disarray by the sight of naked limbs flailing about in the sea and histrionic women in fits of embarrassed apoplexy would have littered the sands. Based upon these implied assumptions it is hard to countenance a greater degree of seaside nudity than we are comfortable with today, among a people who were reputedly so sexually repressed that piano legs had to be covered up in order to avoid causing offence. But what if this was a twentieth century myth, a popular fallacy? Successive generations have done such a good job of impugning Victorian prudery that we have accepted as serious a nineteenth century joke against the perceived over-refinement of middle-class Americans. The notion of piano legs clothed in frilled pantaloons became a sort of shorthand for excessive sensitivity across the pond but, as historian Matthew Sweet has revealed in his book

Inventing the Victorians, there is no evidence that housewives on either side of the Atlantic had recourse to drapery for any other purpose than to protect valuable furniture from damage. Posterity has reworked this ridiculous fiction with impressive solemnity; the Victorians have not simply become the butt of their own joke, the joke itself has disappeared under the scrutiny of academics and psychoanalysts.

So maybe our great-great-great-grandparents deserve a reassessment. On summer beaches the ripple of moral objection was insufficient to halt the rising tide of visitors. That is not to say it was irrelevant; from the 1860s local authorities were compelled to take action to segregate the sexes and force men into bathing drawers but even then the making and enforcing of by-laws turned out to be two very different things. In fact, the persistence of complaints demonstrates that men chose to bathe naked for much of the nineteenth century and women chose to leave the protection of the modesty hood. Day-trippers chose to rush from excursion trains into the sea stripping off as they went, and the assembled crowds of promenaders chose to watch. People made their own moral judgements but the number writing huffy letters to local and national newspapers represented a small proportion of holidaymakers. Refutations appeared less frequently because the people charged with indecent behaviour were too busy enjoying themselves.

Rumbles of discontent about English bathing practices were in evidence by 1800 but the male rejection of clothing was already sanctioned by tradition; none of the bathers depicted at Scarborough in 1735 were wearing a stitch. Health implications also had to be considered. Although the medical imperative lost ground to the pleasure principle during the nineteenth century, the idea that bathing was good for you survived in the popular consciousness. Physicians continued to theorise on its benefits for as Dr Augustus Granville claimed in the early 1840s, 'some of the active principles of sea-water penetrate into the body through the skin'. His belief in human osmosis was backed by personal experience: 'For some hours after bathing in the sea have I often noticed a continuous taste of salt in the mouth...

Men bathed naked throughout the nineteenth century and the practice was still common enough to appear on comic postcards like this one from the Edwardian period.

although not a drop of water had entered the lips during the operation of bathing.' The evidence was clear and the process of unwitting ingestion was, he declared, an admitted fact. Granville's logic reached a compelling crescendo: 'if absorbed, is it likely that a fluid charged with so many distinct and powerful agents shall remain inactive in the midst of life, and within the vortex of animal secretions, and excretions, and circulation? Certainly not.' Hindering this 'mechanical absorption' of marvellous minerals by wearing clothes in the water could, therefore, be considered prejudicial to health.

There was also an undoubted element of machismo in the habit of nude bathing. Bathing in clothes was for girls. According to Romantic aesthetics, the competition between man and ocean could be viewed as a test of virility, so much so that female onlookers were supposed to be impressed rather than affronted by displays of aquatic dash and daring. As the nineteenth century progressed, aggrieved complainants regularly referred to the vastly preferable arrangements in force at French resorts where bathing in drawers was the norm. To the patriotic Englishman, heir to centuries of cross Channel antipathy, this could hardly be seen as much of a recommendation. Bathing in clothes was for girls *and Frenchmen*.

Parisian author and cultural tourist, Francois Wey, sampled the bathing at Brighton during a visit in the early 1850s and confessed his surprise – 'knowing how easily shocked English people are' – at the custom of men taking to the water stark naked. Screened by his bathing machine, Wey entered the sea in this unaccustomed state without trouble; his exit proved to be an entirely less dignified affair. Swimming out so as to enjoy a good panorama of Brighton, the poor Frenchman returned to find that the tide had deserted his cabin, leaving it 'high and dry at fifteen paces from the sea'. More perturbing than this was the presence of three staunch sabbatarian ladies, a mother and her daughters, who, noted locally for their novel means of protesting against Sunday bathing, had settled themselves on camp stools between Wey and his machine. Not wishing to offend these respectable looking women, the unsuspecting foreigner attempted a cautious advance on all fours, 'raising myself by degrees as much as decency permitted'. A brief scan along the beach revealed no seaweed that could be used in place of a fig leaf, and as the serene triumvirate failed to move either themselves or their prayer-books, Wey retreated back to his former exercise. 'But one cannot swim for ever, while one can sit without fatigue for hours.' Torn between the tormentors who

The "Nothing at all" costume!

The downside of nude bathing!

displayed a frustrating repose and a host who, striding along the front whilst making gestures towards his watch, was demonstrating a growing impatience, Wey was forced into action. With a face that would have borne comparison with a well-boiled French lobster, he strode purposely past the three unrepentant ladies back to the shelter of the bathing machine. 'Could one conceive,' he asked his compatriots, of 'a stranger mode of teaching a transgressor to be virtuous or of performing an act of religious fervour?'

Irrespective of medical or macho reasons, the fact remained that many Englishmen genuinely preferred bathing in the buff. The famous diarist Reverend Francis Kilvert visited Weston-Super-Mare in September 1872 and, whilst taking a pre-breakfast dip from a bathing machine, noticed that 'many people were openly stripping on the sands a little further on and running down into the sea'. The lack of a towel prevented him from joining them on that occasion (bathing machine proprietors provided towels as part of the service) but the following day he arrived better prepared; 'There was a delicious feeling of freedom in stripping in the open air and running down naked to the sea, where the waves were curling white with foam and the red morning sunshine glowing upon the naked limbs of the bathers.' More than twenty years later the old custom still had its defenders. 'For a man to thoroughly enjoy a sea bath,' declared one letter to the *Daily Graphic* in September 1895, 'he must be perfectly free and untrammelled from any kind of costume whatsoever.'

But could the enjoyment of the individual be allowed to triumph over consideration for the nation's moral health? If we are to believe the authors of pamphlets and letters against the practice of nude bathing, this was in serious and immediate jeopardy. 'If ladies don't like to see men naked,' asked Kilvert, 'why don't they keep away from the sight?' Concerned husbands and fathers argued that civilised society had a responsibility to protect the weaker sex from such despicable displays. As early as 1818 an anonymous pamphlet made *An Appeal to Common Decency and the Law of the Land Against the Practice of Bathing in Situations Exposed to Public View* arguing against nudity: 'Need more be said in condemnation of such a practice than that it involves a gross insult upon the female part of the community; for it either imputes to them that they are destitute of modesty, or it puts their modesty to the blush.' Habitual exposure to the naked male form would blunt the edges of feminine delicacy and bashful reserve. Once those barriers against barbarism were removed, 'what remains to check the progress of licentiousness and profligacy?' Civilised society would slide inexorably into the gutter all because men refused to swim in drawers. In a letter to *The Times* dated 8 August 1864 a writer going by the pseudonym 'Paterfamilias' compared bathers to South Sea savages, guilty of poisoning an innocent enjoyment and rendering 'what might be recreation both obnoxious and repulsive'. In 1841 one regular visitor to Ramsgate swore never to return after his repeated appeals to local magistrates on the subject were dismissed. He then turned to the Society for the Suppression of Vice who, perhaps conveniently given the scale of the problem, claimed that a lack of funds precluded their interference. Ramsgate was the tip of the naked iceberg.

Respect for the freedom of personal choice kept bathing beyond the realm of legislation for a long time but as ribbons of resort development spread out from the smaller eighteenth century centres the number of complaints about sea views spoiled by the sight of exposed flesh increased. It was all about location, location, location. The 1818 pamphleteer claimed that 'at numerous watering places on the sea coast, in canals, ponds, and rivers, great numbers of men, devoid of all sense of shame, are accustomed to bathe openly, in the immediate view of inhabited houses, or before frequented roads or paths'. And as the number of seafront lodging houses, hotels and esplanades multiplied to cope with rising tourist demand the number expecting to bathe, with or without their clothes, also rapidly grew. In 1809 a young man who maintained his right to bathe where and whenever he pleased was tried before Lord Chief Baron Macdonald. Arguing that the disputed bathing spot near Brighton had existed some twenty-five years before any houses had been built, the defence reasoned that the nuisance was caused not by the indicted bather but by the new dwellings, the residents of which had no right to complain. Although there was no evidence that the defendant had committed any wanton indecency or exposed himself any more than was necessary for the purpose of bathing, the Judge nonetheless urged jurors to consider the seriousness of the case. Wherever houses come, decency must come with them for if this principle be not adhered to, said His Worship, 'these persons might run about naked in Bedford-square, which is modern, and the building of which I remember'. Not wishing to set such a dangerous precedent the jury returned a guilty verdict.

There was no flurry of copycat convictions but, for the outraged writer who recounted the details of this test case, prevention was always better than punishment. Among his bright ideas was the institution of a sort of neighbourhood watch scheme against nudity! Such a plan might have been adopted at Gravesend had the alleged scenes along the shore not ruled out the participation of half the population. On 16 August 1842 a family man staying in the town protested to the Editor of *The Times* that the 'position of the machines close to the only good "marine" walk that Gravesend can boast of is sufficiently objectionable, but when the owners of them permit their customers to create so great a nuisance as to prevent females appearing at the windows of the hotel or lodging-house, to say nothing of the impossibility of walking out, I think it is high time that the supineness of the local authorities should be made known'. Whichever party was in the wrong, the restrictions imposed by well-meaning middle class patriarchs on their families must have made for some very dull holidays.

Moralists had a tendency to lump all bathers together as a bad lot but there were plenty who made the best of the privacy afforded by bathing machines or indeed sought out less crowded locations. This latter option could have its own perils as *The Times* reported on 5 August 1843. Visiting the 'far-famed bathing town of Redcar, Yorkshire' a husband and wife rejected the restrictions of bathing from a machine in favour of taking their 'phaeton to a favourable spot two miles up the sands, the lady providing herself with a bathing dress, the gentleman, as gentlemen generally do when bathing, declining such encumbrance'. The couple undressed on the sands and deposited their clothes in the carriage before wading out into the waves. Well, you know what's coming next. Scarcely had they 'recovered from their first "dip" when to their dismay they observed the horse trot with the carriage, dresses and all, leaving them in the primitive state of our first parents'. The lady, barefoot and bedraggled, walked to Marske to recount her comic tale and secure suitable clothes for her now prune-like husband who remained 'patiently enduring his woeful plight, though up to his chin in the water'. A late nineteenth cartoon in *Punch* suggested that no matter how far away bathers ventured there would always be someone

Modesty hoods were no protection against seaside voyeurism particularly when men used telescopes to satisfy their curiosity.

ready to complain. Under the heading 'A Nuisance', Miss Priscilla observed that she did indeed have a beautiful view from her window: 'But tourists are in the habit of bathing on the opposite shore, and that's rather a drawback.' The Fair Visitor sympathised, 'Dear me! But at such a distance as that – surely – ', 'Ah,' replied Miss Priscilla, 'but with a *telescope*, you know!'

The use of visual aids to spy on bathers has a heritage as long as bathing itself. Telescopes were standard equipment in the Margate bathing rooms and, whilst queuing for a machine in the late 1700s, time could be passed in idle maritime gazing. Of course, the sea was a crucial and busy highway then but even the most innocent eye might linger over the activities of budding mermen and maids whilst ship spotting. Satirists focused upon the less innocent spectators, giving the impression that seaside Peeping Tom-ism was approaching the realms of a competitive sport by the turn of the century. If the bathing machine was a seaside fixture so was the dirty old man – but which was the chicken and which the egg? Both persevered long enough to become the stock in trade of saucy seaside postcards. The Victorians created their own caricature of the aged swell, stationed near the ladies' machines with his stiff curling whiskers and cap perched jauntily upon

THE AMATEUR PHOTO CLUB.
A NICELY DEVELOPED PLATE, (& GIRL.)

As technology developed the telescopes of peeping-Tom's were replaced by cameras.

a balding head: 'How fascinatingly he laughs, then mutters something in a tender voice, and every now and then he raises his eye-glass and looks intently, as a young lady in a brown gown, with long fair hair streaming down her shoulders, jumps up in the water, or runs to meet the waves.' One disgruntled bather, fed up with being ogled at Brighton in 1850, was moved to remind gentlemen (an appeal to ruffians and blackguards obviously being useless) that moving on to rowing a boat between the machines absolutely was NOT appropriate behaviour. Her letter of objection, published in *The Times* on 4 September 1850, had been penned after first hand experience of a man laying down his telescope in order to take up oars, the better to gratify his 'brutal curiosity'.

The relative informality of the beach made it a battleground for sexual politics. Women criticised men; men criticised other men; men criticised women for not being critical enough of other men. Terrible though it was to admit the existence of females who could unblushingly watch members of the opposite sex bathing, worse was the fact that at Ramsgate they were 'respectable-looking' and at Scarborough their sisters were 'elegantly-apparelled'. In autumn 1841 letters appeared in *The Times* disparaging the behaviour of female visitors who, at the former resort, made use of chairs and seats close to the water's edge not far from 'several men bathing, who appeared rather to have pleasure in exposing themselves than otherwise'. There was evidently something disturbing about women who were expected to play the role of shrinking violets coming out into the literal and metaphoric sunshine. From a modern perspective, however, this evidence of holiday spirit makes Victorian beachgoers both more interesting and less alien, not least because when questioned on the subject, local trades people claimed that 'the chairs and benches had been frequently removed to a decent distance from the machines, and had been as frequently brought back again'. Small wonder then that watering places were accused of having a bizarre transformative effect upon English ladies and gentlemen: 'no sooner do they arrive than they seem to give up their decorum with their rail or boat ticket and to adopt practices which at home they would shudder even to read of.'

Behind all the rhetorical outrage were scenes of people having fun. Strip away the moral chagrin and you will find women who not only sat unabashedly close to the oncoming waves but also went out beyond the bathing machines to greet them. According to a letter on the subject of 'Bathing at Ramsgate' published by *The Times* on 25 August 1846, the 'gentler sex'

> ... do not confine their water frolics to the bath under the awning, but boldly, and I must add, indelicately, wander away, and so expose themselves to the vulgar throng, who are all on the look out; they do not take half-a-dozen plunges (which really are all that are required for healthful purposes), but they remain for nearly half an hour sporting like mermaids in the sea, forgetting how unbecoming is their appearance, and that the waves, either coming in or receding, repeatedly force up their loose dresses, and so expose parts of their delicate frames, which, ...to pronounce elsewhere would be considered most indelicate; they do

not go singly, nor in pairs, but actually endeavour to get up
a sort of polka or gallop [sic] in the water.

It is indicative of altered expectations that a young governess visiting
Ramsgate a couple of decades later complained of peeping Toms
hindering her enjoyment as much as offending her modesty: 'the glory
of sea bathing, as you know, is to do as you like in the water, to plunge
about as wildly as you like, and to feel that you are free to do so.'

Women, young and old, were beginning to learn to swim but the old
sack-shaped gowns, whose failings were relished by opera-glass-wielding
voyeurs, were letting them down. Increasing attempts at self-propulsion
were also problematic whilst machines used by men and women remained
close together. Though at mid-century Broadstairs was considered to be
the 'aristocratic bathing-station of Kent', the nine machines available to
autumn bathers were 'huddled together in the harbour, close to the boats
and other craft'. The gap between machines was only three or four feet,
the entire line squeezed into a mere forty-five yards of beach 'from which

SEASIDE PUZZLE
To find your bathing-machine if you've forgotten the number

A *Punch* cartoon highlighting the difficulty of returning to the correct bathing machine
at Ramsgate.

ladies, gentlemen, and children are compelled promiscuously to take their bath'. At nearby Ramsgate (a resort that seems simultaneously to have attracted some of the most and least liberal tourists in the country) the bathing place presented 'a gross mixture of machines for both sexes', partly as a result of rival companies jostling for custom in a bottleneck at the end of a narrow road. Though ladies were pulled out into a designated area near the pier the actual separation of the sexes was negligible; the gap

FORCE OF HABIT.

Shop Girl (to bather who has mistaken his machine):
"What can I have the pleasure of showing you, sir?"

BAMFORTH (Copyright).

Attempting to enter the wrong machine could have embarrassing consequences.

between them and the gentlemen was often no more than the breadth of two bathing machines whilst the ladies' portion of the beach was a spectators' free for all.

If the possibility of physical contact was too far beyond the pale to permit specific mention, the risk that forgetful swimmers might return to the wrong bathing machine became a well-tested theme for cartoonists. The huge embarrassment potential of such a situation was exploited for comic purposes because it could easily happen. As the American journalist J. Howe Adams noted in 1895, English 'bathing-masters follow the ebb and rise of the tide religiously; as a result it is no uncommon matter to find that one's machine has been shifted many feet from its original position, and the bather is then compelled to spend many weary minutes hunting for his own particular van. As the little houses are as alike as peas in a pod, he is likely to ruffle the tempers of the occupants of the other vans, if not his own, by breaking in upon their privacy in an apparently unpardonable manner'. By-laws, such as those enacted at the relatively early date of 1857 in Folkestone, dictated that all licensed bathing machines should be painted with a conspicuous white number on a black background, at least an inch and a half in height. At stretches of coastline packed with machines, numbers were made considerably more visible. Nevertheless, the modest maiden aunt who refused to take off her glasses in a *Punch* cartoon ("My dear, I positively won't take off anything more, I'm determined!!") was probably well advised to maintain every possible advantage in that 'hunt for one's bathing machine [which] constitutes one of the daily joys of English bathing'.

Puffing their way over new rails to the coast, steam engines hauled excited carriage loads of holidaymakers and excursionists to stay for several weeks or just several hours. The sea was the main attraction and it was getting crowded. By the summer of '56 the waters at Margate and Ramsgate were described as 'black with bathers'. Middle-class visitors with disposable income provided a mid-century surge in numbers and bathing machine proprietors looked on happily as newcomers clambered aboard to swell their profits. People lower down the social pecking order also benefited from ever-increasing opportunities to leave the smoggy cities following the success of cheap train tickets to the Great Exhibition of 1851. Artisans from the Lancashire cotton towns enjoyed an established tradition of once yearly mixed, naked sea-bathing. Known in Blackpool as 'Padjamers' they would travel in their hundreds by horse and cart to the Fylde coast. After the coming of the railways they travelled in their thousands; busy July and August weekends in the 1850s might witness twelve times the previous level of excursionists. On the other side of the country a well-worn bathing story went as follows:

There once arrived at Scarborough by an excursion train, or 'chape trip,' as the natives say, a party of miners, two of whom hastened down to the beach to bathe. As they undressed one said to the other, 'Hey, Sam, hoo mooky thou is!' 'Aw miss'd t'chape trip last year,' was the laconic and very significant reply.

Working class visitors from the Midlands put their bums on the seats of trains heading for Great Yarmouth where, in 1860, a local newspaper described them rather affectionately as 'buxom, jolly, holiday-seeking people who picnic on the sands, eat very thick sandwiches, and always tell the folks at home that they have been in a bathing machine'.

But had they really? The boast about using a bathing machine is a telling comment upon the price of this equipment. A half-hour dip could cost the same as the return journey to the seaside. As a result, many trippers who wanted to bathe simply went ahead and undressed on the beach. Established resort users were not happy about this disturbance to their peace. They were not happy at all. Fearful of upsetting affluent visitors to Dawlish, the South Devon Railway only agreed to offer a cheap six-penny return fare to those who caught the first train from Exeter and then caught the first train back. Despite working-class bathers being allowed a maximum of just one hour and ten minutes at their destination, tourists spending their long summer holidays in Dawlish were horrified to find that these poor men and women did not form an orderly queue for the machines. Never one to miss an opportunity for filling his diary with erotic anecdotes, Revd Kilvert confessed his amazement at the behaviour of a crowd of rail-trippers who swarmed onto Seaton beach in 1871. He looked on at the girls, 'with shoes, stockings and drawers off, wading in the tide, holding up their clothes nearly to their waists and naked from the waist down'. Even the sickly consumptives soaking up the warm air of Torquay were not immune to scenes of spontaneous bathing. In August 1887 the quiet of a sunny

Saturday afternoon was shattered 'when a number of working men...
whisked off their clothes and ran like savages into the sea'.

Accounts like these offer up easy stereotypes of the shocked rich
man and the shameless poor man but there was a middle ground
and resort authorities were, for the most part, trying to hang on to it.
The sheer numbers of visitors meant that some sort of intervention
was required and it was often to appease the concerns of wealthy, big
spending tourists that seaside towns sought the powers of local self-
governance. At the most popular resorts pressure on finite bathing
grounds could be immense, especially at high tide. Elite visitors who
hadn't already moved on to the Continent or to more exclusive British
resorts could not be expected to put up with the lack of privacy, the lack
of decency and the surplus of spectators for much longer. In the 1780s
men and women were required to bathe separately at Blackpool. Ladies
took their turn first and any gentleman seen on the parade between the
ringing of the bells that marked women's hour would forfeit a bottle of
wine. Civilised though this segregation was, there were neither bells
loud enough, nor wine cellars big enough, to cope with the influx of up
to 40,000 excursionists at a time a century later. Bournemouth was sure
enough of its customer base to ban Sunday rail trippers until 1914 but
elsewhere commercial and moral issues were harder to disentangle.

Scarborough Town Council was petitioned by local clergy and local
inhabitants to act upon the subject of nude male bathing in the summer
of 1866. Not only did protesters consider the practice morally reprehen-
sible but, they argued, it was also driving away respectable visitors. By
cunningly introducing an economic angle into the debate the moralists forced councillors to pay attention. They were still paying attention
when the bathing machine proprietors submitted a counter petition
stating: 'We know from past experience that first-class visitors object
to wearing drawers when bathing...Scarborough will necessarily lose its
fame for want of good families who have hitherto come here to bathe
according to ancient usage.' Damage to any sector of the lucrative bathing trade was to be avoided at all costs so the authorities came up with

a wonderfully English solution: compromise. A by-law was passed requiring men to wear drawers in the main bathing area in front of the Spa. Unless, that is, they took to the water before seven in the morning or after nine at night when it was still alright to bathe naked. In fact, if they were prepared to bathe anywhere other than the central sands no time limit was set to the custom of stripping for a dip.

As this instance suggests, the draconian regulations lain down

The bathing facilities are limited

Bathing costumes and towels were usually hired with the machine.

in local statute books provide only half the story and, to some extent, represent an ideal rather than an actual record of bathing practices. During the second half of the century, resorts around the country attempted to legislate men into covering up. Rather than compelling bathers to purchase their own costumes, the responsibility for providing suitable drawers and gowns fell to bathing machine proprietors. Given that the standard period of hire was half an hour, these clothes would cling to an awful lot of different shaped bodies over the season. Even if new models could optimistically be expected to appear in July, repeated soakings in salt water and wringings through the mangle must have ensured September bathers a decidedly well-washed look. Enjoying a bathe at Seaton in 1873 Revd Kilvert realised too late that one of the two towels with which he attempted to dry himself was in fact 'a pair of very short red and white striped drawers to cover my nakedness'. Unable to claim ignorance of the 'detestable custom of bathing in drawers', at Shanklin the following year he submitted to the shorts. Neither the clergyman nor the costume emerged well from the experience: 'Today I had a pair of drawers given me which I could not keep on. The rough waves stripped them off and tore them down round my ancles [sic]. While thus fettered I was seized and flung down by a heavy sea which retreating left me lying naked on the sharp shingle from which I rose streaming with blood. After this I took the wretched and dangerous rag off and of course there were some ladies looking on as I came up out of the water.'

Conversion cannot always have been so painful because by the end of the century the majority of male bathers were wearing some form of drawers. Notwithstanding the adoption of this garment, an American magazine reporter advised readers that they were likely to be gob-smacked by the 'remarkable garb of the bathing Englishman. This costume is nothing but the familiar swimming-tights worn by American boys when they slip away for a quiet swim to some unfrequented spot on lake or river'. J. Howe Adams described stepping out semi-naked in front of 5,000 Brighton beach goers as embarrassingly unforgettable. He conceded that feeling the reaction of salt water on the skin was an advantage but 'an American boy in an English suit would hide in the bushes on the approach of a passer-by'. And women's costumes in 1895 were no less startling to the Stateside visitor.

Over the previous forty years improvements had been made to the basic bathing gown, dictated as much by an increasing fashion consciousness as by concerns of modesty. Amelia Bloomer's eponymous gathered trousers were not a success on the city streets but by the early 1860s they had become the standard bathing-dress on British and French beaches, worn with a knee-length or thigh-length short-sleeved jacket. Blue and red were popular colours for those who could afford to make a style

statement when step-
ping from their bathing
machine. Thick fabrics
such as flannel or serge
were generally used be-
cause flimsy silks and
cottons clung too re-
vealingly to the body.
That this was an impor-
tant consideration for
purchasers is clear from
the fact that most bath-
ing dresses were adver-
tised as 'not showing
the figure when wet'.
By the end of the next
decade straight knee-
length trousers had re-
placed 'bloomers' and
fashion writers were
dispensing advice on

A deliberately titillating view of women's bathing costumes from the early twentieth century.

what the well-dressed bather should be wearing. In 1870 drawers tied below the knee with scarlet ribbon were all the rage. Seven years later deep pink and blue were the colours of the season. The discomfort of a shingly beach was relieved by the excuse it provided to wear the fashionable footwear of flat ballet shoes tied on with ribbons around the ankle.

As female costumes got progressively smaller, male costumes got bigger. By the 1880s both sexes were wearing a similar one-piece garment that came down to the knees and elbows. This decade saw women aspiring to an extremely slim silhouette so for a few years corseted costumes became fashionable. Visiting Great Yarmouth in 1888, William Miller was struck by the number of ladies who 'fancy the tight-fitting pink bathing dress'. At Ramsgate he gazed at the sea 'filled with a heap of mingled pale-faced and rosy nymphs in scanty and dripping attire, and all sorts of little cockneys...sans gloves, sans well-brushed hat, sans slender silk umbrella, and sans almost anything'. Keeping up with the latest trends is only really worthwhile if other people are aware that you are doing it and female bathers quite clearly knew that they would be observed by men lounging on the beach as well as by their sister bathers. So as the necklines of evening dresses plunged towards the *fin-de-siecle* so did those of bathing costumes. J. Howe Adams noticed how 'these suits are cut, as a rule, quite low in the neck, frequently being as low as a décoletté ball gown, necessitating considerable care on the part of wearers to keep them from being washed away by the waves'. The ever present moralists also realised that such attire was not designed simply to decorate the inside of a bathing machine and for this reason they remained reproachful despite the existence of laws to segregate the sexes whilst bathing.

There was no universal standard for the accepted distance that should be observed between bathing machines. Folkestone specified just twenty feet whereas Lowestoft, praised by *The Daily Mail* in July 1896 as 'one of our best managed, most orderly and most lavishly adorned' watering places, stipulated that 'a person of the female sex shall not, while bathing, approach within *one hundred yards* [300 feet] of any place at which any person of the male sex, above the age of *twelve years*, may be set down for the purpose of bathing'. Some resorts had coastal geography on their side. Dawlish designated separate ladies' and gentlemen's bathing beaches although the latter, at Coryton Cove, was only approachable by walking along the former. Bathers at both beaches were also subject to the passing stares of rail passengers travelling along one of the Westcountry's most scenic lines. Probably the most effectively segregated bathing areas were to be found at Ilfracombe, a circumstance that makes the North Devon resort's reputation as the 'The Mecca of Honeymooners' all the more surprising. Walls were built up at The Tunnels to connect rocks and create two large pools separated, each from the other, by an extending arm of the cliff. Mrs Anthony Trollope expressed her satisfaction at the ladies' pool: 'It is a deeply-sheltered cove of exquisite beauty, looking so sacredly apart that it is impossible to enter it without feeling that Diana and her dainty train might here indulge in playing with the cold, clear water for ever, without fearing any audacious hunter's eye or fisher's either.' A guide book of 1897 asked if anybody would ever 'discover the reason why Ilfracombe creates for itself such a subtle magnetic charm in the minds of the newly-married?' Magnetic or otherwise, it certainly had nothing to do with the bathing arrangements.

The political will to forcibly divide husbands from wives, sons from mothers and fathers from daughters was a phenomenon of the second half of the nineteenth century that seems incomprehensible now. Whether the proscribed distance was tens or hundreds of feet, family bathing was essentially prohibited. Mr Howe Adams wrote plainly that the 'English bath is stupid and unpleasant'. Having visited various resorts on behalf of his American readers, Adams considered that the claim to privacy represented by sexual segregation was, in practice, largely pointless: 'the English, being only human, have not carried out their ideas as consistently as they might have done. The bathing-grounds of the two sexes...are, as a rule, only a few hundred feet distant from each other; consequently, each set of bathers is in plain sight of the other, while the beach at each point is often crowded with men and women watching the bathing.' As a result, he concluded, 'as far as any seclusion or privacy is concerned, the bathers might just as well use the same grounds'. There is certainly evidence that some English tourists agreed and, as prosecutions seem to have been extremely rare, the authorities, having mollified the moralists with strict words, frequently failed to enforce their apparently harsh by-laws.

Margate Town Council finally gave in to pressure for regulation in 1862, decreeing that all bathers wear costumes and that a distance of not less than sixty feet be maintained between male and female machines. This would have been a triumph for supporters of the local

Modelling the latest style at the door of a bathing machine. Costumes were increasingly designed to be seen but could be quite revealing when wet.

newspaper campaign that compelled the Council into action had these new by-laws not been routinely ignored. Two years later the *Observer* dismissed the rules as 'mere waste paper' and in 1866 protested that the sexes were still bathing together, that for every man wearing drawers there were ten who did not, and that 'the authorities were openly set at defiance...for the simple reason that offenders know they will not prosecute.' Nor did the threat of punishment hang heavy upon the lady at Broadstairs who, in 1874, delighted 'in swimming to the head of the pier with her nude and whiskered friend on her back'. Even at a fashionable, high-class resort like Bournemouth, bathing remained difficult to police with the limited resources available. Men who declined to wear drawers were a commonplace and in 1885, a visiting Scotsman noted that there was a great deal of unofficial mixed and family bathing (with costumes) taking place amongst people who could afford to hire machines for the purpose.

In its designation of separate male and female bathing areas Brighton made an early start, passing by-laws in 1825 and stating a distance 'long enough one would think to meet the scruples of even the most prudish and fastidious'. Forty years later the resort authorities further stipulated that after seven in the morning nobody was permitted to bathe from a machine without suitable clothing. This sort of legislation always presupposed a level of income that left working class visitors with a hugely unfair choice between giving up their desire to bathe and committing a crime. Recognising this problem, some resorts did create public bathing stations, usually away from the most populous areas, where people (ie. men) were permitted to undress on the beach. At Brighton this facility was restricted to the hours before eight in the morning and after eight in the evening when it was expected that drawers should be worn. Despite these constraints the bathing stations were extremely well used – though not entirely according to the regulations. 'It is estimated that during June, July and early August, on an average, 8,000 persons bathe from the beach per week, or an average of 500 daily from each of the stations. Fully one-fourth of this number bathe without any covering whatever.' With such large numbers it was almost impossible to enforce the no drawers, no bathe rule. 'Two or three of the most efficient and best disposed constables in the force are powerless to deal with the impatient and undiciplined [sic] crowds, who nightly throng our public bathing places during the warm summer nights, and it may well be doubted whether double the number of policemen stationed there would be one whit more efficacious.'

Concerned to alleviate a situation that in 1871 saw the law 'almost as much honoured in the breach as in the observance', a writer who adopted the pseudonym 'Piscator' suggested that one answer might be the provision of cheap, stationary bathing machines 'which have become quite popular at many of our watering-places'. The by-laws fixed the fares chargeable for machine hire but 'many of the better class of mechanics and artisans, who cannot afford 6d., or even 3d. for a bath, would not begrudge 1d., or even 2d'. Expanding the principle of Benjamin Beale's modesty hood, Piscator also proposed that temporary awnings could be stretched over the bathing station as an inexpensive and practical solution. But what is most interesting about this pamphlet is the attention it pays to the neglected subject of a working-class woman's equal right to bathe. Putting aside Piscator's disclaimer against the more general movement for women's rights and his dubious opinion that women are better adapted to the exercise of swimming because 'their bodies are generally of less specific gravity, and consequently float more easily whether in fresh or salt water', this author nevertheless asserted that women, like men, had the inalienable right 'to life, health and happiness without barrier or restriction' and, furthermore, that it was their unquestionable right to use the public bathing stations.

And yet they were provided with no suitable accommodation; whereas 149 machines were provided 'for the class fortunate enough to be able to pay for them', not one was within the reach of their less favoured sisters. This disgraceful state of affairs precluded thousands of poorer women from contact with the sea, thereby depriving them of the means for 'complying with the Gospel injunction – "Wash and be clean!" In a seaside town of more than 100,000 inhabitants there were three bathing stations for men but none for their wives and daughters. 'Women in this matter have apparently been deserted... Only occasionally, and then in out of the way, obscure corners, has a voice been raised on their behalf, and even this in a feeble deprecatory, shamefaced sort of way, that augurs little real interest in, or regard for, the cause it espouses.'

As far as Victorian bathing practices were concerned men undoubtedly got the better deal; their freedoms were certainly the least curtailed. Yet it would be wrong to see the bathing machine purely as a symbol of sexism and prudery. However much these wheeled wooden huts carried the weight of new and restrictive by-laws they did not, on their own, possess the power to circumvent the activities of people seeking to enjoy the experience of bathing. François Wey, the unfortunate Frenchman on the receiving end of a peculiar sort of evangelical moralising, commented upon the inconsistency of English

prudishness. 'In reality it is mostly offended by *words*.' Body parts that
were considered too delicate to speak of were, for most of the century,
regularly exposed up and down the coast. 'An Innocent Spectator',
annoyed by the misguided protests against Brighton bathers in 1846,
questioned the motivation of these Mr and Mrs Grundys in a letter to
The Times of 10 September:

> ...I should like to know who are the people that see or feel
> anything improper in looking at a man or woman enjoying
> a bathe? Are they moral, well-principled youths? – are they
> innocent and pure-minded maidens? No. I will answer
> for it that the man whose mind is ever filled with impure
> thoughts is the one who sees immorality and indecency in
> this innocent amusement. There is so much of this false
> delicacy in the present day, and yet I doubt if we are a whit
> more moral than our ancestors, who spoke of things as they
> were, and called a spade a spade.

The Victorian era was not one unmitigated period of sexual
abstinence – we would hardly be here if that were true. The sliding
scale of moral standards may have encompassed a more profound
disapproval of contact between men and women than we can conceive
possible today but this was by no means universal.

The cultural tensions evident in different people's bathing habits
demonstrate just how complicated the situation was – and just how
unprepared many people were to submit to the imposition of ridiculously
restrictive by-laws. The Victorian beach was a much livelier place than
the black and white images of serried bathing machines would lead
us to believe. Visitors from abroad were genuinely surprised by the
licence exhibited in English bathing practices but there is something
reassuringly familiar in Monsieur Wey's analysis of our national
propensity to contrasting values: 'When English people are not icicles,
they are apt to become shameless...So decency is a mere convention –

the expression is guarded and language intolerant, but in reality, it is only censorious not sincere. You will find English girls talking of love without more scruple or emotion than a housewife discussing jam-making or spring cleaning.'

Chapter Nine
Whitstable to Eastbourne

Whitstable beach huts can be expensive but £75,000 is definitely well above the going rate. For that price you'd expect something a bit special. What Charles Saatchi got in 1999 was not a prime seafront plot, or any sea at all, but a work of art that had once been Tracey Emin's weekend retreat. Paint peeling from its dark blue sides and a plywood patch above its door, the battered hut was installed in the white space of Saatchi's gallery with photographs of the naked artist placed inside and the title 'The Last Thing I Said Was Don't Leave Me'. In Whitstable's tourist information office the lady behind the desk proudly told me of the town's claim to BritArt fame. She didn't believe it was a coincidence that there were more new huts than ever on Tankerton Slopes. Tracey Emin might have removed her hut from the beach but she'd still managed to make the ones she left behind cool.

On the train from London my first glimpse of the coast was accompanied by huts; the track into Whitstable ran directly behind West Beach. Although these were not the first huts along the North Kent coast they were the most visible and the most accessible for city dwellers reliant upon public transport. Geographically close yet distinctly remote from its up-and-coming Oyster Festival-holding neighbour, Seasalter lay on the western outskirts of Whitstable, a ribbon of post-war bungalow development between marshland and a pebble-strewn beach. Though it could boast a holiday camp and sailing club, Seasalter did not look especially appealing on a dull day. A battered sign on the beach warned that the sand beyond was private, presumably for the sole use of people inhabiting the motley line of beach chalets. Just a couple of months before my visit the sale of one of these, with UPVC cladding, double glazing and a fitted kitchen, had led to a bidding war. The new owner would be able to make it his permanent residence for up to eleven months of the year and had paid £71,000 for the privilege, a handsome £16,000 over the guide price. Past the chalets was a row of green day huts so I turned trespasser and went to take a closer look. All ten of them were shuttered and locked, a fact not lost on the cavorting couple just visible in the distance. I had to look twice but, yes, there was a naked bottom pumping in and out of view. If Tracey Emin had unwittingly assisted in the smartening up of Whitstable I couldn't help thinking that she would be pleased to know it still had some ribald edges.

The best place to see the West Beach huts was from above. I'd walked in front of the two stubby-legged rows but enjoyed the panoramic effect from on top of the railway bridge more. Immediately in front of me was a green bunkered strip of golf course and then snaking above the shingle came the huts in multiple shades of blue with intermittent reds and yellows. Lots of them looked new but for such an apparently popular spot there was a lot of mud between the huts and the sea. I'd seen glossy photo spreads showing some pretty bijou interior decoration down here and was hoping to get at least a glimpse of the stripy curtains and retro furnishings so beloved of magazine stylists. Unfortunately a grey Monday morning proved completely the wrong time for this kind of nosiness. Only a couple of huts were open and from what I could see they had failed to adopt the trendy urbanites vision of beach hut living. I hoped to have more luck on Tankerton Slopes, where Canterbury City Council was running a 'Best Kept Hut' competition as part of the Oyster Festival.

The town centre was busy, with its independent shops seemingly doing good business. By trading on its strengths Whitstable had managed to make the enviable transition from old-fashioned to fashionable seaside resort. The parallel had even been drawn between artsy New Yorkers heading to the Hamptons and cool Londoners escaping to seaside boltholes at Whitstable. Like at Southwold, beach huts seemed to be a big part of that. So much so that the Hotel Continental had bought up several old fishing huts and turned them into luxury beach hut guestrooms. For those who favoured a grittier location – quite literally – there was a short line of gabled huts in the shadow of the harbourside 'blacktop' plant, where they'd been mixing raw ingredients into tarmac since the 1930s. Its twenty-five metre high tower dwarfed the huts offering a starker, more industrial backdrop than the rolling grass slopes and detached seafront houses at Tankerton.

There the huts were wider than they were deep, with front verandas and stumpy legs which helped them climb the gentle incline away from the sea. Among the rows, often three or four deep, were lots of new huts, some still in the naked colour of their timber construction. Others wore much brighter shades but my vote for Tankerton's 'Best Kept Hut' went, without question, to the superbly striped 'Upper Deck', near the far end of the front row. The walls were red and white, each horizontal plank of wood carefully coloured; on the balusters of the veranda and the planks of the window and door shutters the stripes were in a contrasting vertical. Under the hut, the stilted platform was French navy blue with the same colour applied to the stair and balcony rails. It must have taken ages, a real labour of love and, of all the huts I'd seen, no other had embraced the nautical possibilities of colour with such vivacity. Forget Tracey Emin, *this* was a work of art.

Whereas the future looked rosy for Whitstable huts, the same could not be said at Swalecliffe. Along the coast towards Herne Bay, chalet owners were campaigning to save their community of mini-holiday homes from extinction. It was the East Mersea battle all over again; people who cherished their little wooden huts and landowners who looked at static caravans and saw pound signs. Strange how, in such close proximity, day huts at Whitstable and their holiday camp cousins at Swalecliffe could be facing such different prospects.

With that thought in mind I was pleased to see the familiar hut line on my arrival at Herne Bay. I hadn't been back since the trip in November 1998 when my affair with beach huts began so, to savour my return, I decided to make my walk along the shingle in the early sunlight before breakfast. It was absurdly exciting to be back. Life-changing experiences are rare and even if beach huts aren't an obvious catalyst I knew that seeing them that winter's day had influenced me in a way I could never have foretold. It sounds implausible; I couldn't really explain it nor, as it turned out, could I replicate it. Walking along the row for a second time I willed that original feeling to return but it didn't. My first reaction had been emotional and wholly irrational; perhaps I knew too much to be so impressed second time around. I knew, for example, that the 300 Herne Bay huts were relatively unusual for being on the actual beach but I also knew that in terms of design and construction they were pretty typical. I took some more photos and, as I made my way back towards the town, my attention was drawn to on an odd little building out at sea. The derelict kiosk, topped by an oriental onion dome, had once been the end of Herne Bay pier. Now it was marooned, little more than an over-sized bird table, never likely to be reunited with its landward end. Over the past week I'd walked along the two longest piers in the country; in its glory days Herne Bay had been the third but I wouldn't be making that particular promenade. It was time to visit the bays of Thanet and turn the corner of Kent's coast.

From Minnis Bay to Ramsgate the map showed fourteen Bays, one Sands and a Gap. Of these, nine could boast council huts all done out in a livery of white walls and either sky-blue or sunshine-yellow doors. Despite this uniform colour scheme I found a surprising architectural diversity, which transformed the Thanet bays into a kind of open-air museum of beach hut design. On the sands there were flimsy bathing boxes no wider than their double front doors; there were huts with broad fronts and low gabled roofs, boxy huts with roofs sloping front to back and sturdier interwar huts with neo-Tudor gable ends; there were 1930s bathing stations at West Bay and Viking Bay; and there were wooden rows with simple verandas, brick, concrete and even pebble-dashed rows. And that's not counting the private huts. It took me a good three days to get around them all!

An odd smell lingered over Minnis Bay and when I arrived the high tide was a strangely dark colour. The water was thick with seaweed, so soupy that when the waves hit they made a schlock rather than a crash against the concrete defences. I watched a man who'd been in for a swim come out, put on a fluorescent jacket and pick up his sweeper's trolley and brooms. He told me that the Council filled trucks with the weed then dumped it back out at sea but it always found its way back. The locals were used to it and there was clearer water beyond the waves.

'It's quite bad this year,' a woman on one of the eighty individual hut plots agreed, 'but it usually comes at some point in the summer.'

She brought her children down to the beach every day during the school holidays and it didn't sound like a bit of seaweed would put her off. The gang of teenage boys on the slipway didn't seem too upset either; they were flinging great handfuls of weed at each other with the abandon of evident enjoyment.

At Minnis Bay I got my first taste of the council-owned huts, three different freestanding wooden types and a couple of more permanent rows with red brick end walls and pebble-dash fronts. West Bay had a similar variety although behind the central promenade there was also a concrete colonnade of squared arches, each gap filled with its own built-in beach hut. Next was St Mildred's, rather narrower than West Bay but squashed with huts. Two stood out along the privately owned row and I went to talk to the owner of number twenty-two about her patriotic paint job. The hut was mostly white but a bright red cross was clearly visible across its open front. An integral shutter was hinged horizontally above the entrance so that it could rest on the double doors to provide extra shade for the middle-aged lady who was sat outside in her swimsuit.

'I've got the Cross of St George,' she told me, 'and number twenty-six, painted with the Italian flag, that one belongs to my brother.'

They were big football fans in her family: 'We painted mine this year because of the World Cup, you know, to show our support.'

She'd had the hut for six years and was happy to reveal it had been a present for her fortieth birthday. 'I'd always wanted my own beach hut.'

In the middle of the promenade was a row of brand new huts, their timber still showing the greenish tinge of very new wood. The lady at number twenty-two told me how they'd been built by prisoners in Liverpool who'd been bussed down to Kent to erect them on site. I'd heard of plenty of beach huts being used for recuperation purposes but these were the first that were part of a rehabilitation programme.

My final bay of the day was Westbrook, in shouting distance of Margate and location of the sadly derelict Royal Sea Bathing Hospital. By now the tide was out revealing a wide arc of beach, albeit with a high-water fringe of that noisome seaweed. The yellow and blue council huts were concentrated in groups below the grassy cliff while on the sands a wonky collection of old bathing boxes and private stained-wood huts sat with their backs against the seawall. In a simple white hut with a not-quite-flat roof, I met Ron who'd been coming to Margate from York for the past thirty years.

'I come the same four weeks every year and go home before the school kids come down,' the Yorkshire man told me. 'I really keep coming back for the people.'

Two gents at the other end of the bay confirmed the strong sense of community among hutters, be they locals or holidaymakers like Ron. Both men were retired and claimed to enjoy the beach hut as an escape from their wives.

'I don't know what we'd do without the huts,' said one.

'We'd have to decorate or mow the lawn,' chipped in the other.

The next two weeks would be really busy with an influx of visitors at the beginning of the school holidays. It sounded like Margate still had a loyal following even if it was less numerous than in the past. The first man looked me in the eye:

'If you'd told me, aged twenty, that I was going to move to Margate and spend my days in a beach hut I'd 'ave knocked you round the head. I definitely wouldn't have believed you. Thing is, I love it.'

Unfortunately, Margate's appeal was harder to see now than at any point since it became a tourist resort in the early eighteenth century. I was disappointed to see that the only huts on the main Marine Sands were for deckchair hire. The bathing empires of Hancock's and Pettman's were long gone. Benjamin Beale, inventor of the bathing machine, was remembered in the name of a pub on Fort Hill but the pub was closed and boarded up. The Cliftonville Lido had been filled in with sand and the fantastically confident 1930s brick cinema of Dreamland was offering cash bingo. Behind it the wooden scenic railway, one of Britain's oldest surviving rollercoasters, stood alone in a vast sea of concrete where once there'd been an exciting and vibrant amusement park. My landlord at the curiously named Luxor Hotel complained about how the town had turned into a dumping ground for immigrants and outcasts; people with social problems were easier to forget on the coastal edge, a fact mostly tragically illustrated by Margate's claim to having the highest number of children's homes in the country. It would be too generous to suppose these troubled youngsters were transplanted to the seaside in order to benefit from the healthy air. Margate badly needed some positive investment and I hoped it would get it.

The next morning I set out for Broadstairs with a detour via Kingsgate Bay. The bus dropped me off on a quiet wooded road and I walked the rest of the way beside the North Foreland golf course, accompanied by the unlikely sound of parrots from the trees above. On the high chalky headland of Kingsgate Bay a sham castle had been built for Lord Holland in the 1760s, with flinty walls and stone crenellations. In the 1950s it was turned into flats and about the same time a brick row of beach chalets was built at the edge of the castle grounds. All the blue and yellow doors were closed but peering through one window I spotted some buckets and spades. It was a steep descent to the beach and I wondered if this secluded spot was really very family friendly; a notice on the chalets asked people to 'Please note that the nearest public toilets are situated at Joss Bay' – that is, the other side of a rather large cliff!

Broadstairs had a very different feel to Margate. In the nineteenth century it was known as Kent's 'aristocratic bathing-station' with a star summer resident in Charles Dickens. Locals weren't shy to promote this literary association as a journalist visiting the beach in 1853 found out when he was asked to 'look, sir; them's Mr Dickenses footmarks, and them's the footmarks of Mr Dickenses dog'. Long dead but still a tourist draw, Dickens has a festival and two museums in the town, one of them in his old holiday home, Bleak House, where he wrote *David Copperfield*. In Margate they were hoping to turn the town's fortunes around by promoting the link with J. M. W. Turner who was not only the pre-eminent painter of his generation but also a repeat visitor. It had certainly worked for Broadstairs, although Dickens did come as part of a very attractive package; four sandy beaches, a pretty and historic seafront and a compact town centre with interesting independent shops. Where Margate had amusement arcades and cheap chain stores, Broadstairs had antique shops and second-hand book dealers.

It also had plenty of beach huts. At Stone Bay the beach was scattered with colourful family groups and windbreaks. The sun was out so the air was noisy with chatter and laughter. Most of the huts were the private stained wood type but in the centre were two breeze block rows with flat roofs and council coloured doors. Viking Bay, the town's main beach, was also busy. There were boats, children and lilos bobbing in the aqua waves of high tide. Below the verdant chalk cliff a line of private huts and council bathing boxes faded into the background when compared to the long two-tier bathing station that filled the space between chunky sets of white zigzag stairs. Built in 1935 with sixty-six changing cubicles and thirty-two day chalets, it was a strong contender for the biggest of its type in the country. At each end steps led up to a flat roof deck designed for promenading and sunbathing. West into Louisa Bay then Dumpton Gap the huts continued to be a melange of private sheds and council huts built either individually of timber and plywood or grouped in short concrete runs. None of these held very much interest after the statement of interwar bravado that near-filled Viking Bay. I was tempted to visit the town's vintage clothes shop for a pre-lycra swim suit from the window display then lay down £13.50 to hire a chalet. Maybe next time...

Broadstairs library was next to the station so I popped in while waiting for my train. In the local history section I found a postcard showing the beach in black and white before construction of the bathing station; in its place there were huts and lots and lots of tents. On the back Margaret wrote to Enid: 'It's marvellous down here! The sea's warm, the sun hot, and the sand yellow! We're lazing on the beach at present and all we seem to do is eat ices. We had 3 yesterday, and 1 already today. A man just came up and took our photo. I got talking to a nice boy in the sea this morning and there's another nice one, tall and fair, at our boarding house. We're having a wonderful time.' And she didn't even mention Dickens.

I'd read so much about Victorian Ramsgate that I decided to stop off on my way down the coast. Unfortunately the beach station that famously spewed trippers straight onto the sands was long gone so when I got off the train it was a mile inland. I asked a lady waiting at the bus stop if she could direct me towards the town centre.

'Margate?' she asked.

'Er, no, Ramsgate. We're in Ramsgate.'

'No,' she replied without a hint of irony, 'I only know Margate.'

I managed to find my way to the seafront but most of the beach seemed to have been swallowed up to make way for a flashy new marina. I got back on the train heading for Deal.

My next two hut destinations had been tipped for big things in the early twentieth century but never quite lived up to expectations, probably because of their inaccessibility. Deal wasn't one of them but I had to change there for a bus to Kingsdown. The shingle beach lay below the main village and in the afternoon sun the sea ahead of me shone a bright aquamarine. My guidebook from 1921 described

Kingsdown as 'one of the quaintest and quietest places imaginable; its cottages all at right angles to the beach, the shore littered with capstans and sheds, odd bits of sail, ropes and nets, spars and planks, and all the miscellanies of the fisherman's calling.' It also foretold an end to this peace due to rapid development: 'at no distant date Kingsdown will probably be a flourishing seaside resort.'

Well, it wasn't and it isn't. In front of a cluster of small boats twenty-four beach huts of varying size and colour were assembled. And, as if to comply with the old guidebook writer's description, the second hut from the left had a veranda decorated with tangled fishing net. Woven into a thick green cat's cradle of net were thin strands of orange and on the other side of the hut a battered lobster pot hung from a rusty hook. Midway along the beach hut row was the HQ of Kingsdown Angling Club. On their notice board congratulations were offered to J. Sheppard and B. Smith who had respectively bagged the most cod and whiting during the 2001 angling festival. While I sat watching a group of children play among the boats a man emerged from one of the huts clad in wetsuit and life vest ready to go windsurfing. That was Kingsdown, ever quaint and quiet.

Even though they were also under the remit of Dover District Council the fourteen huts at St Margaret's Bay were quite different. At the base of steep chalk cliffs covered with greenery and dotted with large houses the huts sat on their own plot, complete with garden gate. The two blocks of seven pointed towards each other at a forty-five degree angle, each hut unit stepped back from its neighbour so that they had an unusual zigzag profile. Built in the 1970s with breeze block ends and flat roofs, the huts were painted alternate shades of pastel orange, pale peach next to pale tangerine, the doors in contrasting tones to the walls. Against expectation, these colours worked remarkably well with the lush trees and brown shingle. And with so few of them there was a long waiting list.

The only one open that morning had finally come to its occupants after a four-year wait and they weren't giving it up.

'When you close that gate behind you the wind just drops, even if it's breezy on the prom,' said the lady in hut ten.

She had family connections to the area because her mother had been born in Deal. Not to be outdone, her husband revealed his own story:

'I was evacuated here during the war,' he told me. 'I always thought they must have been trying to get rid of me sending me here!'

The Channel was too hazy to reveal the French coast opposite but from St Margaret's Bay it was just twenty-one miles, or thirty-four kilometres, across the narrowest point on the Straits of Dover. In World War II this pretty strip of coast became 'Hellfire Corner', occupied by troops shelling France with heavy guns – probably not the most obvious place to send an evacuee.

Still one of the busiest shipping lanes in the world, the English Channel affords a constantly changing seascape, a silent highway below those famous white cliffs. On a clear day you could see the entire opposite coast from Calais to Boulogne, though you'd probably need a pretty strong telescope to spot the hundreds of beach huts raised on stilts along the Calais sands. Had the Victorians pursued their idea of a Channel Tunnel when it was first mooted in 1874, St Margaret's Bay would have been the starting point. Instead it developed as a small but fashionable resort with picturesque villas, flower-beds and tennis lawns. Ian Fleming, the creator of James Bond, was a past resident, as was Noel Coward, whose beach house he bought. The most recent addition to the seafront was a large barn of a beach hut. Rows of tightly packed wooden shingles had been used to make a maritime-themed roof that curved down from the ridge to about a foot above the ground. The designers were clearly playing with the idea of turning a boat into a hut but the longer I looked at it the more I realised how supremely unseaworthy such a shape would be. Upside-down the prow and stern would be gaping holes, their diagonals cut into the hull rather than away from it. Thankfully the students responsible for this were studying architecture rather than shipbuilding. The hut was the result of a project run by the Prince's Foundation for the Built Environment, a foretaste, perhaps, of what Poundbury-on-Sea might look like.

Picnicking at a borrowed hut at Felixstowe, Suffolk

The brightly painted bathing machine rescued from an Eastbourne allotment and restored by Julian Martyr, manager of the Langham Hotel

Cream huts around the bowling green at Felixstowe, Suffolk

Raised above the waves are the brooding huts at the Whalings in Frinton, Essex

Colourful huts at Southend-on-Sea, Essex

Looking from the railway bridge over huts on Whitstable's West Beach

A close-up view of the vast 1930s bathing station at Broadstairs, Kent

Millionaire's Row at Folkestone, Kent

Huts in use on a hot day at Bexhill-on-Sea, East Sussex

The concrete block of West Marina Bathing Station, St Leonards-on-Sea

The late July day had turned into a real scorcher by the time I got to Folkestone. Away from the harbour and port, beyond the helter-skelter of the Pleasure Beach and the run-down Regency facades of Marine Terrace I walked along the Lower Leas Promenade towards Sandgate. Above me on the cliff top The Leas had been developed from the late Victorian period as the fashionable heart of elite Folkestone. Described by one guide book as 'indisputably the finest marine promenade in the world' this was where ladies in expensive dresses would stroll in front of huge red-brick hotels like The Metropole and The Grand. Local builder and Folkestone Mayor Daniel Baker was on a mission to use innovative construction techniques at The Grand so the building was among the earliest to have a steel frame which was infilled with reinforced concrete. When the first beach huts were built at the base of the cliff about 1910 they were also made of concrete. The walls were cast with an exterior pattern meant to look like timber-framing, the pitched roofs laid with diamond-shaped asbestos tiles and the gable barge boards were decorated with dentils, little teeth meant to represent the ends of timbers. Some were built with their gables facing the sea, others were sideways on, with two windows looking out across the Channel. Inside, the huts had wood panelling up to dado level then plaster above. We're talking sophisticated beach huts here, designed for the rich clientele of exclusive hotels. During the interwar years more huts were added to the row, simpler concrete boxes with flat concrete roofs; the last building phase came in the 1960s. By the early Eighties the wealthy hutters were long gone and the council was ready to call in the demolition contractors.

Thankfully Don and Julia Gordon stepped in, spent a significant sum in bringing the neglected huts up to scratch and guaranteed lessees that all repairs would be done the next day. Their dedication saved these unique huts. In 1992 they handed the mantle onto Peter and Joanna Kemp. When I met Peter he had plenty of stories to tell, not a few of which involved amorous liaisons in and around the huts. There was the successful local businessman in his fifties whose chalet (complete with mattress in the roof space) was shared with a succession of attractive lady friends. And 'Ruth' the masseuse who, for a few years, had used a chalet as her business premises, refusing to give Peter either her surname or address. The most memorable tenant during his first summer was Mrs Turner.

'We were down there painting,' recalled Peter, 'and I have to admit she was gorgeous, a real stunner. One of my painters called me over to her hut; said I *had* to come and have a look at it.'

Inside there was a bed built up on stilts and above it the gable was lined with mirrors.

'I remembered that when some time later I saw this man coming up from the beach with a mirror under his arm. When I went down to the chalet the door was like matchwood. After making some enquiries it turned out her husband had been down there!'

According to Peter, Millionaires Row was the most desirable hut location. Eight post-war chalets stepped up the cliff, four on either side of a central staircase and each with its own private terrace. The doors were painted primrose yellow like all the other huts but they opened towards each other leaving space for windows on the front seaward walls and, whereas the other huts had stone-coloured walls, these were bright white. With their flat roofs these chalets wouldn't have been out of place on a Spanish beach. I asked the man sitting outside number seventy why people loved beach huts.

'As to your question, I can't answer it,' he replied. 'Some people they want complicated lives but for me this is enough. I like the mornings and evenings best. When people walk past some look away but others will stop and chat for hours.' He made it sound very sociable.

Other chalet residents told me how they sat and timed 'The Walkers', a couple who kept fit by walking up and down, up and down, sometimes for hours at a time: 'Its about eighteen minutes between sightings.' Then there was the very cheery woman I spoke to who had made such an effort on the interior design of her hut, with mosaic wallpaper left over from her bathroom, cast off fishing net, driftwood and shells, that an American couple walking past had exclaimed 'Wow' and asked if she was selling things from her shop.

I kept walking along the promenade until the smooth path ran out and then continued across the shingle. On this more remote beach the sunbathers had shed their inhibitions (which, from the sounds of things, weren't very strong here in the first place!) and their clothes with them. I'd stumbled across a favourite spot for nudists and what a contrast between those totally unencumbered souls and myself, trudging along with a sweaty back pack on the hottest day of the year so far.

When I got there Sandgate proved to be lacking in beach huts and Hythe, where the short row of eleven huts was run by Peter Kemp's son, looked miles further away than it actually was. In the mid-1980s it had been so difficult to find tenants for those huts that Peter had allowed Bill and Nell, a mother and son tramp duo, to stay in one for a couple of months.

'The whole time they stayed there neither of them had a bath. They'd sit outside cooking their tea around a fire and when I was down there it looked quite good. Bill offered me a cup of tea and I ended up drinking it out of the corner of a margarine container! The place stank when they left but at least they provided a bit of security.'

Hythe huts were rather more popular these days but I'd already decided to take temporary leave of the sea by staying with a friend in London for the night so I turned around and made my way back to Folkestone station.

Having finished with Kent I set out next morning for East Sussex, glad that I was not going to Brighton. The weather was gorgeous which meant that, it being Sunday, half of London was heading for the coast. Victoria station was crammed with beach-goers, dressed in shorts, sundresses and flip-flops, waiting for delayed trains. For the first time I got a sense of what it must have been like to be a nineteenth century tripper. The rush for the excursion train was genuine; when the first Brighton service was called the crowd seethed forward and the

concourse miraculously cleared. If there was standing room only on
that train imagine how much worse it would have been dressed in your
Victorian Sunday best? After a tortuous queue for tickets I boarded the
late-running service to Bexhill-on-Sea.

By the time we finally arrived the midday heat was stifling. The really
hardcore sunbathers were sprawled on the pebble beach but everyone
else was seeking shade. On the balcony of the De La Warr Pavilion I
found a cool spot to eat some lunch, surrounded by toe-tapping diners
keeping pace with the Hooe Village Brass Band who played below us
on the new shell-shaped band stand. It was thanks to this pavilion
that Bexhill could claim a place in international architectural history,
something few other seaside resorts could manage.

When the competition for a new entertainment centre was
announced in 1933 the brief demanded a design that was 'simple,
light in appearance and attractive, suitable for a Holiday Resort'. The
winning partnership consisted of a German, Erich Mendelsohn and
a Russian, Serge Chermayeff, who together gave Bexhill a forthright
statement of Modernism with large expanses of sheet glass opening up
the interior to sea and sun on three levels. The interior accommodated
a large theatre, restaurant, library, conference room and lounge, while
outside there were terraces for sunbathing and listening to music with
a rooftop sundeck where visitors could pretend they were on an ocean
liner and play games like quoits. Had the funds been available this
iconic building would have been linked to flats, a hotel, cinema and
shops, creating a brand new Bexhill Amusement Centre. And to top
it off, in front of the pavilion the architects proposed a large circular
bathing pool, surrounded by dressing boxes and sunbathing decks,
from above which a slender double-decker pier would have extended
into the sea itself.

Expectations had changed a lot since the 1930s but the sun still
brought crowds to the beach. Yet, for all these people, there was an
uncanny stillness in the air. Looking out towards an indistinct horizon
the sea was almost flat, normal waves were barely visible and even less

audible. It was like a lagoon, so appealing in the heat that I regretted my lack of bathing suit. A little too dedicated to my cause, I stayed on the prom walking to the end of De La Warr Parade and the line of Russell's Beach Huts. Their construction looked somewhat on the flimsy side with white plywood walls, blue double doors and darker blue canvas stretched over the shallow pitched roof. Nonetheless, an apologetic notice in the window of Russell's Kiosk left no doubt that they were popular: 'Sorry,' it read, 'no more Beach Huts available for this season.' Kevin and Lori Doswell were inside tidying up during a brief lull in ice cream and cold drink sales.

'We've got the sign,' said Kevin, 'but we still send two or three people away every day asking about the huts.'

He and his wife had taken over from Mr Russell in 1999, intending the huts as a retirement project but running them as a second job in the meantime. During the week Kevin worked as a carpenter.

'Mr Murrell had the huts for about fifty years and when Mr Russell took over in 1976 I built the kiosk for him. His wife said that when they gave up the huts I could have first refusal and they stuck to it.'

Kevin told me how this year he'd applied to the Council for permission to erect another ten huts, giving him a licence for forty-two in all. Mr Russell had apparently been rather less troubled by protocol and put up as many as he could on the amount of beach left after the winter storms. Mr Russell sounded like a bit of a wheeler-dealer, using 'recycled' timber from demolished houses to build the huts that Kevin was now gradually replacing. To ease the twice-yearly move in and out of winter storage, Kevin was building the new type with a collapsible roof for the sake of flat-packing.

'We're choosy about who we let them to,' Lori told me, 'but people just don't give up their huts. There was a lady who'd had her hut for fifty years and unfortunately she couldn't manage anymore. It's nice that we've been able to let some to young families recently.'

Lori's reference to families was significant because Bexhill generally catered to an ageing population, seafront apartment blocks providing high-density retirement residences along what had become known as the 'Costa Geriatrica'. For the people who lived here beach huts supplied crucial outdoor space, as witnessed by the merry group of grey-haired friends outside one cream cabin I walked past. They were chatting and milling around, making themselves comfortable after a dip in the sea. Their soggy swimming costumes hung out to dry – five belonging to ladies but only one lucky pair of gents' trunks – and hooked over the top of the open door were two walking sticks.

Walking west along the prom I passed other wooden huts and larger concrete chalets buzzing with activity. The late afternoon heat was more tolerable so I kept going towards Cooden Beach, the ritzy end of Bexhill. As I got closer the detached properties above the seawall got grander and irrespective of their age they all shared a characteristic bigness. Where they ceased a short run of twenty-seven white huts began. In front of the verandas was a springy strip of grass then the shingle beach; the road ran directly behind. Midway along, the charred skeleton of a hut made for a sad sight, the singed roof perched on one blackened and three see-through walls. The next-door hut had come off even worse, its remains limited to a charred window frame, some melted glass and a few broken bits of crockery. Weeds were already beginning to grow through the ash. As I stared at this proof of a beach hut's vulnerability a lady walked past with her dog. 'Not your hut is it?' She seemed relieved to learn it wasn't and I guess I was too.

Retracing my steps to Bexhill I noticed that the sea had disappeared, leaving a glimmering expanse of sand and rockpools. The pink evening light was beginning to fade but I paused in front of a row of concrete chalets raised on steps above the promenade. There were nine in total, all but two of them painted in vibrant colours: jade green followed royal blue, then came candy pink, mint green, Wedgwood blue, bright orange and fuscia pink. I took a photo that I knew would never come out and as I put my camera away the occupants of the middle blue hut called me over. I told them about my trip and asked about the white huts at the end of their row.

'We have our own beach hut association,' the lady with long grey hair told me. 'It's run as a company and we were all supposed to agree on the colour scheme. When they used to be white the lady at the end painted her two avocado green but then the others went coloured and she went white!'

There was clearly some animosity but we quickly moved onto other subjects.

'Why don't you sit down?' said her husband. 'Would you like a glass of wine? We've just started a bottle of rosé.'

The fleeting colours of sunset rippled through the clear liquid and I sat down to watch the last traces of day disappear. The couple's baby grandchild slept in a rocker while her mother handed out cold barbequed sausages and juicy slices of watermelon. Across the distant headland the lights of Eastbourne gradually flickered on and as the last dog walkers and hutters disappeared, candles were brought out and set in wine bottles to illuminate our comfortable scene. It didn't seem necessary to exchange names; we just talked as if we'd known each other for years, aware that we were unlikely ever to meet again. My hostess spoke of quiet Cooden with its view towards Pevensey Bay as her idea of beach hut heaven. For me it would be that night, when I sat by the English seaside wearing only vest sleeves till eleven o'clock, sipping wine and enjoying good conversation with complete strangers.

Next morning I set out early to walk to Hastings along the beach. Kevin and Lori had exposed a pretty major omission in my route and I'd promised to go backwards to see these unlooked for huts. It wasn't much of a hardship. Though I'd never considered myself much of an outdoors-type, after nearly a month on the road I felt fantastically healthy. The weather was still good and not far beyond Russell's huts I came to more white sheds at Galley Hill. Rounding the sandy cliff, a few more came into view at West Glyne Gap. Trains ran directly behind these before passing through a tunnel in the cliff to hurtle past yet more at East Glyne Gap. This eastern variety looked bigger than average and the man in number seventy-six, who also owned hut number twenty-eight next door, told me they were a maximum of sixteen by eleven feet. The second hut was for his grandchildren but the numbering required a little explanation.

'Well yes, there's only twenty four left but there used to be about 280 in a continuous arch along the beach. The grandchildren's hut used to be in the front row and this one was at the back in the third row.'

Over the past thirty years he'd watched the headland recede by almost a foot a year and had to move his hut back three times. His wife showed me inside to a space which, she confidently assured me, could seat sixteen people. The décor was homely in a sort of 1970s way. On the outside deck two holes had been drilled for parasols, one to provide shade from the morning sun and the other for the afternoon. Although home was just fifteen minutes away near Hastings Castle they seemed perfectly content in their peaceful spot.

'I've never been abroad and I don't want to,' he asserted. 'There's a great camaraderie amongst the hut owners. And all of this for just three pounds a week – what a bargain!'

I was walking on to St Leonards so the man in seventy-six recommended the huts at Bulverhythe, otherwise known as Bo Peep and/or West of Haven.

'When you get there, ask for Jack Cork and tell him that Peter sent you. We were in the fire service together, now he's the boss-man caretaker. He'll be there. He's there eight days a week!'

I found the Bo Peep huts beyond a cluster of black felted fisherman's huts and the sinuous hull of the beached Mona Liza. A line of traditional huts stretched along the beach, predominantly white but with intermittent hints of newly sanctioned colours. Behind were two more rows.

'Excuse me,' I tentatively intruded upon the gossip of two couples sat outside hut forty-nine, 'do you know where I can find Jack Cork?'

'Yes,' all four of them replied in chorus. They directed me towards his blue hut in the front row.

Dressed in navy blue shorts and a vest that showed off his tanned body, it was clear the beach life kept Jack fit and healthy. He invited me into his hut where we sat at a table in front of the window. The side walls were panelled in varnished pine and the ceiling was painted yellow. He told me that the hut owners association had been lobbying the council for a couple of years to get them to allow colour. Some people had objected because the huts had always been white but his was the first to turn blue and so far more people had picked that colour than any other.

Jack told me that the beach had been cleared and declared out-of-bounds during World War II. When the huts did return it was his father who built the first one in 1947. The following year he built a second. Now Jack had taken over the mantle acting as builder, handyman and estate agent for the community.

'I've got a list of 157 people who want one but there are only 150 here! They'll be vacant in the morning and gone in the afternoon.'

Some people bought pre-fabricated garden chalets to erect on the beach but Jack didn't think much of these, not being built with coastal weather in mind.

'I can put one up on my own in about ten days,' he revealed, 'but I needed help after the 1987 hurricane. Although the tide was out at the time the wind took twenty huts. Two or three were found half a mile away. After that I had to build a dozen.'

'And are you here every day?' I asked.

'Every day, even Christmas Day. I'm the local beach bum,' stated Jack with some pride. 'Last Christmas I got forty bottles of whisky and 3,500 cigarettes from people whose huts I look after.'

Jack was clearly not short of work or friends. I left him re-felting the roof of number 112 and walked on along the shore.

St Leonards came into being as an early nineteenth century seaside new town. James Burton, the London builder who had worked with Joseph Nash on Regent's Park, started laying out the classical terraces, villas and colonnades on farmland from 1828 and his son Decimus continued to add buildings into the 1850s and 60s. The resort was specifically designed for a wealthy aristocratic clientele but the Grecian-style Crown House, identified by a plaque as the villa borrowed by Queen Victoria when she was still a princess, was now a pub and a rather seedy-looking one at that. A century after its creation St Leonards enjoyed a second architectural flourish, this time in concrete rather than stucco, under the guardianship of Sidney Little, Borough Engineer. It was Little who created the huge open-air pool in 1933, the West Marina chalets near Bo Peep and the double-decker promenade into Hastings. The West Marina chalets, which I came to first, had an extraordinary industrial look, their two levels of sky-blue doors punctuating a long horizontal block of concrete. The flat-roofed upper chalets were set back so that the roofs of the lower level became their sun terrace. If the Folkestone chalets had a Spanish feel then these were more reminiscent of something from Soviet Russia. They were the gutsiest huts I'd seen, no nonsense functional buildings from a period when concrete was sufficiently full of wonder to need no embellishment. I could see they wouldn't be to everyone's taste but several were in use.

Along the seafront of St Leonards proper there were more concrete chalet rows in the shadow of Marine Court, a huge block of flats with the look of an ocean-liner. They were cleverly built into the promenade between the upper, roadside walkway and the lower beachside path. Wandering past more sky blue doors I rounded the corner to look along the shore at the double-decker prom that ran all the way to Hastings Pier. The covered lower path with its built-in seats and rounded observation points carried an upper deck with elegant Modernist shelters which would all have been nicely retro were it not for the drunks. Notices threatened prosecution to anyone consuming alcohol on the prom but within a few footsteps I saw a man wrenching the ring pull from his third can of beer having discarded the empty second onto the pavement. It was mid-afternoon on a sunny summer's day but I felt faintly intimidated as I walked along the front. Poor St Leonards had definitely lost its genteel edge and Hastings was so down at heel that even the Oxfam advertised 'Super Savings'. The potential was there but like at Margate, it would take a good deal of investment to reinvigorate these sister resorts.

Before leaving Hastings I went to look at the famous net huts, the skyscrapers of the beach hut world. They shared the same basic shape but the impressively elongated black sides were built tall and thin for drying hemp fishing nets. The 'Stade' where the fishing fleet was still based had been given its name, meaning 'landing place', in Saxon times. Although the net huts were not so ancient, the oldest could be dated to the sixteenth century, well before sea-bathing became a popular pastime. It would be nice to say that this was the place where beach huts were *really* invented but that simply isn't true; the net huts were always functional rather than recreational. Nowadays they weren't even that, having been turned into redundant tourist attractions at the end of a car park. I walked onto the beach to see the colourful boats surrounded by their paraphernalia of pots and nets. Modern nets made of nylon overflowed from plastic bins; they didn't need to be hung up so the fishermen had built much shorter huts, tarred like their predecessors, but just as likely to be made of breeze block as wooden clapboard.

Next day I was back on track, continuing my journey westwards. A sign outside Eastbourne welcomed me to the 'Sunshine Coast' but overnight the weather had turned and was stubbornly refusing to comply with this advertising slogan. With its majestic Victorian pier, the seafront was actually wrapped in a low mist. As the first spots of rain began to fall I made for the Lifeguard Station midway along a corridor of fibreglass changing cabins. It was midday and the station, staffed by a young team of seasonal employees dressed in sporty red and yellow uniforms, smelt of fish and chips. One of the lifeguards introduced me to Garry who'd recently taken over the job of looking after the bathing cabins. Like most of his colleagues, he was working over the summer to pay for a winter's worth of global backpacking. Garry rooted around in a pile of papers and handed me some stapled sheets headed 'Bathing Cabin 5 Year Plan'. I flicked through while he outlined the strategy for replacement of the small turquoise and white huts.

'We've got rid of fifty per cent on West Beach this year and in five years' time all these will have been replaced with bigger wooden cabins.'

'So who uses them?' I asked.

'Most of the seasonal tenants are local but we get holidaymakers too. And a lot more families recently,' he added. 'It did used to be renowned for old grannies down here but the dynamics seem to be changing.'

Past the stubby round Wish Tower (a former Martello fort) the promenade extended in the direction of Beachy Head. Where the path ran out at Hollywell I found another short line of fibreglass cabins, their rather squat forms overawed by the high chalky cliffs behind. On the way I'd passed rows of brick bungalows, exquisitely well-kept with doors, windows and dividing screens still fitted with multiple small panes of glass. I'd got so used to seeing shuttered blank walls that being able to enjoy the original unaltered design was rather refreshing. It also said something about Eastbourne that these conservatory chalets could survive just metres away from a very pebbly beach. Above the door of number two a discreet sign recorded that 'this chalet was used by their majesties King George V and Queen Mary in the month of March 1935'. Visiting on a four-week break from official state business, the royal couple, noted the *Eastbourne Chronicle,* displayed a clear partiality for the parade between the Wish Tower and Holywell when taking their morning constitutional. And as the royals prepared to leave the local press proudly announced that 'the King's health has greatly improved; he has slept well, his appetite has been good, and his weight has increased by several pounds – a sure sign that the sea air has done him good and that he has been happy and contented'. Maybe Eastbourne just had that effect on people. As I rode on the little land train back to town everyone along the prom smiled and waved and behind Royal Parade I overtook four elderly gents giggling in the street, actually creased up with infectiously raucous laughter. If that was the Eastbourne effect it was pretty impressive.

My own route to happiness and contentment came with the opportunity to see a bathing machine. I'd only ever seen them in pictures but here in Eastbourne they had the real thing restored to full working order. Under normal circumstances I should have been able to turn up at the Langham Hotel, where the machine's owner Julian Martyr was managing partner, to see the red and yellow striped vehicle parked outside. Instead I had to go on a bizarre mission to Eastbourne Lawn Tennis Club.

I met Julian at the hotel where he told me about the difficulties involved in becoming a twenty-first century bathing machine proprietor. The authentic cabin had been recovered from a friend's allotment where, having been coated with the council's favourite shade of green paint, it was being used as a potting shed.

'When we lifted it up the bottom fell out!' said Julian.

'It sounds like a real labour of love.'

'Oh it was! We wanted to use as much of the original structure as possible but we had to let it dry out for several months to see what was salvageable. The chassis had to be entirely recreated but the trickiest bit was the wheels.'

The entire project had set him back some £3,000 but the biggest expense was those wheels.

'There just aren't that many wheelwrights around anymore. We found a man in Hooe but it cost over £2,000. He based the axle structure on a contemporary Romany caravan then we had to work out how big the wheels would have been. Because the beach is so soft they have to be heavy duty and each one's got a four and a half inch metal rim.'

Impressed with the trouble Julian had gone to in getting the right workmen and the right colours, discovered after taking a series of paint scrapings, I really wanted to see the machine.

'Can you come back tomorrow?' he asked. 'The machine was filmed for a TV appearance last week and it's not come home yet. Should be back tomorrow morning.'

The next day was rainy but I hung around until mid-morning before going back to the Langham Hotel. The machine's usual spot was still empty. By now I was running out of time so Julian drew me a map and directed me towards the tennis club. On the back of a compliment slip he scribbled his permission with the words 'Allows bearer to visit

Bathing Machine', just in case anyone questioned what I was up to. The map worked but the permission slip proved less useful because the machine was locked up near the service entrance, the other side of the bright green courts. The man with the key was on his lunch break – could I come back later? I started to explain why this was less than ideal but the maintenance man wouldn't answer his pager so there was no choice. Since the rain had stopped I sat on a bench outside the museum eating ice cream with an elderly couple who were happy to talk to me but seemed to have had enough of talking to each other. I tried the tennis club again and finally got up close with the bathing machine that I had spied earlier from a distance.

It was huge! A full size beach hut mounted on wheels that came up to my eye-level! The cabin sat right in the middle of the chassis but because the axles were fitted at the very front and rear less than a quarter of each wheel turned against the sides. The interior was spacious but the shuttered openings on either side were so tiny that even with one of the two doors open it was pretty gloomy. In the middle of the floor there was a loose board that could be lifted out to wash away any lingering sea water. The space was covered on the underside by another panel to make sure no one could 'accidentally' peer inside from below. Having satisfied myself with a good look over the machine, I stepped back to make a clumsy sketch of its construction. Behind me the outer gates swung open and I was greeted by two rather surprised-looking removal men come to take the machine home on the back of their truck. Given the chance I would have ridden along with them then taken the machine onto the beach to give it a try. Regrettably that wasn't an option so as they set off I did too. Like the stripy Eastbourne bathing machine, it was time for me to go home. I had a month's worth of laundry to do before I set out again to complete my coastal journey.

Chapter Ten
Life vests and stripy legs

When bathing machines were first introduced, few people who used them could swim. By the second half of the nineteenth century a new relationship was being forged with the sea, one in which self-propulsion came to be seen as important for safety's sake but also because it allowed for fun and games. In the summer of 1878 pairs of would-be champions took to their boats at Scarborough equipped for the latest sport of water jousting. So that spectators could be confident they were cheering for the right knight, each man wore a 'brilliantly-coloured blouse' over his bathing costume. Somewhat at the mercy of their boatmen, the combatants were rowed into position and, with as much swagger as they could muster, each found his footing on a plank placed loosely across the bows of the boat from where he poked 'with a padded-ended pole at a similarly attired and equally adventurous man on another boat.' As the waves continued their perpetual motion and the padded lances were swung with varying force, it took just one well-aimed blow or one unusually heavy swell to shatter the improvised equilibrium and condemn one, if not both of the knights, to the home of the fishes.

Although the dipping ritual was still advocated by some Victorian doctors, spectacles like this Yorkshire water tournament were proof that the sea had been transformed into a holidaymaker's playground. The coast itself was steadily becoming the pressure valve for a nation that, according to the 1861 census, now counted more of its population as urban rather than rural dwellers. Small wonder, given this historic statistic, that each summer the seaside attracted more and more escaping city dwellers: 'People hear the surf in the rumble of the omnibuses, and instinctively sniff for the smell of seaweed in the hot choky vapours of the narrow street; bathing machines become gorgeous dreams of expectancy.' Although escape was made possible by the railways even cheap excursion tickets were no good to workers who lacked free *time*. Things were changing on that score too; in 1871 the Bank Holiday Act not only sanctioned traditional holidays, it added to their number: the weekly half holiday became widespread in industry: the number of manual workers granted an annual holiday was growing and the idea of holidays with pay was beginning to gain acceptance. But, as the number of seaside tourists grew so did the number of accidents. During the 1860s and 70s reports of drowning reached unprecedented levels. Thus it was that in a period when moralists were trying to make the beach *decent*, other campaigners were trying to make it *safe*.

The bathing fatality. A stereoview from the 1860s when drownings were on the increase.

While staying on the Isle of Wight in 1849 Charles Dickens witnessed the effects of a strong swell upon his good friend, the *Punch* artist John Leech. 'The sea has been running very high and Leech, whilst bathing, was knocked over by a bad blow from a great wave on the forehead. He is in bed and had twenty of his namesakes on his temples this morning.' Dickens' friend made a full recovery but others were not so lucky. In June 1867 a sixteen-year-old girl died while trying to save her mother at Silloth in Cumberland. This seaside resort on the English side of the Solway Firth, about twenty miles from Carlisle, attracted many Scottish tourists including the widowed Mrs Greig and her daughter, who were visiting from Selkirk. The ladies had not been in the water for more than a few minutes when rough waves knocked the mother off her feet. While trying to reach her, Miss Greig was also carried out of her depth. The mother survived but her poor daughter could not be resuscitated. The year before, at Sheerness in Kent, a non-swimmer put his own life at risk trying to save a fellow bather from drowning. Lifeguards were yet to be thought of and the bathing machine attendant proved less than helpful, unable to render assistance even after the rescuer had dragged the unconscious victim near the shore: 'being nearly exhausted I lost my hold, and could not again rescue him. I called for a rope, but unfortunately there was nothing of the kind to be found.'

These were just a few of the many cases that showed how easy it was for bathers to get into trouble and how ill-prepared resorts were when life-threatening situations arose. In August 1873 the *Pall Mall Gazette* railed against resort negligence: 'Day after day instances are recorded of either narrow escapes or fatal accidents when bathing; but the same recklessness is displayed by bathers, and the same *insouciance* prevails among the local authorities of the villages and towns on the sea coast as to the fate of the visitors by whom they make such large profits.' There were all too many quotable examples of this carelessness: 'Last week a well-known solicitor of London was drowned in the Isle of Wight. This week we hear of two young ladies being drowned together at Ilfracombe, and next week probably will bring the account of some other tragedy of a like nature.' The apparent epidemic of accidents even touched the royal family when Prince Arthur had to be saved from drowning while on holiday at the French resort of Trouville.

Articles like this provoked an increasing sense of anger at the inadequacy of life-saving equipment, yet complaints continued throughout the 1860s and 70s, suggesting that few seaside authorities acknowledged their responsibility or took action to help safeguard members of the public. Bathing Women, the heirs to eighteenth century dippers, continued to find work around the country and their presence must have saved many a nervous bather. The superlative example was Mary Wheatland, famous for her impressive life-saving record during a sixty-two-year career at Bognor Regis. Dubbed the 'Grace Darling of the South Coast', Mary was born in 1835 and began work aged fourteen. Three months before her sixteenth birthday she rescued a lady called Mrs. Woods who had got out of her depth. By the time she retired at the age of seventy-four, Mary had saved thirty lives and been awarded two medals. She proudly wore these pinned on the bodice of her rough blue serge costume and, on the walls of her neat bathing hut, Bognor's local celebrity displayed the two testimonials she had received from the Royal Humane Society. Always photographed wearing the battered sailor hat that bore her name in gold letters, the brave Mary Wheatland also had a sense of humour; her party trick was to stand with her head in the water, waving her button boots in the air!

Bathers with the wealth to match their anxieties could always invest in their own life-saving equipment and, as early as 1804, a report in *The Times* described how Margate bathers were using 'an apparatus of cork, which enables them to swim with ease, and is an effectual protection against the dangers of drowning. The seafaring people here call it the seaman's friend'. Multiple other devices were logged in the nineteenth century patent books, often variations on the same cork-filled theme. Whole garments were designed to be stuffed with buoyant material; even dress bodices and corsets could be provided with 'ornamental puffings' full of charred cork or a similar form of vegetable cellulose. Of

The disarray caused by a particularly high tide at Boulogne in August 1875 as depicted by *The Illustrated London News*

course, even if these things actually made it into production they would have been out of reach to the majority of bathers, especially those for whom a dip in the sea was an expensive, once yearly, treat.

The *Pall Mall Gazette* may have berated seaside resorts but it also admonished bathers for their own recklessness, recognising that there was often a real gap between a holidaymaker's aspiration and ability to swim. From a historical perspective this could almost be viewed as an improvement. At least now people *wanted* to swim. Until the sixteenth century, swimming was considered an immoral pastime, something only the ill-mannered classes would do. In his 1587 manual *De Arte Natandi* or 'The Art of Swimming', Sir Everard Digby rejected this prejudice and attempted to reclaim swimming as an essential attribute of the Tudor gentleman. Digby favoured breaststroke above all others and his influence helped ensure its pre-eminence (his other claim to fame was to be executed in 1606 for taking part in the Gunpowder Plot to blow up King James I and Parlia-

Ropes were attached to the end of bathing machines for the benefit of non-swimmers.

Mary Wheatland was a Bognor celebrity having saved numerous lives in her career as a bathing woman.

ment). If social conventions were a hindrance to popular swimming, then another historical problem was the widely held notion that it was downright unhealthy. The writer Tobias Smollett was a notable eighteenth century fan of swimming but when he swam in the Mediterranean in 1763, doctors from the impoverished French town of Nice gave a prognosis of 'immediate death'!

Attitudes turned progressively more favourable over the ensuing hundred years until in 1875 swimming was raised to a matter of collective national pride. In that year an Englishman, Captain Matthew Webb, became the first person to swim the Channel from Dover to Calais. The publicity surrounding Webb's achievement encouraged other people to take up a sport that had already been growing in popularity at the seaside. The Brighton Swimming Club held its first races in 1861, open only to male competitors wearing drawers. In Devon, the Dawlish Swimming Association was established in 1864, its competitions developing into a highlight of the summer season, attracting crowds to the sea front where bands provided musical accompaniment. Five years later, at the German Gymnasium behind London's St Pancras Railway Station, representatives from several city clubs founded the Metropolitan Swimming Association. Within a month they had agreed standards in measures, strokes and distance that put swimming on a more scientific footing.

Brighton Swimming Club c1900.

Up and down the coast swimming also evolved into a form of entertainment. Novelty aquatic acts were provided by self-styled 'Professors of Natation' whose fame was often based on diving prowess; Professor Osbourne would regularly dive off the roof of Thoms Tea House at the end of Southport Pier while Professor Reddish made his reputation riding off Brighton's West Pier on a bicycle! The popularity of water performances was such that Professor Parker's show at the Ilfracombe Hotel Baths in 1883 attracted up to a thousand spectators at a time. R. D. Blackmore, author of *Lorna Doone*, was in the audience at one of these galas and watched with amazement while a 'male and female professor of the natatory art took afternoon tea at a table floating in the middle of the water'.

Wowed by these magnificent demonstrations, tourists could then sign up to have swimming lessons from the professor himself. Contradictory though it sounds, lessons were normally given on dry land. Even diving could be rehearsed in this way with the fully clothed student suspended by webbing over a sand pit. The ultimate aim was to mimic

Ilfracombe's champion swimmer and Professor of Natation, Harry Parker.

the leg action of a frog so pupils would almost certainly be required to practice lying on their bellies on a table or chair whilst simultaneously studying pictures of frogs or, even better, live examples kicking their way around a jar or tub. When tuition did take place in the water it was no less bizarre. Rudyard Kipling learnt to swim 'in the accepted manner' while he was a pupil at the United Service College at Westward Ho! between 1878 and 1882. A belt made of webbing was arranged under his armpits then attached to a long pole: 'with Foxy, the gym instructor, in person at the safe or shore end of the pole and our sweet singer in his belt at the danger or fish end, the instruction proceeded.' Immersed in the water Kipling, 'strongly upheld at first by the faithful Foxy, would make valiant strokes on what he supposed were correct principles. Gradually the helpful support would be slackened as the pupil became more self-sustaining. After half a dozen lessons, a partial independence was won'.

At the turn of the century the proportion of swimmers in the population remained relatively small, partly due to persistent double standards. Although female bathing costumes were designed for more active use by the 1880s, women were still less likely to be able to swim than men. John Hulley, Vice-President of the Athletic Society of Great Britain, described the situation as he saw it in 1864 suggesting, in a letter to *The Times* of 6 August, that improvements could be made by following the Continental model:

> English ladies, as a general rule, on leaving their van are rather timid in the water, not having the advantages of a male protector. They cling frantically to the rope attached to the van, and disport themselves in a most extraordinary fashion. The height of perfection seems to be the possession of a sufficient amount of courage to give the greatest number of low curtseys in the water, so as to immerse entirely the head and body. It is very seldom we find them go into the water more than 24 inches in depth, while those who go to that depth are generally considered good bathers and possessed of remarkable courage. The majority stay about the wheels of the van in, say, about six inches of water, or a little above the ankles. Now, I do not hesitate to say that all this absurdity would be got rid of if ladies had proper bathing dresses, and if the manners of our bathing-places were so modified as to permit them to avail themselves of the help and aid of their husbands, fathers, and brothers.

Although this paternalistic view may strike us as sexist, by the standards of his day Hulley was actually seeking to liberate women's bathing habits. He had been to Biarritz, the French Emperor's favourite resort, and seen 'gentlemen walking down to the water with their wives on their arms, and their daughters following them'. Surprised at first by this unfamiliar freedom, Hulley soon came to see Biarritz as a model of pleasurable and healthy bathing. The adoption of similar freedoms in Britain would not only make bathing more enjoyable it would also

Biarritz Pittoresque

ATTENTION ! ON NOUS PHOTOGRAPHIE ! - N° 52

Cliché

Mixed bathing at Biarritz. The three men wearing hats are official bathing guides.

help save lives as girls could learn to swim with their brothers, wives with their husbands.

In the 1860s this sort of reasonable argument was premature and easily dismissed by moralists. Yet, over the next three decades, accounts of foreign bathing would routinely appear in the press with the aim of exposing the backwardness of British practice. As John Hulley realised, a pre-requisite for mixed bathing had to be decent costume for *both* sexes. Unlike in Britain, where male nudity had become entrenched as a customary right, the French had made clothing obligatory for everyone from the earliest days of their seaside history. In 1811, a child was condemned at Dieppe for bathing naked in the sea. The punishment is unknown but the principle was remembered, not least because it came so soon after the French discovered sea-bathing. This chastisement came just three years after the Comtesse de Boigne visited Dieppe to take the plunge. She was one of the first grand Frenchwomen to adopt the English bathing habit on her own coastline. Dieppe was a seaport totally unprepared for this innovation and the Comtesse suffered the indignity of being followed about by a large giggling crowd who nicknamed her 'l'Anglaise'. By the time a member of the royal family, Marie-Caroline, Duchesse de Berri, visited in 1824 local businessmen had realised there was money to be made from bathing. Their new casino could boast rooms for billiards, reading, dancing and cards; it even hired out bathing-dresses. As the beach was too steep for bathing machines they were never used at Dieppe, instead rows of little striped tents were provided for undressing and dressing. By this point, bathing was already more regulated than in England. It was illegal to bathe without a *guide-baigneur* in attendance, the French equivalent of a dipper. These individuals, who patrolled the beach in striped jerseys and leather hats, consequently did very good business.

As standards of living rose in the second half of Victoria's reign, more middle as well as upper class Britons could afford to leave their crowded native coast in favour of French seaside resorts. On 24 August 1871, *The Times* published a letter comparing the bathing tents of Dieppe to the bathing machines of Britain and found the latter sadly wanting. The British machine was 'a damp dark box', a 'frightful prison' from which the 'shivering inmate, whose shins have already been scarified against the benches during the journey down by the exertions of the horses', emerges to undergo 'a similar process against the steps by the agency of the waves, with the addition of feeling that decency, in reference to the persons sitting a few yards back on the beach, is almost impossible'. The actual experience of bathing was no better, referred to as 'a few minutes' struggle in the turbid water, perhaps under a dismal awning which keeps off the fresh sea air' before retreat into the machine and 'the huddling on of clothes [which] is soon after rudely disturbed by the jerks of the horse'. To add insult to injury 'a gross sum is demanded which makes bathing much dearer than in France'.

At Dieppe the experience was far less terrifying and there was none of the 'rattle and roughness of the machine, and the darkness suddenly changed for the frightful vignette of steps and waves before mentioned'. Hire of a wooden framed canvas '*tente*' cost twenty-five centimes or two and a half English pence. 'The door faces the sea...at the back, is a good broad bench, and there are pegs, a small shelf, a looking-glass, and little windows, seaward and landward, which may be opened and shut at pleasure. A line of boards in front, and another at right angles, leading over the shingle to the sea, protects the feet of the bather, who may also wear straw-soled shoes.' Men and women kept to separate bathing areas but all were fully attired. The letter writer, an old Etonian swimmer, confessed his uncertainty about the French costume ('similar to that of our acrobats') but accepted it as 'preferable to the ludicrous and ineffectual half-attempts at decency which one witnesses in England'. Here the point was less about safety than comfort; the Dieppe example showed that bathing machines were unnecessary because people could change first then simply walk across the beach.

From a twenty-first century point of view this sounds obvious. Not so in 1871. Perhaps the most interesting thing about this letter was the response it elicited in *support* of the English system. The following day an unimpressed reader dismissed the 'highly-coloured comparison' of English and French bathing by pointing out that the Dieppe tents were immovable. The experience of the unfortunate Monsieur Wey, described in chapter eight, comes vividly to mind when this writer talks of having to walk to the water's edge at low tide as well as high tide 'over the shingle, very often without shoes, generally without any plank, and always through groups of critically curious women seated on the beach between his tent and the sea.' He preferred to choose his own time and tide at Brighton, where he could 'have the machine wheeled on to the sands, and so avoid jolting and criticism'.

If this might be called the traditionalist response, the letter sent by Jabez Streeter published in *The Times* on 28 August showed that more innovative arrangements were already in place – and had been for a decade – at Littlehampton in Sussex. 'Your correspondent...has certainly not visited this pleasant watering-place on the south coast during the last few years, or he would have seen in full force in England what he admires so much in France – the bathing tents.' Alongside existing bathing machines the local board had provided twenty canvas tents, six feet square in size, with solid wooden floors which, going one better than at Dieppe, were mounted on very low wheels. 'When the parties have taken their places inside, these tents are pushed down over the shingle into about six inches of water on to the hard sand, where the bathers can walk out into the water and disport themselves at pleasure.' The price of 3d. per person included hire of the tent, a clean towel, a bathing dress and, if desired, instructions in swimming.

Improvements along French lines had also been made to the fleet of Dawlish bathing machines. An article from the *Exeter Flying Post* of 13 November 1871 described how:

> ...they are constructed entirely of wood, and stand upon two fore wheels with rests behind. They are about six feet in height from floor to roof, and three feet six inches square, each being furnished with carpet, boot-jack, and looking glass. By means of a pair of removable shafts – a single pair sufficing for a long row of machines – the boxes can be lifted up from behind, and wheeled forward or backward on the beach as the state of the tide makes it convenient, thus removing the objection raised against the French stationary tents, to which, when the tide is out, the bather has to walk in a costume more or less unsuitable for "taking his walks abroad".

The new design was introduced by a local artist and engraver, Frederick Davies, who had visited Boulogne and used the bathing machines there as his prototype. Mindful of safety concerns, the company responsible for these vehicles also provided life buoys and diving stands free of charge, as well as a rescue boat.

Behind the generalities of difference there was a lot of regional variety to bathing in England and France. The real cross-Channel division concerned whether men and women should take the plunge together or separately. From a non-European perspective bathing in both places was essentially private. By contrast, American journalist J. Howe Adams described how in his country it was a public activity like 'rowing, riding or other athletic sport'. For him, the difference in behaviour had its roots in something more fundamental: 'abroad, the old idea of exclusiveness still prevails: at home, the ocean bath is the essence of democracy.' Bathing machines were

The Delightful Process of Dressing in a Bathing Machine.

By the late-ninteenth century people were growing tired of the discomforts associated with changing in a bathing machine.

provided as standard at English *and* French resorts, designed to allow a discreet transition from changing room to ocean waves. Even where the accommodation was stationary, as at Trouville, Adams noted the same principle of privacy: 'each bather, it makes no difference whether male or female, is furnished with a *peignoir*, which is in this case only a white muslin sheet which envelops the figure from head to toe: this sheet the bather leaves on the shore on entering the water, and wraps around him again before returning to his bath-house.' According to the American this modesty garment had the unfortunate effect of making its wearer look 'like a somnambulist!'

Within Europe, the differences between English and French bathing styles were so readily apparent that the mixed bathing area at Scheveningen, the Dutch coastal resort of The Hague, was described as offering ladies and gentlemen the opportunity to bathe together in the 'French style'. This former fishing town, dubbed 'the Brighton of Holland' in its first official guidebook, was a relative late-comer to the seaside scene only getting its smart entertainment pavilion, the *kurhaus*, in 1885. On the sands below there were cosy tents and the distinctly Dutch wind-chairs, described by one writer as consisting of 'wickerwork made in the shape of a huge peanut shell hollowed out on one side'. Here the bathing arrangements were, in fact, a kind of Anglo-French amalgam. Bathing 'coaches' were available for hire with or without an awning (presumably like Beale's modesty hood) and charges were dependent on the choice of large or small vehicle. Scheveningen prided itself on operating a convenient system without queues. When bathers paid to hire a machine they were given a numbered metal counter; their turn came when the number was called. Yet, like in England, the sea remained divided – albeit into three areas rather than two – for 'Ladies' baths; Gentlemen's baths and *Bains-mixtes* (mixed-baths). In the baths reserved for gentlemen only, the ordinary bathing-drawers are allowed, whereas in the mixed and Ladies' baths all bathers are obliged to don a bathing costume. That the mixed-baths find favour, the annual increase shows. A great number of families prefer them to the other baths'. This situation endured from the early 1880s until at least 1910. Visitors came predominantly from the Dutch and German hinterland but their overall number was tiny when compared with the English resorts. In the 1890s Scheveningen attracted roughly 20,000 tourists a year. During the same period, the small North Sea resorts of Redcar and Coatham could play to host to that many Teeside trippers over one Bank Holiday. By 1884 Blackpool was already entertaining up to 40,000 excursionists at a time.

The Belgian royal resort of Ostend had a longer history, beginning its career in 1831. By the end of the century it welcomed between 40,000 and 50,000 visitors a year, mainly from Belgium, France and Germany. When John Henry Cardinal Newman, head of the Catholic Church in England, visited in August 1863 he noted 'shoals of people', all well-to-do Belgians following the King who spent a six-week season by the sea. There were few English people in the crowd but there were hundreds of bathing machines: 'Bathing machines without end, and bathing all

Rows of machines lined up on Ostend beach during bathing hours.

day; a continual landing, more or less dextrous, of the clumsy machines, drawn by clumsier horses scarcely in harness, from the pier into the level sea-line of deep ploughed up sand.' As the resort became more cosmopolitan the variety of changing accommodation also grew. In 1901 bathers could choose from a basic 'Voiture Ordinaire' with a time limit of forty minutes for one franc or a superior 'Voiture Spéciale' for three francs. On the east beach, where the locals went to bathe, a machine cost just seventy-five cents. Whatever the choice, a knock with a whip on the top of the vehicle signalled that the horse was being attached. On the busy west beach, particularly during the most crowded hour between eleven and twelve o'clock, bathers were advised to take careful note of the number and colour of their machine, which could and did move. Once reunited with his or her machine the bather pulled a string inside and a little red flag popped up on the roof to show attendants the machine was ready to be pulled back up the beach. Confident enough of its elite clientele, in 1905 Ostend introduced the ultimate 'designer' bathing machine. Called the 'machine de luxe', this moveable saloon had picturesque views etched on its be-curtained windows. It took two horses to pull it and could be hired for the vast sum of twenty francs.

As was the case at Scheveningen, Belgian bathing arrangements were a hybrid of French and English customs. There was no separation of the sexes at Ostend but guidebooks stressed that the strictest propriety was maintained by each bather being provided with a costume. Although an area known rather provocatively as 'Paradis' was set aside for gentlemen who preferred to take to the waves naked, some visitors were shocked to find that the distinction between the two parts of the beach could be negligible. As in Britain, the tidy guidebook descriptions were rarely matched by the actual behaviour of bathers, not least because the official striped neck-to-knee *maillot* often clung revealingly to intimate bodily contours when wet. Local artist James Ensor, caricatured the beach in his controversial 1890 drawing *Les Bains à Ostende*. In the spirit of English eighteenth-century artist Thomas Rowlandson, Ensor portrayed a teeming sea with all ages and both sexes cavorting in front of a line of bathing machines that functioned mainly as sites of voyeurism or assignation. The barely concealed sexual practices were totally at odds with the elegant, sophisticated image Ostend sought for itself.

The same could be said of Trouville as depicted in French writer Guy de Maupassant's 1888 novel, *Pierre et Jean*. Having taken a boat trip to the most fashionable and expensive watering place on the Normandy coast, Pierre arrived at bathing time to find the beach transformed into a 'garden full of gaudy flowers. All along the stretch of yellow sand... sun-shades of every hue, hats of every shape, dresses of every colour, in groups outside the bathing huts, in long rows at the margin of the waves, or scattered here and there'. Walking among these 'immense bouquets on a vast meadow' Pierre came to the conclusion that the wide shore was 'no more than a love-market, where some sold, others gave themselves – some drove a hard bargain for their kisses and others promised them for love. All these women thought only of one thing, to make their bodies desirable – bodies already given, sold, or promised to other men. And he reflected that it was everywhere the same, all over the world.'

This point of view was exactly what British moralists chose to resist. Yet what did it say about our wealthiest citizens that their presence, in great numbers, was remarked upon as a prominent feature of continental resorts? This movement began in the 1870s and by 1889 one fifth of Boulogne's resident population was made up of English ex-pats. The northern European coastal resorts were relatively easy to get to so it is not surprising they were cited as paradigms of polite mixed bathing. In America the practice was even more heartily embraced but fewer tourists made the long trans-Atlantic boat journey. Accounts in the early days made excuses for the mingling of men and maids as in James Stuart's description of bathing at Long Branch in 1829. 'Because of the swell, females are often afraid to venture into the sea with a female bathing woman, and on that account prefer the assistance of a man. This custom, which is very far from being general, has given rise to ill-founded stories of want of delicacy on the part of American females. The fact is, I believe, exactly as I have stated it, and the parties always go into the water completely dressed.' This last statement needs to be qualified a little; when bathing together men and women were fully clothed but at mid-century naked submersion was still allowed during the gentleman's post-luncheon bathing hour. As this practice gradually died out, mixed bathing gained in both popularity and acceptability.

Bathing machines at Boulogne had distinctive rounded ends.

Although Winslow Homer pictured bathing machines in his drawing of *The Bathe at Newport* (1858) this apparatus lacked widespread appeal in America. The alternative practice of changing in static bath-houses at the top of the beach meant walking to the water's edge in full view of everyone on the beach and therefore led to a foreign idea of the American bathe as very bold and exposing even if patriots like J. Howell Adams preferred to call it 'democratic'. In fact, foreigners like the English woman Amelia Murray who witnessed mixed bathing at Newport in 1854, were amused rather than shocked, infected by the enthusiasm of participants. She described ladies, young and old, frolicking among the waves with the aid of strong male arms to save them from being knocked over in the surf. These gentlemen 'handed about their pretty partners as if they were dancing water quadrilles: it was very droll, very lively, and I daresay very amusing to all engaged.' In 1860 Dr S. Thomson, a self-confessed arbiter of British resorts, reported that at the great American watering place of Cape May, 'ladies and gentlemen, from the grave senator or merchant to the miss in her teens, promenade the waves together'

Regulation of British, mid-nineteenth century bathing practices was a hard-won victory for moralists but it tended to apply only to the main beaches of the main resorts. The misconception that strict segregation was enforced *everywhere at all times* paints a conveniently black and white picture of Victorian attitudes and hides a whole spectrum of greyness. To redress this requires an acknowledgement of historically different ideas about male nudity. In 2006 a survey into unacceptable public practices registered nudity as the greatest modern taboo. Thirty-seven per cent of those questioned put it top of their list. We have so far dispensed with embarrassment in the social discussion of sex that it has become a commodity for daily consumption and yet we still expect people to cover up in public, even on the beach. This is not something for which we can blame the Victorians. Sea-bathing began earlier in England than in Europe or America. It began as a means of improving health so exposure of the whole, unclothed, body was considered important. Purists still took this view at the end of the nineteenth century and there were enough of them to warrant some form of separation between men and women. Was this to protect women from a perceived offence or was it to protect the male right to nudity? Perhaps it was both, because although Continental mixed bathing was usually portrayed as more liberal it should be remembered that costume was always obligatory. Even those Englishmen who stood up for naked bathing did not go so far as to suggest that their wives and daughters should

This moustachioed gentleman looks well pleased by the removal of restrictive by-laws designed to keep the sexes apart whilst bathing.

indulge with them. So they were, by our definition, sexist, and their resistance to neck-to-knee bathing costumes meant a long opposition to mixed bathing. But by looking at it in a different way, perhaps the fact that this opposition was not overruled sooner means that fewer people were ashamed of public nudity than they are now.

And, besides, mixed bathing was never outlawed in the way historians have led us to believe. In 1947 J. A. R. Pimlott, the first man to chart the history of the English holiday, claimed that the momentous change back towards mixed bathing occurred in 1901 when Bexhill was in the vanguard of moral trend-setting. The sport of Victorian-bashing was *de rigueur* in the post-war period so the date of 1901, year of Queen Victoria's death, was deeply symbolic for an act that apparently demonstrated the loosening of social mores. In fact, Bexhill was following rather than leading the way. As historian John Travis has shown, growing disillusionment with segregated bathing led to a national press campaign in 1895–96; petitions were organised and local newspapers were bombarded with letters demanding the relaxation of restrictive by-laws. What this concerted effort revealed was that, though it had been marginalized, mixed bathing was still happening. Its survival was reported at places as far apart as Newquay in Cornwall, Felixstowe in Suffolk, Littlehampton and Deal on the south coast, Seaton in Devon, Barmouth and Tenby in Wales and Seaview on the Isle of Wight. One correspondent who wrote in to support *The Daily Graphic* campaign pointed out that most letter-writers had wrongly assumed that there were 'but one or two spots where the sexes can mingle in the water, or none at all'. He emphatically stated that this was not the case and that men and women bathed 'together in almost every part at the country except at the larger resorts'.

Apparently there *was* a choice and those families who sought out spots beyond the legislative reach of resort authorities, even at select towns like Eastbourne, simply got on with enjoying each other's company in the water without publicising it. In August 1896, the *Daily Mail* demonstrated just how absurd the situation was with reference to the still popular resort of Margate. Printed notices on the main beach warned male and female bathers to keep to their allotted areas, while, just beyond the control of the town council, at one end of the resort, 'men and maids' could 'swim in company without any sense of indecorum'. This was not a singular case: 'In many of the smaller bathing towns, where there are no bathing machines and possibly no town councils, family bathing parties are the rule.' Add to this the arguments about saving lives by teaching women to swim, as well as the decency of Continental precedents and something official had to give. An increasingly forceful economic argument tipped the balance.

In 1895 Llandudno became the first British seaside resort to officially reintroduce mixed bathing on part of its beach. Subsequent pioneers

The novelty of mixed bathing ensured it was a popular subject on Edwardian postcards.

included Paignton in 1896, Cromer and Dawlish in 1897, Worthing and Bognor Regis in 1899 and Bridlington and Torquay in 1900. These were predominantly resorts that prided themselves on a reputation for exclusivity; they pitched themselves at the upper end of the market, to people who had the wherewithal to take their business onto the Continent. One letter to the *Paignton Observer* asked:

> Why do we not adopt the Continental idea of mixed bathing? And why should not Paignton, with its unrivalled sands, be a pioneer in this matter? I feel confident that, were the experiment tried, many, who like myself now take their wives and families to French watering places, would flock to Paignton.

His hunch proved to be right. After the Urban District Council permitted the sexes to bathe together in neck-to-knee costumes, business boomed. Neighbouring resorts had to follow suit when their patrons began shifting loyalties.

An article in the *South Coast Quarterly* of 1899 referred to the proclaimed 'freedom and harmless *abandon* of the bathing' in France and the ease with which it could be enjoyed. 'And the journey, why it's nothing...You leave Victoria at ten, Brighton at ten thirty, and you're at Dieppe at three.' Full of fighting talk, the article went on to promote transport improvements making access to south coast towns just as easy. But reducing journey times alone would not combat the middle-class drift abroad. At the same date, A. R. Hope Moncrieff's book *Where Shall We Go: A Guide to the Health and Holiday Resorts of Great Britain*, noted that 'a burning question at many of our seaside resorts is as to whether a place shall be set aside for "mixed" or family bathing, on Continental models; and this is still so far unsettled that we have not been able to give precise statements in each case, but at most towns where the authorities interfere with such matters, the innovation seems likely to be admitted'. A certain lack of clarity remained at some places, like cautious Southend where according to a Guide of 1904: 'Mixed bathing is not actually sanctioned by the Corporation but it is not prohibited.' In the same year a lady visitor to Dovercourt Bay, also in Essex, wrote to the *Free Press* alleging 'indecent bathing upon the part of the male sex' and criticising the habit of mixed bathing. The *Press* enquired and found that 'there is a share of male nudity, yet so there is of female...but nothing to warrant such a strongly worded epistle'. It then suggested the building of wooden huts on the foreshore and the idea was soon taken up. Change was gradual but the days of the bathing machine were numbered.

Chapter Eleven
Brighton to Mudeford

Central Brighton had a buzz despite the gloomy sky. Though bits of the seafront had been done over with public art and an imaginative children's play area, the derelict West Pier was a woeful reminder of recent, less fashionable days. Seagulls wheeled around the two abandoned pavilions, so vulnerable now on their spindly iron legs. The oriental bandstand was fenced off and along Madeira Drive, east of the piers, rust impinged a little too heavily on the ornamental railings and lattice arches running below the seawall. These imperfections seemed to suit Brighton's shifting fortunes yet the short row of twenty-three beach huts surprised me. I'd nearly given up looking and almost missed them. Battered wire mesh enclosed the bit of beach in front of the huts, which were built as a single brick building under a flat, slightly sloping, roof. What little wall showed between the consecutive sets of double doors was painted cream and the metal poles that held the roof out beyond the front were coppery green, the same combination as on the metalwork of Madeira Drive behind. All but one of the huts was shut up. Most had white doors but the open pair was green. Their owner, a slim middle-aged man, sat inside reading the newspaper with a big black motorbike parked next to his deckchair. I suppose I was expecting more panache from these Brighton huts but perhaps their relative anonymity was a refreshing bonus to residents. After all it wasn't the sort of place you'd expect to see someone as famous as Sir Lawrence Olivier, former occupant of number one, or actress Dora Bryan, who'd had the hut next door.

Further eastwards, midway to Eastbourne, were the 1950s brick chalet blocks at Seaford and closer still the brick blocks at Saltdean. At Seaford the rows were enlivened with brightly alternating doors in green, red, blue and yellow. Under the chalky cliff at Saltdean the doors were more subtly subdued, shades of pale greens, blues and greys succeeding each other in no particular order. But back in the city it was the Hove huts that made the biggest impression.

For administrative purposes Brighton & Hove had morphed into one place but a historic sense of snobbery continued to give meaning to the old boundary. Locals joked that Hove should be called Hove Actually since this was the well-used reply given by residents when asked if they were from Brighton. Where Brighton was the wayward, rakish seaside resort made famous by the pleasure-seeking Prince Regent and his cronies, Hove had grown from a little fishing village into a separate, elegant destination for wealthy visitors who preferred tranquil tree-lined boulevards. Victorian trippers picked Brighton over Hove; so did the Mods and Rockers. And so did the trendy students and club owners who were dragging Brighton – often in drag – to a vital new heyday. Just the week before I arrived DJ Fat Boy Slim had played to a bigger than expected crowd on Brighton beach, a beach that was apparently now out of bounds because of all the pint glasses and alco-pop bottles crushed on the shingle. It was fun, people had a good time but by reputation it wasn't the sort of thing you'd expect residents of Hove to want on their quieter doorstep.

And yet the Hove huts were bold, with far more sass than their Brighton sisters. It wasn't their shape, which was the standard four walls and gabled roof; it was their decoration. The council dictated a basic scheme of burgundy bottoms topped with a bluish-green upper half so that from behind uniformity reigned; from the promenade the four hundred-odd huts were a spectacular rainbow. As long as the private owners stuck to one bold block of colour they were permitted to paint their doors according to individual preference. Matching the front to the sides hardly seemed to matter. 'Tardis' had a fuchsia pink entrance and next door 'The Nap Hut' was golden yellow. More than one had a little notice with a phone number for 'The Beach Hut Man', Hove's answer to Jack Cork; every day of the year Bernie Foster was somewhere along the line guarding, repairing or replacing the huts. I was walking the twelve or so miles to Goring-by-Sea and by the time I got to Shoreham Harbour it was clear I'd missed him.

The estuary of the River Adur meant cutting inland past gravel spewing machines and a noisy main road. Then a footbridge crossed over the freshwater channel onto the spit of Shoreham Beach where the long line of West Sussex beach huts began, mostly white, some with verandas and some without. The couple in hut 41a told me how the wooden shacks and converted railway carriages of Bungalow Town used to stretch along the shore.

'In the war they were worried the Germans would come ashore and hide in them so they were bulldozed.'

When peace returned they were replaced by permanent houses with proper planning permission and only day huts were allowed on the shingle.

'A lot of the beach was washed away in the Great Storm of 1987,' went on the man, 'and towards the end of these huts two old walls with flowerpots on top were uncovered that used to belong to the bungalows. It was like archaeological evidence or something.'

More hut clusters dotted the beach on the way to, then through, Lancing. From a lady hut resident I learnt that in the half century from 1912 the main employer here had been the Southern Railway Carriage Works. It was such a local institution that almost every house – and beach hut – had had benches in it made at the carriage works. At Shoreham people had taken empty train compartments and turned them into holiday homes, at Lancing they'd taken the discarded seats.

Walking into Worthing, I passed plastic palm trees on the beach with stuffed toy monkeys hugging the fake trunks. They were supposed to supply the exotic element for Ju-Jus Coconut Kiosk but the sky had turned grey and people at the café tables were holding onto their parasols. The huts flanking the pebbled octagon of Ju-Jus looked a bit more sheltered, built underneath a long and sturdy slab of concrete roof held up along the front by a widely spaced colonnade of chunky columns clad in those same flinty pebbles which looked as though they'd been collected directly from the shore. Four strips of pale blue crittal windows fronted each hut and on the central clock tower a plaque recalled the 1951 Festival of Britain, giving away their age. Their modern design worked well with the fantastic Art Deco pier buildings. Worthing's other huts were also consistent with their backdrop though neither the boring brick tower blocks nor the white huts, mostly in pairs angled up against each other with felt lids for roofs, had a great deal of aesthetic charm. On some, the Worthing Borough Council initials had been tinkered with, leaving on the first and last a pairing with a rather different meaning.

The 285 white huts at Goring-by-Sea returned to the traditional gabled shape, albeit with some odd front appendages that reminded me of four-poster bed frames. These strange scaffolds stuck out from the sides, built from wooden batons nailed under the roof and above the floor joined to upright posts. Filled in, they would almost have doubled the hut's floor space but none of them *were* filled in because it was evening and everyone had gone home. My best guess was that Goring hut owners set up temporary windbreaks and sunshades when the weather called for it or when they wanted privacy from their neighbours. It was a peculiarity I found nowhere else. Not even at neighbouring Ferring where, on my last stop of the day, the short line of coloured gables enjoyed an unencumbered outline and an informal, villagey feel. The middle-aged couple outside number eleven had just set light to a disposable tray of charcoal when another couple arrived with bottles of Chardonnay to join them for a seafront supper. I found out the next day that it wasn't just a barbeque that burnt that night; two huts were destroyed and two others were damaged in a fire caused by vandals.

In the 1820s Littlehampton was recommended as a good place for families and a century later this so-called 'Children's Paradise' was routinely chosen by noble and wealthy parents as *the* place to send nanny and the little ones. It was the south coast Frinton. When I arrived girls and boys were leaning over the promenade near the mouth of the River Arun, trying to bait crabs with bacon lowered in net bags originally designed for washing powder tablets. Beyond the prom were jolly crescents of colour co-ordinated beach huts in combinations of Cornflower Blue, Garland Green and Aztec Yellow, their unpainted wood interiors still displaying the pallor of newness. Sitting on the blue decking of a blue hut I met an elderly lady in her second year as a council tenant. She'd lived in Sussex since 1963 and remembered how, despite the obvious paradox, the council used to erect plastic 'igloos' on Littlehampton beach.

'They weren't sturdy enough though and in gales they'd end up across the road.' Her new blue hut was much better even if she had to share it with field mice in the winter.

'I must have left food in here,' she reasoned, 'but I'm a country girl, I can cope with that. They don't bother me in the summer.'

As the bright huts ran out the large Victorian building of Rustington Convalescent Home gradually came into view. This seaside getaway set up in 1897 to help working men return to fitness was still welcoming people in need of rest, recuperation and respite. A hundred years ago there were so many of these facilities it would hardly have been worth mentioning. Now there aren't and it is. Is convalescence an outmoded concept? Can you get a pill for it these days? Or is that what daytime TV is for? I'm not sure it's such a good exchange. A couple of weeks in a beach hut might do the trick but if the convalescent home owned one along the line at Rustington they weren't advertising it. Most of these were on a private beach hidden from the rest of the world by a high hedge of juniper bushes. Deep growls of thunder were beginning to upset the August afternoon and spits of rain began to fall on my bare arms. There were only four other people on the beach, Pauline and Mark and their hut neighbours Ivor and Hazel.

'Come in,' urged Pauline as we all followed her towards the folding chairs set up inside the white hut. She and her husband lived in

Cambridge but stayed with parents just up the road. They had bought their hut five years ago from a lady called Betty who wanted to sell to people who loved the sea as much as she did.

'There are no amenities here,' Pauline pointed out, 'so we just come to swim, that's all you can do.' Her brown hair was still wet from the last dip and she wore a sarong that matched her bright red swimming costume patterned with pink flowers.

'You can only swim when the tide is high. There's a three hour window,' added Mark. 'There's sand when the tide goes out but it's not deep enough to swim.'

The couple consulted tide tables before booking time off work to guarantee a pre-breakfast swim. Ivor and Hazel lived locally so could get away with less planning.

'This is our twenty-first visit this year,' Ivor told me. 'A couple of weeks ago I came down and we'd got some beautiful graffiti over the hut. Thing was, the spelling was atrocious!'

'So where have you been on your travels?' Mark asked me.

I began to talk about the places I'd seen so far and the people I'd met.

'You mean there are lots of us?' He sounded faintly surprised. 'I didn't know we were part of a socio-economic group!'

We all exchanged smiles but he did have a point.

At nearby Angmering there were white concrete hut blocks, the design of which Pauline likened to public lavatories. In the other direction, past Littlehampton, I found more yellow, blue and green huts arranged across a wide strip of lawn below the seawall at Felpham. Nearer Bognor Regis rented huts lined up sentry-like in a uniform of deep navy blue. The view of Bognor itself was dominated by the white-tented roof of Butlins, a kind of pneumatic meringue wired taught above the holiday complex. In its shadow I walked past the last survivors of another Edwardian bungalow community, the original railway carriage shells just visible underneath extensions and UPVC additions.

Past Butlins and past the pier I came to Aldwick Beach where the hut hamlet included individuals, pairs and quads, some gable-on, others side-on to the sea. In the early evening light the concrete rendered walls in pale shades of green and orange blended with the mixed tones of the shingle. A few brown wooden sheds had infiltrated this line and one stood open, missing its door. Inside there were wood shavings on the floor and Cliff Richard posters on the wall. My personal favourite captured the 1980s bachelor boy sporting a pair of unfeasibly large, round glasses. Could this have been a drop-in shrine for local fans? With slightly ironic reverence I leant in and stuck the peeling corner of one picture back on the wall. And that was the highlight of my visit to Bognor.

The next morning I went into Chichester and out again on a bus bound for West Wittering. In the front seat a well-spoken older gentleman chatted to the driver and as each new passenger stepped on he handed them a foil-wrapped mint. Everyone seemed to know him. He was on his way to spend the day at a lady friend's beach hut. It was impossible not to eavesdrop:

'I've been to M&S to get some things for a picnic,' he told us all, pulling a little bottle of red wine from a carrier bag between his legs. Then, as it always should do on an English bus, the conversation turned to the weather. Was it really fine enough for a picnic? We all looked out of the windows as if intending to join in the debate. It *was* a bit gloomy.

'They said it was going to turn nasty so I've put my raincoat on over my shorts,' the gentleman assured us.

When we both got off at the same stop I followed him towards the beach.

On the first hot weekend of the summer the road onto this almost-island was notoriously packed, bumper to bumper all the way from Chichester. It was quiet as I made my way past the colourful beach huts but I could see why this was a popular spot. For a start, the beach actually had some soft sand on it, something I hadn't seen much of since leaving Thanet. And because of the wiggly coastline there were also open views on three sides; sailing boats whipped across this panorama round from Chichester behind me, past Hayling Island to my right and then out toward the Isle of Wight in front. To get a hut here the best chance was inheritance because thanks to the tradition of handing them through families it was extremely unusual for more than two to come on the market each year. And even then the market wasn't an open market. As owners of the beach, the West Wittering Estate kept a waiting list of wannabe hutters but had closed it at 105 names since, with only 156 huts, the people at the bottom would be waiting a good fifty years on current form. Which made me wonder, not for the first time, about all those locked doors; the retired couple sitting outside hut 126 could only remember seeing their neighbours about three times in twelve years. They themselves routinely walked down to the beach from their home in Chichester on Sunday mornings after church. Perhaps their neighbours didn't have time to spend days drinking tea from a thermos flask and sunning their shins below rolled up trouser legs but it was a shame the hut wasn't in regular use.

I found the same situation at East Wittering even though the short row of huts sat on the metaphorical doorstep of seafront houses and flats. Their boundary was marked by a signpost: 'PRIVATE property reserved for occupants of hut sites only', but there was no-one in the huts to take issue with my presence and a few of the doors were being overtaken by pretty beds of daisies.

From East Wittering I bussed through Havant onto Hayling Island. Regency speculators had planned a resort here to rival Brighton but two smart terraces were all that remained of their unfulfilled dream. The urban setting for these town houses never materialised but they made a nice backdrop to the beach huts. I set out along the lines and U-shaped configurations of West Beach and Beachlands where the privately-owned huts guaranteed a nice diversity of colour and size within the basic gabled form. In Block B I met Derek who told me he knew everything there was to know about beach huts. Derek's father had brought him down to Hayling Island as a boy and now, in his fifties and a little more rotund, it was the place where he and his wife spent most of their time. They described some of the local characters, including Chick and Brenda from America who had been the first to completely clad their hut in UPVC and put mahogany stain on the floor. It would have been good to get their perspective on the British love of beach huts but Chick and Brenda had gone back to Oregon. Derek suggested I visit the Beachlands Office instead. The man responsible for the huts wasn't in but I was permitted a quick glance at the charts covering the walls of his control room; studded patterns of different colour pins described each of the 358 hut locations in this nerve centre of beach hut activity.

Perhaps it was all those dots that had a subliminal effect or my competitive nature that made me want to prove I was more of an expert than Derek. Something that day caused my one and only beach hut nightmare. The rain had started to fall as I left Hayling Island and during the night a torrential downpour woke me from my stressed subconscious, an alternative existence where the beach huts stretched into infinity and I could never hope to see them all. I was at a crossroads trying to decide which street of bright beach huts to go down first, each extending so far into the distance that it seemed impossible that I would ever come back to my starting point. The choice was paralysing. How could I complete my mission? In my dream nothing seemed more important yet I couldn't move. According to my approximate calculations I'd already clocked up more than 11,300 over the past five weeks so it was pretty amazing my sleeping hours weren't perpetually overrun with huts. Mostly the sea air just knocked me straight out. But not that night; whatever the trigger for my dream, I woke up in a funny mood.

It was still damp when I arrived at Portsmouth; by the time I got to the seafront there were proverbial cats and dogs tumbling from the sky. Stepping off the number twenty-three bus at South Parade Pier I scanned both directions from under my umbrella and decided to head east. Either side of the entrance to Southsea Rose Garden there were flat-roofed blocks of chalets which I found offered some shelter from the rain slanting off the sea as long as I squeezed my body right up into the right-hand corner of the row. Remarkably, the diagonally panelled brown doors of hut number ten were open, the lady inside drying off not from the rain but from her morning swim. She was thin with a tanned face wrinkled like parchment from years of being outside. From the breeze block walls of her hut there hung clothing suitable for all weathers. It wasn't a decorated space but it was definitely lived-in. She claimed that it was always warm in her hut so, as the rain, which had eased off, began to fall again, she invited me to join her for a cup of coffee. The cheap granules and powdered milk dissolved into a bland yet pleasingly warm liquid, which we sipped together while puddles formed outside and the guttering discharged rivulets off the roof. She was an original tenant, one of the two left from thirty years ago when the chalets were built. Her story from the Sixties sounded surprisingly familiar.

'First of all we had a dalek hut on the beach nearer the pier. It was like a plastic cone with portholes in the sides. Then we got on the waiting list for a hut here. Seven years that took and every year we'd go to the Beach Inspector and ask how far we'd moved up the list. When we got to be sixth my husband went and counted the new huts and there were six extra so we would have made a fuss if we hadn't got one.'

The council were knocking down the dilapidated wooden huts to build solid blocks so the couple got the keys to a brand new one. Widowed last year, the lady kept her hut on because, she said, her husband would've wanted her to.

Back out in the rain I trudged on along the exposed promenade getting increasingly soggy, particularly on my seaward facing right leg, which bore the brunt of the squally precipitation. I was glad to see a row of tall pale green, pink and blue beach huts, on the other side of the road and tried in vain to find shelter under their verandas. They were new and attractive but the toilet block next door was warmer and equipped with electric hand dryers that I could blast towards my hands and face. Back outside I dipped my head and kept walking until the end of Eastney

Esplande where, behind a row of dark and light blue huts, I finally lost it. What the bloody hell was I doing? Yes, it was only a bit of rain but I was cold and wet and I really began to question my sanity. Of course, I knew my obsession with beach huts was a bit nutty but in that moment it felt totally ridiculous instead of just a bit eccentric. Who cared how many beach huts I saw? And yet, when a male cleaner came into the next set of loos with his mop and bucket I still couldn't help asking whether he knew of any other huts, concerned in case, after all this effort, I might have missed some. There was really nothing for it but to turn around, get my left leg as wet as my right and move on to the next huts.

Thankfully the weather cleared and so did my mood, mostly as a result of talking to Malcolm and Lynn. I managed to hop on a tourist bus with running commentary on all the sights between Southsea and Portsmouth Harbour, then jumped on a ferry for the three-minute crossing to Gosport. From there I took a bus to Stokes Bay. The thirty huts I'd come to see were in two blocks, brick built with cream painted walls and full-height green doors. On the other side of the bay at Lee-on-Solent there were fifteen more in the same style. They weren't architecturally distinguished, all of them were shut up and it was quite a walk between the two places, mostly on my own across a pebbly beach that made my legs turn to jelly as soon as I returned to a flat path. In the distance though, I could see a line of about sixty green huts curving along the top of the beach in front of trees interspersed with a few big houses. I had to keep going.

It was outside number thirty that I met Malcolm and Lynne. They'd had their hut at Monks Hill, Fareham, for a year but like the Southsea lady they'd waited seven years to get it.

'We're total converts,' said Malcolm, 'but it was like getting used to a different culture. With the hut we inherited a piece of carpet and we were going to throw it away but then we found out it was an essential piece of equipment. It's the first thing you do when you get here; the laying out of the carpet in front of the hut, it's like marking territory.'

In the past they'd been 'squatters', the name given by hutters to the people who camped on the shingle and got chased away by the rain. Now they could sit in the hut with the doors open and enjoy the widescreen view. Malcolm ushered me in and showed me how the outside was framed by the hut. Everything, especially the grey sea and the cloudy sky, became sharper for having edges.

'While we were on the waiting list I painted the inside of our garden shed up as a beach hut. It had the same white and blue colour scheme we've got here and I created a seaside garden in front of it too.'

'We've let the boys put their bikes back in there now,' remarked Lynne. 'They tell people we've gone to our shed on the beach but actually most of our friends have stopped asking!'

As they talked I got a sense of the strong community here and with it all the politics and gossip of village life. Malcolm recalled the speculation that their arrival had occasioned with good humour.

'I used to have long hair so when people were trying to guess my profession they decided I was a potter. Actually I mend dustcarts for the council so I think they were a bit disappointed!'

Whatever their differences everyone shared a love of beach huts and when it was necessary the community pulled together. Recently there'd been a particularly touching example when an old lady who'd had a beach hut for years died. All the owners went to her funeral and the hearse actually drove past the huts, down the road, turned around at the bottom and went back again like a last goodbye.

'So what do you do when you're down here?' I asked.

'That's just it,' replied Malcolm, 'it's relaxing because there's not much you can do. I read, do a bit of painting but the best thing is just looking at the view. In winter we close one door and put the gas heater on behind it; we move the wicker sofa in front of the other door and it's fantastically snug. It's like reverting to childhood; like living in a big Wendy house.'

I noticed that everything in the hut had a seaside theme.

'We collect things and friends and family look out for stuff too' Lynne explained, pointing out the curtain rings shaped as beach huts that I secretly coveted.

'Everyone has a colour scheme. We're blue and white, Doreen is red and white, next door are Roy and Joy,' Malcolm paused. 'No, honestly, that's what they're called, Roy and Joy!'

After my wobble this morning Malcolm and Lynne made me feel much less bonkers. Malcolm was unashamed about his love for the seaside, for rock shops and lilos, even confessing that he liked how the smell of suntan cream wafted up from the crowds when the beach was busy. He was clearly in his element.

'I suppose you know that the normal culinary rules don't apply in beach huts?' His wife smiled at this. 'It's like men and barbeques. I hate cooking but down here I've invented a new dish – *oeufs à la mer*. Next time you come I'll make you a plate.'

It was the end of Cowes Week and the regatta always closed with a bang. Malcolm and Lynne, and several of their neighbours who had also rolled out their territorial carpets, were getting ready to watch across the water for the fireworks display on the Isle of Wight. Triangles of white sail cloth were massing in the Solent, performing a maritime ballet for beach hut owners on both shores.

Ahead of me the Isle of Wight was floating off the Hampshire coast like a jigsaw piece waiting to complete the puzzle. An interwar guide likened its shape 'to a diamond placed horizontally, and, with greater exactitude, to a turbot'. The mainland let go of this big fish many millennia ago but thanks to its presence the channel and inlets of the Solent experience four tides a day, a phenomenon unique in Europe. There were beach huts near all four points of the diamond: on the turbot's head at Puckpool Park, near Seaview, St Helens, Bembridge and Foreland; on its top fin at Gurnard and on the turbot's tail at Colwell and Totland Bays. The greatest concentration, however, was on the side of the fin pointing toward France where, for about two miles under the greensand cliffs, huts lined the route from Sandown to Shanklin. I'd visited earlier in the year and counted eight different types along that esplanade, the bright blue private huts sticking together in a row between the various colour-strips of operators who offered their huts for hire. At Shanklin there were yet more, both summer-only beach sites and more permanent ones like those on the Western Esplanade painted in shades of beige.

Four miles on, over the cliff path with its stunning views back to Shanklin, I reached Ventnor and the island's most antique huts. Coated with a fine shingle reminiscent of dried red lentils, the town's beach sat below an 800-foot hill onto which generations of builders had contrived to create a theatrical townscape. The sea was the stage and every house looked upon it, soaking up the southern prospect. Reputed as a warm place even when everywhere else was cold, Ventnor enjoyed world-wide fame as a winter health-resort to the extent that my 1931 *Red Guide* had to reassure potential visitors that the 'town is *not* crowded with consumptives.' The huts, with their cream walls, curved green roofs and different pastel doors, had certainly seen the end of that trend although members of the Blake family, their proprietors, must have served many a tourist seeking the tonic of mild sea air since they began business in 1830. Now you could pay the current generation £4.50 to while away a day in a real bathing machine; well half of one, without its wheels. I learnt that the sand at Ventnor was too soft for horses so in its prime each machine had been equipped with its own capstan. The Longshoreman's Museum, run by Mr Blake Senior, had models in glass cases of the white carriages fitted with black wheels that were bigger at the back than the front because of shelving sands. The wheels had come off in 1920 when fashions changed. In the museum there were photographs, advertising signs and even examples of the Edwardian bathing costumes embroidered with the initials 'JB' from when J. & B. Blake hired them out with their machines. All of it came from the family collection, a collection that was surely as unique as the four tides. Here was the ultimate example of handing beach huts through the generations, an impressive succession that had lasted for more than 170 years.

The eastern tip of the island was interesting for its beach huts too. I'd read about railway carriages reused for holiday accommodation and had seen the vestiges of a surviving few but along the seawall at St Helens there was almost an entire train that had been turned into beach huts. A gradual make-over was clearly underway because new timber cladding covered the first few carriages nearest the café. The shape of the narrow arched doors had been kept but there was no sign of the old windows either side. Further along the line, the original panelled carriages were much more obvious under a peeling coat of red paint. It was a shame that the rhythm of windows and doors would be hidden but at least it looked like the carriage huts were staying.

At Bembridge the huts looked new and purpose-built. Left of the lifeboat station, behind a neat wooden fence they were dotted across a sloping lawn, most wearing bright shades of green or blue. Net curtains hung in the windows. All of which formality was a world away from the Foreland huts. Around the blowy headland the beach was much wilder, littered with shells and sun-bleached driftwood. There was no concrete promenade to build huts upon so they had been constructed amid the trees and bushes at the base of the cliff. Some were well-hidden by all this vegetation, others were only accessible by ladders lain against the sandy bluff. It was a little flotsam and jetsom community, the sort of place any castaway would have been pleased to call home. Locals had been escaping to huts here since well before the Second World War but only the first two, barely visible behind high hedges, were of that vintage. Some had been used by fishermen but others were year round dwellings, like the one occupied by a sickly London child and his mother in the 1930s. Due to a serious chest illness the little boy had been advised to live a completely free and open life by the sea, which his father saw to it that he did for ten years in a chalet here. It clearly worked because the boy, now an elderly gentleman, still lived in the village. Few of the original fifty-six plots were really secure because of cliff erosion but there was still a waiting list for these pretty tumble-down huts.

Back in Hampshire I'd spend another few days looking at the Isle of Wight from a mainland perspective. On the Saturday after Cowes

Friday I left Fareham for Hill Head, also known as 'ill ead' according to one butchered road sign. Below a pub called The Osborne View green huts followed the curve of the bay facing toward Queen Victoria's island summer house. The rain storms of the day before had cleared so I could see the Monks Hill huts to the east and, on the other side of Southampton Water, the vertical landmark of Fawley power station's cooling tower. That was where I was headed next. As ever, the journey was convoluted including a bus, a train, a ferry across the estuary from Southampton then a ride by miniature railway along the 2,100 feet of Hythe pier. The boat ride was a useful shortcut but most of the time I saved was wasted at the bus stop in Hythe. It probably would have been quicker to walk the last few miles to Calshot Spit.

With the 1960s oil-fuelled power station behind them, residents of the 170 council huts surveyed a busy waterway, thronged with sailing boats that were regularly dwarfed by the luxury cruise liners leaving Southampton. Surprisingly few of the huts were open but one male twenty-something owner had set himself up for an afternoon of sun worship. Prone against the shingle, with a radio playing tunes against his mop of blonde hair, he lay in front of his hut, the walls of which were adorned with posters of buxom beach babes like a sort of low rent bachelor pad.

I walked westward along the orange-pebbled shore of the Solent as deciduous trees began to fill in the background and block out the cooling tower's presence. Beyond a sign announcing the start of a private beach, the small day huts gave way to a row of twenty larger beach bungalows complete with bunkbeds and bookshelves. Most were occupied; people, chairs, boats and windbreaks filling the space outside each hut. I felt very conspicuous walking along the empty space between them and the outgoing tide, sure that in such a small community everyone must know everyone else.

There had once been an RAF base at Calshot. I knew that because Bert, the hut owner I'd met at Southend, had been stationed here in the last war. The locals were able to fill me in on more of the details and confirmed that there had been a few huts on the beach in 1913 when Winston Churchill took his first flight in a seaplane from the newly created Calshot Naval Air Station. The base became synonymous with seaplanes, playing host to the Schneider Cup Trophy Race twice in 1929 and 1930. First held in 1912 and founded by the French industrialist, plane and balloon pilot Jacques Schneider, the competition was conceived as a spur to the development of seaplane design which was lagging behind other aircraft. Calshot was due to be the venue again in 1931 but Ramsey MacDonald's government declared that there were insufficient funds available to enter a British team to defend their title. Lady Fanny Lucy Houston, reputedly the richest woman in England, stepped in with £100,000 and had a hut built on the beach to watch the planes. The French and Italian teams pulled out at the last minute but the British team raced for the right to retain their trophy, setting a new air speed record of 340mph in the process. With its distinctive row of six windows along the front, each split into nine small panes, and a petite dormer over the door, Lady Houston's hut lives on. Current owner Mike did his National Service at the Calshot Air Sea Rescue Unit and bought the historic hut in 1987.

At the end of the row I met Kath, Penny and Marie, owners of the penultimate three huts. My instinctive sense of a strong community down here was borne out by their observation that it could take half an hour to get from car to hut because of saying hello to everyone on the way. I joined the ladies for a gin and tonic outside Kath's sea-green hut and they told me how their children had all grown up together on the beach. Over the years they'd become one big extended beach hut family.

'At Christmas time we all do our own thing with our families,' said Penny, 'but to make up for not seeing each other we have a Christmas dinner in the huts every August. There's holly and present-giving and a flaming Christmas pudding.'

A couple of their teenage children were around and everyone had been together the night before when there'd been a bonfire on the beach for all the people who came to see the Cowes Week fireworks. As we sat chatting a vast cruise ship sailed serenely out of Southampton Water, lit bright white by the late afternoon sun. It was the second of the day.

'When the children were young we'd put them at the edge of the sea when the Townsend-Thoresen ferry sailed out' Marie remembered. 'It caused such a huge wash you could see it coming like a tsunami. It used to pass by at 7.05; that was bath time.'

The majestic mass of the QE2 was another regular sight. As was the milkman. Until about ten years ago the local shop had delivered milk, orange juice and newspapers to the beach. Though that service had been discontinued the postman still came, which was probably a good thing for Kath who always spent her August birthday at the hut.

My phone rang. Mum had just pulled into the car park. She was coming to join me for a few days so I directed her to the far end of the beach. When she arrived the gin glasses were topped up and chocolate cake was offered around the table. It was all so wonderfully sociable I could see why, despite having travelled around the world, these three friends maintained that there was nowhere like Calshot Beach.

Mum and I spent the night in Lymington, gossiping and eating vinegar-soaked chips by the harbour. Next morning I introduced her to my beach hut regime. We continued along the New Forest coast beginning at Milford on Sea where the battered looking concrete blocks of chalets had been given cheery painted doors and window shutters. Wispy white clouds were scudding across the blue sky but within half an hour they'd been replaced by a blanket of grey. The huts looked out towards the most westerly point of the Isle of Wight where The Needles extended their chalky stacks into the Channel. At the end was a red and white striped Victorian lighthouse but the most important lump of rock, the tall pointy one that actually had needle-like qualities, was long gone. Known as Lot's Wife after the Biblical misadventure of the woman whose glance back to the destruction of Sodom got her turned into a pillar of salt, the chalk column collapsed during a storm in 1764. The name had stuck even though the remaining Needles were rather too short and squat to properly qualify for the title. At Hordle Cliff the copiously colourful huts were layered at the top of the shingle and behind on the cliff itself. It was as if seeds had been scattered and hundreds of gabled huts had grown up wherever they could find space. The beach was the only promenade; there was no hulking concrete seawall so the wobbly lines of huts blended organically into the landscape. At Barton on Sea the lines of flat-roofed wooden huts were more autumnal in their colour palette but the browns and greens complemented the sandy clifftop as if they too were meant to be there.

We drove onto Highcliffe. Mum recalled holidaying here as a child, staying in a beach hut with her parents and four younger brothers and sisters in 1961 or '62. Forty years on there was no sign of any huts.

'I'm sure it was here,' she said as we stood looking down from the cliff top for some confirmatory evidence. 'The hut belonged to a colleague of my Dad who, as usual, was very hard up but still wanted to give us all a holiday. We came by car because by then he'd bought a Morris Traveller, which was a very big, very turquoise, heavy estate car. Even so it was a squeeze for five of us in the back.'

'So where were the huts?' I wanted to know, keen to find out about this surprising new evidence of family hut history.

'Ours was about halfway down the cliff – a long way to the beach and a long way to the toilets, which were at the top. We definitely had a cooker and sink but no toilet.'

She described how they'd walk along the back of the row of huts and, to save time, as the steps were a fair way along, scramble up to the top between the huts. That was probably how my Uncle Andrew had broken his arm.

'I remember there was a boy in the neighbouring hut who was excited because he'd been to see a group called The Beatles. I was about eleven or twelve and had my first pair of sneakers; they were really coloured lace-up plimsolls but I felt they were the thing to wear.'

'Seven of you in the hut must have been pretty cramped.'

'It was. My mother hated it and I'm not really surprised. We had basic teas like baked beans on toast and she would use two giant tins of beans for all of us – even making enough toast must have been a nightmare!'

Sunlight was beginning to brighten the sky and from our lookout we could see Dorset's first huts on the western side of Christchurch Bay. At Friars Cliff there were 139 council huts; the white ones stood out most strongly but there were blue and brown gables along the row too. After a short gap a second run of huts began, all of them either green or rusty-brown. Although Avon Beach was part of Mudeford the really famous, expensive Mudeford huts were visible on their sand spit the other side of the channel running into Christchurch harbour. I'd made an appointment to meet Tim Baber, editor of Mudeford Sandbank News, the following day so contented myself with a closer inspection of the nearest huts. At Friars Cliff the council had erected a new terrace of uniform wooden sheds obviously mindful of their earning potential. Neighbouring Avon Beach, however, was private; run as a family business since 1934. In the souvenir shop I found a little plastic beach hut attached to a key ring and whilst paying for it, took the opportunity of asking about how long the real ones had been around. There had been 140 since before the war, always green.

'About 1940, when invasion threatened, the army took over the beach,' said the man behind the counter. 'They didn't give my father time to find storage for the huts they just burnt most of them. We only managed to salvage about fifteen.'

After the war there was a timber shortage so most of them weren't replaced until about 1952. Now, of course, they were in demand. Vic Derham, current owner of the beach, handed me a flier that set out the hire costs for different periods. Seasonal leases were the most sought after. Only two had been given up that year so to ensure they got them when bookings opened on 2 January, two would-be hutters had slept in their cars the night before. Mr Derham compared it to queuing for the January sales. In 2006 Alan and Valerie Day topped that by spending four days and nights in their car, braving icy winds and rain just to get their Avon Beach hut. They described their eventual success as 'like winning the lottery'.

Ironically, I'd probably *need* to win the lottery before I could afford to get my hands on one of the bigger huts on Mudeford Spit. Before meeting Tim the next morning, Mum and I visited the local estate agent Humphrey's and Orr. Even in the ailing property market of 1992 the grandest huts could go for as much as £30,000, though a figure of about half that was probably more likely. For someone who'd bought just five years earlier, to sell then would have meant a tidy profit; to sell now would guarantee a considerable nest egg. There were four huts in the estate agent's window priced at between £59,950 and £70,000 for a space measuring sixteen feet by ten feet, plus front platform. Two were marked 'SOLD'. In the face of such outside demand locals were selling up to buy holiday flats in Spain. The numbers were getting silly and I wondered if a simple hut could ever really be worth that kind of money.

We took the ferry across from Mudeford with other passengers carrying windbreaks and fishing nets. There were two rows of huts, back to back, even numbers looking across the shallow harbour to Christchurch Priory, odd numbers facing out to sea. Side by side the 350 coloured cabins made for a diminutive skyline. The lack of *any* hinterland, be it dunes or cliffs or seafront, lent this place a blissful remoteness; the sandy finger of land was surrounded by water on three sides and on the fourth was Hengistbury Head, a headland rich in wildlife and archaeology that acted as a scenic buffer against the spread of Bournemouth's urban development. Tim's white hut was number 156, easy to find because of the narrow canoe parked in front emblazoned with the red-painted words 'THE MUDEFORD SANDBANK NEWS'. There was a clock mounted in the gable and, perched on two poles in front of the hut, were carved wooden sailors with blue and white striped bodies, following the changing moods of the sea breeze with red and yellow flags in their hands. These mascots were the work of Tim's father, the man who had built the hut when Tim was just a year old.

Now in his mid-forties and a semi-permanent resident at the hut, Tim was keen to share his files of beach hut press cuttings and talk about the place he loved. Inside he directed us to a table under the harbour-facing windows.

'I've got lots of things that will interest you,' he said, sitting down in front of a pile of papers. 'Have you heard about this?'

He held out an article on Beach Space Deprivation Syndrome, a phrase recently coined to describe the trauma of fighting for space on overcrowded beaches. Otherwise known as resort rage, it was not a condition suffered by hut owners who seemed to enjoy a blissfully stress-free beach experience.

'Of course, you know the great thing about the huts on this beach is that you can live in them? I live in mine from March until November. For six years I lived here all winter as well but I got what they call cabin fever so now I winter in a house with friends.'

A few huts appeared among the dunes in the 1920s and by the time Tim's grandmother came in the next decade there were over a hundred. In those days the spit had no fresh water supply or toilets but tea barges would come for the summer season and moor up against the piers to offer refreshments. Though they had the benefit of a permanent café, twenty-first century hutters still shared communal showers, toilets and standpipes so in that respect living here was a lot like glorified camping. The council huts that used to be available for lease were mostly sold off under Margaret Thatcher and the day huts that Tim remembered from his childhood had disappeared. Modern owners were also liable for council tax.

'The huts used to be a way of having a cheap holiday for the lower middle class. Now they're worth a fortune; you've got to be either lucky or rich to have one.'

Having inherited his hut, Tim fell into the lucky category. As a college librarian he couldn't hope to get one any other way, not these days. When he'd first moved in the walls were hard board and the windows were single glazed. There was condensation everywhere so he quickly had to ventilate and insulate.

'I put everything on wheels,' he told us proudly. 'I'd put the whole thing on wheels if I could. The interior's all done to suit me, one man living a slightly eccentric lifestyle.'

Apparently there'd been a girlfriend who wanted to put up Laura Ashley curtains but she was now an ex-girlfriend. Tim described his home as a machine for living in: 'Everything has to earn its place. I've used pretty much what I can get my hands on from skips, tips and car-boot sales.'

This wasn't just about the cost. He seemed to be genuinely pleased by the idea of taking something others had deemed useless and making it useful. Like the laboratory-bench sink made of solid mahogany in the kitchen and the cork floor tiles salvaged from his work place. That was where his old Apple Mac Classic came from too, the computer he'd thought of turning into a fish tank until he found it actually worked and he began work on his local newsletter. With electricity from a solar panel on the roof he'd never looked back. In summer 1998 the first issue sold 2,000 copies and Tim had now launched sister publications the *Hengistbury Head Times* and the *Christchurch Harbour Chronicle*. I had a full set to take away for bedtime reading.

After a tasty lunch of quiche and salad from the rescued fridge, Tim walked us over the headland. The sun was warm on our backs and from the top we looked back on the line of huts with water on either side. Descending again near the landward end we could see more clearly how the back-to-back rows were in fact built along a curve, the serpentine spine of this sandy spit. We wandered back down through the ferns and purple heather so that Tim could introduce me to some fellow owners. His mother had provided a feminine touch in the décor of David Limebear's hut recommending a sunny colour scheme of yellow and gold to complement the varnished pine walls. Even the teapot was yellow. David worked as a personnel management consultant in London but came down to the beach for at least a month every summer. He'd been coming consecutively since 1946 and reckoned that probably made him the longest serving hut resident.

'I was six years old when I first came,' he told me. 'My father was a university lecturer and we came for the summer holidays. I finished school on one day and by six o'clock the next morning was at Mudeford. We stayed the whole six weeks, leaving at ten o'clock on the last night so I could start school again the following day.'

The family didn't have their own hut at first but on Easter Saturday 1948 an envelope dropped through the letterbox of their London home stating that their application for a site licence had been approved. David's father was on the spit the very next day to put up their first hut.

Rob Townsend sold his inherited hut in 1990 but had been a regular visitor since July 1939 when he stayed for the first time aged three. The long trip from Hereford had been prompted by the fact that his father's best friend married a lady from Christchurch.

'After the war Dad bought a second-hand garage off another friend of his, which he transported from Hereford to Mudeford. Altogether it cost £30 to buy it, move it and put it up. We called it "Got-a-lot".'

Like David, Rob spent his summer holidays at the hut with his mother and two younger brothers. His dad came down at the weekends.

Continuity certainly seemed to be a positive virtue down here. David's next door neighbours had been coming to Mudeford for forty-five years and another near neighbour, John Timms, could boast fifty-two years, only four less than David himself.

'There are two sisters with a hut further down; I played with them as little girls. It's like a village where an awful lot of people know an awful lot of people.'

'But you must have seen some changes in your time?' I asked. David thought about it.

'Hardly any,' he replied, then thought about it some more. 'The biggest change is that there are no cars allowed anymore. We've had the land train since 1968 but before that cars came right onto the beach. And second is the ferry, which replaced the rowing boats. There used to be two fishermen, Jim and Ron, who would row people across the Run.

Often you'd have to wait half an hour for them to come out of the pub!'

After more cogitation David also remembered the long salmon season, which had been curtailed because of over-fishing.

'It's still like it was in the Fifties really. People here like to say that it's Christchurch where time is pleasant and Mudeford where time stands still.'

Many journalists had been seduced by this place in the past, not to mention those people wealthy enough to push the prices up so far that long-standing members of the community feared for its survival. If there was a fourth change then it was a social one; professionals had moved in. It was like commuters taking over a Cotswold village with the same inherent paradox. Attracted by the nostalgic charm and strong sense of community, these incomers had a tendency to erode the very thing they paid so highly to become a part of. After a day on the sandbank I could see why visitors pushed notes under hut doors offering to pay any price for a hut but I could also see why that was problematic for existing owners. Someone had told me about the Mudeford magic and I knew, as I walked back towards the ferry, that I'd fallen under its spell. The huts were bathed in a pinky-orange glow as the sun began to sink below the horizon; people were sitting in front of open doors on their front decks, reading, strumming a guitar, chatting. There was a little party outside 'Ticketyboo' and the happy men in shorts raised their beer cans as we passed. It was still warm and the water lapped gently at the sides of the boat as we climbed on board with the residue of day-trippers. We waved at Tim.

'Remember,' he called out, 'it's a 360 degree experience!'

Chapter Twelve
Home from home

G oing through my files of beach hut cuttings I came across a jaggedy-edged square of newsprint that had been torn from a weekend supplement. On it was a photo of a beach tent with striped sides in thick and thin rainbow colours. The four vertical walls were topped off with a pyramid roof in the same fabric. Dimensions, price and stockist details were provided in the accompanying blurb, which began by reflecting on the early twenty-first century cost of permanent beach huts. In this context praise was due to the 'clever Conran Shop' for producing a 'personal portable shelter.' But how much more convenient must it have seemed one hundred years ago when holidaymakers could opt for this type of tent instead of a bathing machine?

In 1900 a guidebook described the sands of Swanage in Dorset as 'besprinkled with bathing-boxes and white tents.' Schoolboy J. S. Wayne, who visited the quiet Yorkshire resort of Filey with his parents in 1908, walked along the beach on the last day of August and recorded in his diary that 'there were bathing tents for ever, and young women skipping down to the sea in neck-to-knee costumes'. At Broadstairs a turn of the century guide proclaimed that bathing tents 'have to a large extent replaced the orthodox vans, adding greatly to the picturesqueness of the scene.' Pettman's bathing establishment was proud to offer all the latest facilities at Cliftonville, including a considerable number of tents that could be hired for changing at 4d. per person or rented by the day or week. Just to have this choice was a new thing. Bathing machines did

Beach tents made family bathing a more enjoyable experience providing a permanent base on the sands. This Edwardian group look as relaxed as it was possible to be in so much clothing!

not suddenly disappear, not even at Broadstairs, but on any given day they were used by a succession of different people, each for a short time. The special advantage of a hired tent was that, once bathing was over, it could be used as 'a lounge for the family during the day'.

Like mixed bathing, beach tents were associated with the Continental way of doing things so it's no coincidence the two things appeared at the same time. Temporary tent towns sprang up around the coast and the Suffolk resort of Felixstowe apparently felt so confident of its place as an up-to-date European destination that it published a version of its guidebook in French. At Bexhill-on-Sea enough sumptuous hotels had been built before the direct rail link arrived in 1902 to set the resort's select tone and guarantee refined bathing arrangements. 'Below the promenade a long file of tents and gaily-coloured cabins betokens the preference of Bexhill visitors for Continental modes of bathing. There are plenty of the orthodox machines for those who like them, but families who are making a stay of any length generally find it cheaper and more convenient to hire one of these useful little structures.' Most hotels and boarding houses kept cabins for their guests' use while tent prices varied from 3s. 6d. to 5s. per week. This bought 'a shelter from sun, wind and rain, and...a kind of "home-from-home" for the little ones. Many people pass practically the whole of their day on the beach. By means of a spirit kettle and a few cups the high function of afternoon tea may be celebrated with the minimum of inconvenience, and some enthusiasts even go to the length of collecting the material for wood fires and frying steaks and other toothsome dainties on the spot'. Though there may have been no thought of skipping the English ritual of afternoon tea, a new relaxation was definitely on the menu: 'You may bathe almost when, where and how you please, and nobody minds, or is any the worse.' Instead of dreaming up an elaborate roster of restrictions the Bexhill authorities decided to place their faith in the good taste and common sense of the public. It helped that the 'public' to which Bexhill catered was notable for an almost total absence of 'trippers'.

The smart resorts were first to embrace beach tents; the sands at places like Blackpool and Margate were too busy with working class bodies to attract people with the money for weekly hire charges. Had tent users existed in any number in 1884 Bernard Becker would probably have included them in his book *Holiday Haunts* under the category of 'anti-trippers'. 'There is a very large class of English folk,' wrote Becker, who 'enjoy our magnificent English seaside resorts and inland baths so long as these are kept fairly clear of the "tripper", who brings in his train the donkeys, the brass-bands, the organs, the Punch and Judy, and other nuisances – at least esteemed as such by the "anti-tripper".' In our days of easy international travel the 'anti-tripper' has been superseded by the 'anti-tourist', whose destinations become ever more remote in order to keep one step ahead of the holidaymaking crowds. The need to escape turned the anti-tripper into a pioneer, 'ever on the look-out for fresh sand and billows new...ever moving on, driven away and away by the railways and "trippers".' This constant searching led to the development of many new watering places the success of which, to this audience at least, also meant their failure. 'As they become popular the ingenious 'anti-tripper' moves on and opens up a new Filey to every Scarborough, a new Lowestoft to every Yarmouth.' Increasingly he took his tent with him.

The harder it was to get to a place the more likely it was to appeal. On this basis Cornwall managed to retain an air of exclusiveness until well after the Second World War, when more holidaymakers began to make the long trip by car. In 1852 a lady named Caroline Pearce from Launceston introduced readers of *The Englishwoman's Magazine* to her favourite bathing spot at Bude, on the northern coast of her home county. There were no bathing machines at Crooklets Beach so alternative changing arrangements had to be made. Two local women, Nanny Moore and her daughter Harriet, were happy to be called upon at their beach-side cottage to act as dippers and could supply coarse flannel or serge bathing dresses for those who lacked their own. They were also responsible for "The Tent".

Three poles are joined on a hinge. These are stuck in the sand at such a distance from the tide as will insure safety from its intrusion. An old, rough, and pieced covering, a sort of barras, or sailcloth, is adjusted over the poles. The ends are weighed down, and the whole is kept steady by a heap of sand thrown on the long skirts of these curtains. But the scanty furniture still leaves an open entrance; and ladies cannot feel quite secure yet from impertinent curiosity; so an old shawl of Nanny's is pinned across, and this done, the mysteries of the toilette may be carried on in confidence and repose. Within, are two important articles of furniture; a camp stool, and a large basket to hold the clothes.

Strangers were grateful for the shelter of this makeshift structure but Caroline Pearce called them 'poor prisoners' compared to the 'old Bude-bathers, who have had some experience on the beach, [and] will manage as well behind a good rock'. As a self-confessed '*rockite*', Caroline required

An advertisement for sun shades and tents from the 1890s.

the assistance of a maid to unfasten the numerous hooks-and-eyes, strings and buttons of mid-nineteenth century costume but claimed that the job could easily be accomplished between the shelter of a rock and 'an enormous, old and *old-fashioned* cotton umbrella'. Bathers at other remote beaches must have found similar solutions meaning that basic tents were already in use well before their Edwardian heyday.

Nanny's Bude tent was obviously homemade but by the end of the century round bell tents were becoming a common sight on quieter beaches. After a long history this wigwam shape was adopted by the Victorian army, being used by soldiers in the Crimean War and later campaigns including the Boer War of 1899–1902. A bell tent could sleep up to fifteen men, one for each canvas panel. Heads were arranged around the circumference with feet concentrated at the central tent pole, bodies radiating out like the spokes of a wheel. It may be that some of the bell tents photographed on beaches as far apart as Woolacombe in North Devon and Mablethorpe in Lincolnshire were army surplus;

the market for civilian camping was certainly very small at this point. A sign of things to come was the establishment, in 1894, of Britain's very first holiday camp near Douglas on the Isle of Man. A decade later the Cunningham Holiday Camp, named after its teetotal founders Joseph and Elizabeth Cunningham, could boast 1500 bell tents filled with enough beds to accommodate up to 12,000 young men.

On the beach, bell tents became just one in a wide range of different designs. People could pitch their own whether it was stitched at home, bought from the local hardware shop or ordered from the pages of a national department store catalogue. Whatever they looked like, private tents began to change the way the beach was used. As portable domestic space they became the focus for a more family oriented holiday experience.

The artist Vanessa Bell, a member of the Bloomsbury set and sister of the writer Virginia Woolf, often dealt with the theme of domesticity in her paintings. One of her most important works is *Studland Beach*, a powerful, almost abstract image from c.1912 that has been described as one of the most radical English art works of its time. Against a deep blue sky, rising from the pale yellow sweep of sand, Bell painted a bright white beach tent. It is this tent that attracts the eye first, drawing the gaze towards a group of children digging in the sand. Next to the tent stands a woman, perhaps looking at the structure, perhaps looking past it. In the bottom left corner of the painting sit two figures in straw hats. They have their backs to us because, like us, they are watching the little family clustered by the tent. It is the strength of this connection between the tent and the family that is important. Even now there is isn't much at Studland, just some beach huts, a National Trust shop and a few signs indicating where the naturist beach begins. The following description was written in the 1920s but remains apposite today: 'there is no sea-front, no pretence of a quay. Blackberry bushes and bracken come boldly to the astonished beach, but the brown creeper-covered cottages hide snugly away in the thicket. Studland indeed declines to be maritime; it turns its face from the sea to bury it among its myrtles and fuchsia bushes.' Vanessa Bell and her

3   *SEA VIEW (Isle of Wight). — Bathing-Tents. — LL.*

By the 1890s tent bathing was already favoured at the quiet sea resort of Seaview on the Isle of Wight. In the background is part of Seaview's distinctive Chain Pier.

young family holidayed at this anti-trippers paradise in Dorset between 1909 and 1911. Through her paintbrush, Bell converted the beach tent from a place to change and shelter into an iconic symbol.

Tent settlements, like those at Seaview and Bembridge on the Isle of Wight, were often described in picturesque terms. At Seaview bathing was *en famille* and according to a guidebook of 1897: 'Whoever is responsible for the substitution of bathing tents for the hideous machines that disfigure most sea-side places, deserves the gratitude of the community. Very pretty these many-coloured tents look from the water, with their crowd of many children on the sand in front, and their dark green setting of foliage behind and eastward.' The only noise at Bembridge was the laughter of children, the only daylight occupations were bathing, boating, fishing and golfing; there were nothing to do in the evening. It was labelled an 'unconventional spot' because of its limited amusements but, as with Studland, the visitors who chose Bembridge did so for that very reason. By 1920 the Bembridge tent community was still amusing itself; the resort had not grown, evening diversions remained non-existent and the updated guidebook warned that it would not be to everyone's taste.

Bathing bungalows were built along Bournemouth's Undercliff Drive in 1908. As these
Edwardian holiday snaps show they quickly proved their success as a 'home-from-home'.

At exclusive resorts like Bexhill, tents demonstrated a preference for
carefree Continental habits. At unconventional Bembridge they stood
for a kind of anti-establishment independence. These implications

were not lost on the bigger resorts but there was a gathering momentum for change. The tent acted as an intermediary between bathing machines and beach huts; as a more portable and light-weight structure it continued to be a popular option well into the post-war years. Sometimes, however, the difference between a tent and a hut was minimal as at Felixstowe where, since at least 1895, there had been 'Tents', which were 'not tents at all but wooden structures' used in place of bathing machines. Visitors could take a weekly or monthly rental of these 'snug and pleasant rooms', which were considered so innovative that they still inspired the fulsome prose of guidebook writers in 1919:

> One of the sights of Felixstowe in the season is the long array of "tents", each the centre of a happy home circle...Beneath the shade of the wooden roof heads of families lounge, read or work, as inclination may suggest; while the juniors frolic around or stroll in quest of agates and carnelians, of seaweed and shells; or, in juvenile zest, build sand-castles or paddle in the shallows. These Felixstowe "tents", so characteristic a feature of this bright and attractive seaside resort, are now being extensively imitated elsewhere.

On the south coast, Bournemouth was another hut pioneer; this time because of the name it gave the row of structures built to adorn the Undercliff Drive. Begun in 1907, this asphalted promenade and carriage drive was fifty feet wide. It was a major investment for 'The Pine City by the Sea' and needed to portray the right kind of image. With this in mind, corporation employees began building a series of wooden day huts to a standard design that can still be seen beside the beach today. Under the overhanging gabled roofs the central double doors were given glazed top panels with extra windows in the walls either side. These ten-foot square rooms provided families with 'shelter and shade, a storeroom for books, spades, pails and all the impedimenta of seaside life, and facilities for simple meals'. They were called 'bungalows'.

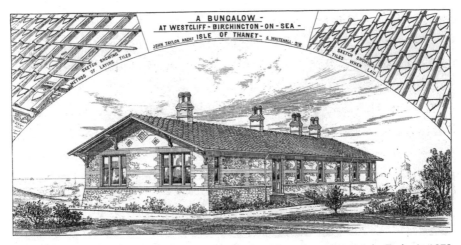

One of the earliest British bungalows built on the Kent Coast by architect John Taylor in 1873.

As a globally ubiquitous form of housing the bungalow has sadly lost its original charm. Pertinent proof of this comes from the decision made by Bournemouth council in 2006 to try and improve booking rates for its seafront shelters by changing their name from beach 'bungalows' to beach 'huts'. Market research showed that people could no longer think of a bungalow as anything other than a single-storey home and a pretty unromantic one at that. It was a different situation for the Edwardians.

The term 'bungalow' originated in India, adapted by European residents from the words used to describe the primitive hut built on a raised platform with thatched roof and veranda, which is indigenous to Bengal. It was first employed to describe a new type of dwelling in this country at Westgate-on-Sea in Kent. The two bungalows designed in 1869–70 by architect John Taylor, on land owned by fellow-architect John Pollard Seddon, invested the term with new meaning; this was the invention of the recreational house by the sea, where healthy sea air and isolation from the masses were given architectural expression. The first purchaser was Sir Erasmus Wilson, Professor of Dermatology at the Royal College of Surgeons and a benefactor to the Royal Sea Bathing Hospital at Margate. Wilson told his architect that: 'I find everybody charmed with my Bungalow and I believe if there were many Bungalows, there would be many buyers. The house is a novelty, very convenient and fitted for a single family and easy as to price...They are novel, quaint, pretty and perfect as to sanitary qualities. The best sanitary home for a family is a Bungalow.'

The next phase of development was at Birchington, next to Westgate, and it was here that Seddon designed 'Ye Tower Bungalows' in 1881–2. These featured low belvedere towers that housed a single bedroom-study for private contemplation of distant sea views. Although the word 'bungalow' traditionally meant a one-storey dwelling, the architects also applied the name to a two-storey house 'under one roof span and of most simple construction'. Yet for all their professed simplicity these were summer homes for the upper middle class with multiple bedrooms and accommodation for servants that included a butler's pantry, larder, scullery, wash-house, stables and coach house as well as an extensive basement housing a large dairy and separate wine and beer cellars. The bungalows were totally self-contained with no communicating links between them. In fact, these detached buildings so enshrined the socially exclusive idea of getting away from it all that each was built in the middle of a one-acre plot on the edge of a fifty-foot cliff, through which a private tunnel led to the beach via a private dressing room. It was the ultimate holiday hideaway for the anti-tripper.

As far as interior decoration was concerned these early bungalows took inspiration from the Arts and Crafts Movement. Indeed their escapist *raison d'être* was perfectly allied to the underlying ethos of the Movement, led by men like William Morris, which turned its back on the industrialising, urbanising trends of the nineteenth century to seek refuge in craftsmanship and the increasingly compelling cult of 'the simple life'. A star publication of this cult was American author Henry David Thoreau's *Walden*, a book first published in 1854, which found new appeal in England at the turn of the century. Now considered a classic, *Walden* recounts Thoreau's experiences of Walden Pond, a place less than two miles from his home town of Concord, Massachusetts, where he lived intermittently from 1845 to 1847. With our heightened environmental consciousness this story of learning to live with nature resonates across the centuries; in a post-industrialised age the idealised simple life is no less attractive. Thoreau's statement of intent is as irresistible now as it was one hundred years ago: 'I went into the woods because I wanted to live deliberately, to front only the essential facts of life, and see if I could not learn what it had to teach, and not, when I came to die, discover that I had not lived...I wanted to live deep and suck out all the marrow of life...' For this experiment Thoreau constructed his own dwelling, a hut ten feet wide by fifteen feet long. It was architecture pared down to its most basic four walls, a home not much bigger than a modern beach hut.

The promise of freedom and enhanced creativity that was part of this philosophical escapism helped inspire Ebenezer Howard's Garden City Movement. It also became a crucial element in the appeal of bungalow living. The seaside offered plenty of unrestricted land for the fulfilment of this fantasy, on top of which were the much-lauded benefits of rejuvenating sea air. Advantageously located on the Thanet coast, the developments at Birchington and Westgate were also within easy reach of London, their promoters being well aware that devotees of the 'simple life' would still require the foil of metropolitan business and amusements. By the time he arrived at Birchington in 1882 the Pre-Raphaelite painter Dante Gabriel Rossetti had had too much of the latter to be cured by the former. Already ill, Rossetti held on for nearly nine months in one of the pre-fabricated timber bungalows and after his death was buried in Birchington churchyard where his gravestone, designed by another Pre-Raphaelite luminary, Ford Madox Brown, can still be seen. Though not the best advertisement for the bungalow as seaside sanatorium, Rossetti's presence nevertheless demonstrates the kind of social circle from which early residents came. The link was established between bungalow living and artistic Bohemian aspirations.

After the successful experiment at Birchington little was heard of the seaside bungalow until the end of the 1880s by which time the idea had moved inland. In the 1890s there were coastal bungalows built at fashionable Cromer but Bohemian escapism was also being embraced lower down the social scale. By the turn of the century there had been major changes in leisure time, probably most important of which was the notion of taking two whole days off a week, the term 'week-end' only now becoming commonplace. Bungalow settlements developed partly because people had new free time that

An Edwardian mother and daughter on the veranda of their holiday home at Shoreham's Bungalow Town.

could be spent away from home on a regular basis. In a move towards what the social geographers Dennis Hardy and Colin Ward have called 'Arcadia for all', clusters of makeshift huts began to appear at self-made resorts, giving a new sense of independence to working people.

The majority of these plotlands grew up during the interwar period but one of the first was founded in the 1890s on the strip of marginal land between Shoreham and Lancing on the Sussex coast. The settlement had apparently begun when a local resident noticed three or four old railway carriages towed to the beach for use as net stores by local fishermen. With entrepreneurial foresight he marked out plots, took rent and arranged for the purchase and removal of railway carriages from the Brighton Railway. Between 1890–96 there were about a dozen; by 1902 there was a continuous line of about 200 and within ten years it had turned into a mile and a half-long settlement dubbed Bungalow Town. It attracted a socially adventurous, avant-garde community, which, thanks to the fast rail link to London, included many West End theatre people who snatched what leisure they could in a whirl of celebrities, weekend parties and extravagant clothes. Their colourful presence brought excitement to what was still essentially a humble collection of holiday bungalows. Star of the music hall, Will Evans, even added a touch of magical theatricality to his bungalows at Shoreham by naming them 'Cinderella' and 'Sleeping Beauty' after pantomimes he'd appeared in.

There may have been less celebrity sparkle to the bungalow developments elsewhere but previously abandoned stretches of coastline were being colonised. At the mouth of the river Exe in Devon, building on Dawlish Warren had begun in the late 1890s. The unregulated expansion of this community moved one local to lament that 'until recently the Warren has remained the haunt of the wild-fowler and naturalist, but now the red roofs of bungalows are beginning to plentifully dot the wastes; and to play at Robinson Crusoe, with twentieth-century embellishments and more or less luxurious fringes, has become a favourite pastime on the once solitary haunt of the heron, the wild duck and the sea-mew'. Just one year later this trend gained the royal seal of approval when Queen Alexandra had a hand-crafted rubble-stone bungalow erected at Snettisham beach, near the Sandringham estate. In true castaway style the interior of the Queen's room was decorated with shells and pebbles from the beach.

The Bournemouth bathing bungalows were designed to capitalise on all these associations. At Walpole Bay near Cliftonville, the Pettman family also realised the potency of this name, adapting some of their huge stock of bathing machines into day-huts. They fitted glazed doors, verandas and canvas awnings to disguise the old wheeled vehicles at the rear and adopted the name Bungalow Town for the long row of dainty dwellings. The real innovation, however, took place at Scarborough where blocks of permanent seaside shelters were created as part of the Peasholm Park development in the North Bay.

These pioneering examples were a clever response by the Borough

Surveyor, Mr Harry W. Smith, to the prosaic need to protect one of
the town's main drains! A promenade having been created for this
purpose, the idea was put to the council to 'make a block of buildings
of as picturesque a design as possible, [to] provide them with their own
little veranda and bit of pavement, and elevate them so that parents
could keep a watchful eye on their youngsters on the sands below.' The
first block of thirteen, made up of twelve contiguous rooms, measuring
about 7ft 6in square with a 4ft 6in open veranda in front, and a central
building for the beach and bathing inspector, was begun in 1910 at an
estimated cost of £303. The huts were fitted with corner cupboards, a
table, two chairs and a large storage space over the veranda. The central
building also had gas and hot and cold water so tenants could make
tea. A report on their history in the *Scarborough Mercury* noted that
'curiously enough the term bungalow was not used in the early days
of their construction. This was because there was considerable doubt
whether an unromantic Government department would allow such
things to be provided for visitors at the expense of the municipality.
Instead they were called "shelter pavilions". When it was found,
however, that the Local Government Board took a sympathetic interest
in these shelters the term bungalow was brought into common use'.
Additional blocks were added in the winter of 1911–12 and again the
following autumn. Their success was such that the South Bay also took
up the idea with the first batch of twenty bungalows being erected past
the Spa in 1911–12. They were even listed among the town's attractions in
contemporary adverts. By 1927 there were a total of 145 bungalows split
between the two bays.

A model for this kind of accommodation could have been found in
America where east coast resorts provided blocks of changing rooms
at the top of the beach, known as 'bath-houses'. In 1896 a report on
'Seaside life in America' described the facilities at Atlantic City, a place
so popular that its 400 hotels (all built of wood) could alone house
50,000 people. People going 'surf-bathing' along this stretch of the
New Jersey coast would turn out around eleven o'clock in bath robes

Blocks of bathing bungalows were first built at Scarborough's North bay in 1910 and were subsequently copied around the British coast.

and dressing gowns, leaving other clothing in their hotel 'so that the small frame bath-house – which takes the place of the English bathing-machine – may not be uncomfortably crowded'. These bath-houses stood 'in long lines, 100 deep, at right angles with the beach'. From here bathers walked across the beach into the sea. A decade later Bailey's Beach at Newport, Rhode Island (the 'Mecca of the millionaire') could boast more solid bath-houses built atop a raised platform. The row of changing cubicles formed a single building under a pitched roof, with a central gable and columns along the front that carried a shallow veranda to shade the individual doors. There is no evidence that these American structures had any influence in the UK but the similarity of design between the blocks at Bailey's Beach and those at Scarborough make for an intriguing coincidence. This block form of beach huts was replicated around the British coast throughout the interwar period and beyond.

The Great War of 1914–18 ushered in huge social changes with implications for how the modern beach would come to be used yet, during the war itself, seaside resorts remained open for business.

There was considerable disruption to the transport networks used by tourists; steamers were called up for war service while trains were delayed and uncomfortable. Despite this, towns like Blackpool and Brighton continued to flourish. Wealthy holidaymakers who could not travel abroad helped keep the home resorts buoyant. Soldiers were also thankful for coastal resorts, whether providing a temporary forgetfulness for men on leave or offering healthy air to those convalescing. Though parents were anxious, bereaved and rationed, the bucket and spade seaside was able to continue much as before.

Some pillboxes appeared on the east coast but the threat of invasion did not loom as large as it had done in the Napoleonic wars, when Martello towers were built to defend our shores or as it would in the Second World War when the beaches were covered in barbed wire and piers were intentionally breached. Nonetheless, pre-war invasion exercises did take place. The military threat posed by the Kaiser's Germany was becoming increasingly apparent as the twentieth century dawned and as early as 1904 the first combined Army and Royal Navy manoeuvres took place on the Essex coast. The journalist Edgar Wallace, who wrote several critical articles in the *Daily Mail,* dubbed Clacton 'The Capital of Letspretendia'. National hero General Baden-Powell and a variety of foreign military attachés joined East End trippers to watch the 'Blue' invading force take on the 'Red' defenders. Bathing machines became impromptu headquarters and to ensure a sporting fairness the King's brother, Field Marshall The Duke of Connaught, played the role of Umpire in Chief. The Blue team successfully landed and pressed inland before being pushed back into withdrawal and re-embarkation by the Reds. Both sides claimed the advantage but the manoeuvres were declared inconclusive.

Thankfully the Kaiser's territorial ambitions were never tested on British beaches but as the threat of war became a reality the residents of Ilfracombe, on the North Devon coast, resurrected the tale of how Germany's powerful leader had once been bested by a local bathing machine attendant. At the age of nineteen Queen Victoria's grandson, Prince Frederick William of Prussia, stayed a fortnight at The Ilfracombe

Hotel. Official accounts portrayed him as a model visitor; bathing early in the morning, patronising all the boatmen in turn, promenading and attending the parish church to hear the Bishop of Oxford preach. But one afternoon in August 1878 the bored teenage prince decided to try a little target practice, aiming stones at the numbers painted on the bathing machines at Rapparee beach. These machines were owned by Mr Price, whose son Alfred took offence at the Prince's game. On stating that he would not allow such damage to his father's property the loyal Devonian got a question for a reply: 'Do you know who I am?' Price bluntly countered that 'I don't care a dash who you are!' and, so the story goes, received a punch to the right jaw that sent him flying backwards onto the ground. A twenty-minute brawl ensued and to the end of his life Price was known as 'the man who fought the Kaiser'. In an effort to cover up this inappropriate incident Prince Frederick's tutor paid Alfred Price thirty shillings to keep his mouth shut.

The Prince did not finally become Kaiser until a decade later and it was at least another decade until he became an object of dislike and distrust to the British public. Nonetheless, when war broke out Alfred Price became a retrospective hero. Ilfracombe shopkeeper W. H. Coates resurrected the bathing machine incident, claiming an alternative narrative behind the outbreak of war in his verses on 'Why the Kaiser Hates England or What Happened at Rapparee'.

> Then Kaiser turned to Alf and said;
> "Mine friend! You'll rue this day,
> For what you've done t'mine poor nose,
> Mine word! I'll make you pay,
> I'll build big ships, and gurt big guns,
> Then one day I will come
> And blow this place t'smithereens,
> And you...t'kingdom come."
> The germ of hate once planted
> In this gentle German's breast,

The "Culture" growed and spread a apace,
He know'd no peace or rest,
He builded Dreadnoughts and big guns,
And gurt airships too,
And teached his soldiers the goosey step,
Impressive sight I trow.
Then gazing out on his handiwork
He said, "Nigh is the day
When I will cross the rolling deep
And make those English pay,
For what that y'ungster did to me
When I was over there;
Mine nose has never been the same,
He bent it...I declare."

It would be interesting to know, as he prepared for battle in 1914, if the Kaiser could even recollect the incident that took place thirty-six years earlier. Ilfracombe experienced no war damage but other English seaside towns did. At eight o'clock on the morning of Wednesday 16 December 1914, the inhabitants of Scarborough were startled by the shrieking of shells and the crashing of buildings. The grim forms of German warships emerged from the winter mist and for twenty minutes they rained missiles upon the resort. Eighteen people lost their lives and around a hundred more were injured; practically no part of the town escaped damage. Three years later a submarine bombardment killed five more civilians. The strategic location of Dover made it a more obvious target and residents there were attacked by Zeppelins, sea-planes, aeroplanes, destroyers and submarines. A total of 185 bombs were dropped on the town but the number of fatalities was blessedly low at just fourteen. Further along the Kent coast, Folkestone should have been another key target as it was from here that most of the British troops set out for the frontline. Over 3.5 million crossed from Folkestone to Boulogne, 2.5 million came back again and a further quarter of a million went each way between Folkestone and Calais. The town's one bombardment happened on 25 May 1917 when a crowded shopping street was attacked from the air. There were nearly a hundred casualties that day.

Terrible though these attacks were, civilians on the Continent experienced far worse conditions. Whole Belgian towns were turned to brick dust and the country's main resort of Ostend fell silent. In an account compiled from the letters of two wealthy British volunteer nurses on the Yser front the comparison was drawn between September 1913 when the blue, red and yellow bathing machines at Ostend were mere spots of colour in a vibrant scene of paddlers and merry holiday-makers and September 1914 when the same vehicles 'stood up forlornly like huge fungi, and no-one used them'. The Kursaal, hub of summer society, was transformed into a hospital as were the great hotels created for more carefree days of the recent past. The bathing machines were removed from the beach and drawn up on a great level space, 'where – like so many little caravans – they were occupied for some weeks by poor refugees from the invaded territory, nomads against their will'. Many of these people crossed the Channel to Folkestone. From 10 September 1914 until 24 March 1915 it is estimated that some 64,500 destitute refugees arrived in the town. French bathing facilities were also requisitioned for the war effort. In the summer of 1915 Calais became a British base and the Casino was turned into a Military Hospital. Members of the First Aid Nursing Yeomanry: The Princess Royal's Volunteer Corps (FANY) camped on a high sandy hill behind the Casino in four bell tents and a canvas hut that had seen better days. There were also several bathing machines, of which one served as an office and the others became sleeping quarters. On Victorian high days and holidays bathing machines had served as overflow accommodation; now they were providing basic shelter for the homeless and billets for nurses.

By 1918 accommodation on the beach had evolved. There were many more options and over the next twenty years huts would firmly supplant machines around the coast.

Chapter Thirteen
Bournemouth to Woolacombe

When Victoria became Queen in 1837 Bournemouth barely existed; by the time she died it was well on its way to becoming one of the most popular of all south coast resorts. These days grey-haired coach trippers and university students seemed to love it in equal measures and alongside the golden sands of its roomy bay some 1,200 huts catered for devotees of all ages. On that basis I was prepared to love it too. But the urban centre was mostly grim, cut off from the seafront by a fast-moving highway and extending its poor architectural standards onto the cliff in the form of a lumpen conference centre and a spectacularly insensitive IMAX cinema. My first visit was in the rain which probably didn't help. When I went back after my day at Mudeford the sun was shining and the real glory of its position became self-evident. One hundred foot high cliffs punctuated by the narrow valleys of numerous chines, zigzag paths and cliff lifts, formed a backdrop to miles of beautiful beach all the way from Hengistbury Head to Sandbanks. With the exception of a few cafés and some entertainment buildings near Boscombe and Bournemouth piers the seafront was free from development, a walkway adorned only by diminutive beach hut residences. As I set out from Southbourne, I began to count my way towards Alum Chine, at the town's border with neighbouring Poole. I was soon defeated by the sheer number of huts.

They were two main types: private sheds painted green with white gables and the traditional Bournemouth bungalows based on an

Edwardian design. Those had black wooden walls with glazed double doors and windows either side set back under the shelter of a white gable. The barge boards and doors were painted red, yellow then blue in jolly succession. There were a few interloping chalet blocks too, the most impressive of which was Boscombe's Overstrand Building, a three-tier bathing station built in 1958. With rounded ocean-liner-like ends, its shabbiness couldn't quite obscure the post-war design quality that included stylised sailing boats and interlocking fish in the bowed metal balconies. It reminded me a bit of Marine Court at St Leonards. Both buildings needed some serious investment, and even the one room bungalows required constant attention so the Council had come up with a few ideas for low maintenance revamping. There was the trial copy-cat chalet made entirely from recycled materials, the first of its kind in the UK. Meant to look and feel like wood, the walls were actually constructed from recycled polystyrene which meant the hut wouldn't rot or absorb water. When the so-called 'green' hut failed to win people over the Council tried re-using the stock they had, reinventing two neighbouring huts and asking the public to vote for their favourite. In a climate of increased vandalism this reinvention amounted to the removal of as many glass windows as possible. It was a brave attempt at cost-cutting that didn't really work. The most popular design proved to be the one they already had.

I crossed the invisible boundary between Bournemouth and Poole to begin walking the three miles that would take me to the end of Sandbanks beach and the entrance to Poole harbour. Although the high cliffs and cloudless sky continued, the thousand or so huts had a different character. There were individual sheds as well as concrete blocks in single and double tiers. At Branksome Dene three rows were layered into the cliff, long terraces of patio doors stepped one above the other that looked very functional when compared to the cream dolls houses scattered along the chine at Canford Cliffs. These had small glass panes in the double doors and side windows with a subtle decorative frieze below the roof line. Usually beach huts are arranged in straight lines but here they sat wherever the contours of the little valley suggested, a rock garden full of bright flowers at the entrance to the community. Blue heads of agapanthus waved in the sea breeze with golden daisies and bright pink petunias setting off the pretty huts behind. Several windows were blocked up with sheets of hardboard, regrettable proof that charm was no obstacle to vandalism.

In the old days Sandbanks looked like Mudeford Spit with summer shacks dotted in the dunes. Now this peninsula had the extraordinary reputation of being the fourth most expensive place to buy property *in the world*. Modern apartments were springing up to take advantage of Poole's new popularity but at Sandbanks house prices were rising exponentially. Striking out to close the neck of Poole's huge natural harbour, land on Sandbanks was strictly limited and as a result was approaching a value of £20million per acre. Several of the apartment blocks along the narrowest part of the spit had their own chalets but the main hut sites were owned by the Council. Yearly hire rates were the highest in the borough but not by as much as might be expected. I turned up after breakfast while sand was being swept from the promenade back onto the beach and at one end of the 1920s Pavilion bamboo-handled fishing nets were being brought out to join other goods for sale. The Pavilion obviously dated from a time when land was cheap because the Doric colonnade holding up the roof above the wide, angular crescent of thirty-nine chalets allowed for a very generous piazza next to the beach.

To either side of it there were double-decker chalet blocks with zigzag roofs and behind them big, but still not quite big enough, car parks. On peak August weekends there were never enough parking spaces and, as far as traffic was concerned, Sandbanks was an unavoidable bottle-neck. The road from Poole was split into queuing lanes, one for the car park and one for the chain ferry to Swanage. Forty-eight cars could cross the harbour mouth in each trip so queuing times were painted on the road – level with the car park it was a ninety minute wait. Locals took the bus because it could queue jump. Boats also set out from here to make the quick journey to Brownsea Island, famous as the location of Robert Baden-Powell's first scout camp of 1907. In National Trust ownership since 1962, Brownsea dominated the view from the only beach huts inside Poole harbour. These wooden sheds at Hamworthy Park backed onto a flat green lawn. On a hot summer's day the place was full of laughter with children making good use of the playground and paddling pool; kites flew above the park and cricket stumps stuck out of the grass.

Like a floating bridge, the ferry carried us across to Shell Bay where the slopes were clad in heather. The next bay was Studland with the white stacks of Old Harry Rocks loitering off its southern headland. Ten thousand years ago they were part of the same chalk ridge as The Needles, running from the Purbeck Hills to the Isle of Wight. Once part of the Bankes Estate based at Kingston Lacy, the three mile stretch of sandy beach was now run by the National Trust and could boast that conservation body's only designated naturist beach. When this arrangement was formalised in the Eighties, accusations were made of Trust land being used for 'trendy' purposes; a small number of members, including a concerned Canon, threatened to cancel their subscriptions. In fact, the first 'nudist colony' was established at Studland in the early 1930s as part of the interwar sunlight craze. It was something the National Trust inherited, just like the timber beach huts that I found nestled under oak trees amid leafy ferns at Middle Beach. As we approached from behind, a little boat with unfurled sail of rust-red cloth drifted past the beach; it was all very *Swallows and Amazons*. Several of the huts were open. One man was sanding his green front doors to take a new coat of paint. The Trust-owned huts at Llanbedrog, in North Wales, were a colourful parade of red, blue, green and yellow but here they had to stay brown; a range of eight subtle shades was allowed for doors and other details.

Although the sky was low with grey cloud it was warm and the sands were filling up. The owner of hut 227 was entertaining his whole family on the fourteen chairs arranged outside his door. He'd been a resident for thirty-five years and thanks to his love of kites he'd become a very noticeable one. High above our heads three specimens danced in the breeze attached to the ground via a line that was decorated with inflated animals. I asked him about the seven cows and four ducks.

'I like sailing and for the same reason I like kites,' he answered. 'The windsocks are there to warn people about the line and I thought I might as well make them interesting.'

The kite man told me that the huts had been put back after the war starting with his neighbour's in 1949. He reckoned people had got taller since then because the doors were no longer high enough for the younger generation. Patriotic bunting hung across his hut, left over from the Queen's Golden Jubilee.

'We had a picnic down here on the beach,' he said. 'It poured with rain but we just sat under umbrellas. That's the true English experience – we don't need sunshine to be happy!'

Before leaving Studland we wandered along to South Beach and, toward Old Harry Rocks, I came across the most romantic hut location of my trip. There were only ten in this secluded spot, mostly a bit faded and showing their vintage. Wooden stairs led up to a shady ledge and I sat at the top of one flight, listening to the waves turning over little pebbles on the beach below. This was the undisturbed Studland I could imagine appealing to artist Vanessa Bell. All the huts were closed but if they remained so for too long they would be overtaken by rampant bramble bushes and honeysuckle. Like the sand-filled huts at Brancaster, they would become even more picturesque in their uselessness.

From that little oasis of calm we got back on the road heading for Swanage. The beach there was busy. In his trademark red and white striped booth, Mr Punch was defeating the green-faced Devil in front of a rapt audience, multiple deckchairs cradled relaxing holidaymakers and at the water's edge a line of pedaloes painted with startled-looking faces was awaiting custom. Beach huts were in plentiful supply around the sheltered bay with some ten different designs ranging from the Council's brown timber bungalows, through traditional gabled huts and a triple tiered 1930s chalet block that was once modern enough to appear in *The Architectural Review*, to a newer stone-clad row complete with *faux* coach lamps and patio doors with net curtains. The Grand Hotel was in the process of adding to its own hut stock with two new blocks protected by roller shutters. It was hard to see these bland new huts as attractive additions to the seafront but the magnificent view would doubtless make up for that as far as future residents were concerned.

On the opposite side of the bay families were sat on the sun-drenched stone jetty, dangling their legs over the edge and tweaking crab lines dropped into the still water of high tide. From here the huts were indistinct shapes below the built-up cliff, which was itself diminished by the green ridge of hills behind. It was like peering into a tinted postcard view.

And lovely Dorset just kept getting lovelier. The road to Weymouth offered tempting detours to eccentrically named villages like Owermoigne, Affpuddle, Winfrith and Poxwell. Then we passed Corfe Castle, its ruined walls spectacularly silhouetted against the sinking sun. Wispy clouds hovered in the haze behind its crumbling mass as the evening moon hung impatiently in the ascendant. Burning stubble scented the air. It was all so abundantly English, something that might just as easily be said of Weymouth's Georgian seafront and nostalgic sands.

It was dusk by the time we strolled along the prom and above us bulbs were flicking on like strings of electric pearls. On the shingly beach was an intermittent row of what can only be described as skeleton huts. The wooden floors were solid and each hut had a flat roof sloping gently from front to back. So far so normal, except here the walls were see-through. In fact, there were no walls; in their place was a minimal wooden frame of upright and diagonal posts. The design was certainly unique but the advantage of a half hut rather eluded me. Further along was a line of sturdier white huts but even these lacked anything so conventional as a front wall, let alone a front door. The backs were incomplete too, the top half open but for some cross bracing. I wanted to know more about these weird Weymouth huts but realised I'd have to wait until morning when the beach came back to life. For now the seafront was quiet, the pedaloes padlocked together in front of genteel Georgian terraces. Away from the bay the main shopping street proved an unexpected contrast, the high street of anywhere and everywhere, littered with chip papers and noisy with teenagers. If walking along the prom felt like taking a trip back to the old-fashioned seaside then this was a pretty abrupt return to the present – and perhaps Weymouth was more real for it.

Thursday dawned to bright cloudless sunshine. The blue water sparkled in the wide crescent bay and the beach looked glorious. People were getting ready for the hot day to come and among them were the first hut occupants. At Greenhill Gardens iron columns ran in front of two 1920s chalet blocks; on top of the first there were tennis courts and above the second was a bowling green. There were gabled hut rows in the Scarborough mode too, set back behind a green hedge their zigzag roofline alternately purple, yellow and peach. The turquoise doors of number twelve were wedged open so I went to meet the lady owner.

'Well, I've had this chalet for twelve years and I've also got one on the beach,' she said pointing towards the skeleton huts below us. 'The green canvas sides are up so you can tell which is mine.'

So that explained it. Around the edge of each canvas panel were eyes to fit over hooks on the hut's frame and at the back was a locker where they could be stored when not in use. It was quite ingenious really, a cross between a tent and a hut.

'My father-in-law put that chalet up in 1924,' she went on, 'and I'm not sure it wasn't second hand when he bought it.' Since then her family had been keeping it safe in a shed every winter so as to bring it out when the summer season began. Walking back towards the central beach I noticed that several of the white hired huts had also been closed in by striped fabric panels at the back and front.

As the sand got finer near the apse of the bay, people were actually jostling to find space for their prone bodies and all the attendant seaside paraphernalia of towels, chairs, windbreaks and beach tents. The sea was dotted with heads and there was a busy, cheerful hum of enjoyment floating up from the beach. In the midst of all this colour and animation were a number of large huts, all painted in stripes of red, white and blue, one dedicated to the sale of shellfish, another overflowing with buckets, spades, windmills, balls, inflatables and stacks of rubber rings that looked like over-sized doughnuts. At so many of the places I'd already visited it was either too chilly or too early in the season for real summer holiday crowds but they did exist and I'd found them at Weymouth.

It was time for Mum and her car to leave me so I was back onto the buses. As I waited on the prom my X53 coach pulled in from Exeter with a full load of day-trippers ready to empty onto the beach. I should have been heading toward the Isle of Portland but I learnt about the huts there too late so boarded the coach and set out for West Bexington instead. It was an idyllic journey. In the honey-coloured village of Abbotsbury the cottages looked like the type that appear on boxes of clotted cream fudge and as the coach rolled past I watched reed bundles being thrown up to a thatcher working on one of the many picturesque roofs. After that the road climbed steeply causing the coach to shudder and shake. It was a daunting few minutes but on the brow of the hill I was rewarded by the view down towards Chesil Beach, a geologically unparalleled shingle ridge stretching for some seventeen miles along the sea edge and protecting a lagoon on its landward side. Beyond the green cliffs it looked barren yet surprisingly beautiful.

I got off the bus at Swyre and took what looked like a footpath through fields to the sea. The sun was at its hottest and, as I walked on and over stiles, my way became increasingly overgrown to the point where the vegetation was as tall as I was. Rather too worried by thoughts of snakes and the threat of stinging nettles against my bare legs I transferred my backpack onto my front hoping it would push aside any prickly things up ahead. And finally I stepped out of the greenery onto the beach. The pebbles under my feet were the size of jelly beans but they'd once been much bigger, before longshore drift had worn them down in the waves between Portland and West Bexington. Walking past the café and car park fourteen large beach huts came into view, the leftovers from a failed Thirties holiday resort. Year round occupation was allowed so, strictly speaking, they were outside my remit. I'd added them to my itinerary because earlier in the year one had broken the beach hut record, changing hands for £120,000. Within the space of fifteen minutes the asking price was doubled as two determined bidders fought over the rare opportunity to own a West Bexington chalet.

Mr and Mrs Llewellyn, the successful couple, got a small sitting room, kitchen, two double bedrooms and shower room but, as they told curious journalists afterwards, it wasn't the standard of accommodation that mattered. They had been regular visitors for nearly sixty years and Mr Llewellyn reckoned he'd stayed in every one of the chalets at some point in his life. The chalets were mostly passed down through the generations, like that belonging to Michelle le Bailly, whose grandmother had been one of the original purchasers in the early 1930s.

'She came from London so how she heard about it I don't know. My grandparents bought it, then my mum and uncle spent a lot of time down here as kids; during the war it was their escape from the Blitz.'

Mr Llewellyn had told Michelle he remembered playing with her uncle when they were both boys. Michelle herself had grown up spending summer holidays with a circle of Bexington chalet friends.

During the interwar heyday of plotland developments local landowners came up with the idea of 'Bexington-on-Sea', a brand new seaside resort that was laid out in 1932 with 'summer bungalows', a tennis court, café, car park, and salt-water swimming pool complete with changing huts. Two years later everything was put up for auction as part of a 400 acre estate. On the sale plan roads were projected over a third of the site with 1,000 building plots. Thankfully no-one else shared this vision and the sale never happened. The 1930s legacy was much more discreet than first anticipated and though the community of summer bungalows had evolved from basic two room timber huts into larger holiday homes with UPVC cladding and double-glazed windows, it had not grown in number. Now with the designation of Chesil Beach as part of the Jurassic Coast World Heritage Site it probably never would. Michelle seemed slightly to regret the move away from wooden walls but was all too aware of the maintenance issues for buildings in such an exposed position.

'They used to look lovely. In the late 60s they were all different colours. It was a point of honour that you didn't paint your chalet the same colour as anyone else's. They did look gorgeous then. They were all the same size and shape and different colours.'

The more I heard, the more these West Bexington chalets had in common with smaller day huts I'd visited, not least because of their owner's devotion. Michelle had never lived permanently in Dorset but she still considered it her home, assuring me that she would part with everything else before selling her hut.

Turning my back on Chesil Beach, Charmouth was next – a favourite place of fossil hunters where the huts were dark brown sheds and a disused public convenience had just sold for more than £37,000. This loo with a view, just fifty yards from the beach, was set to be converted into a rather unusual day chalet. By the time I finally walked into the tourist information at Lyme Regis it was late afternoon and the supply of available rooms was so sorely depleted that I ended up in overflow accommodation. My attic room was very hot, with 1970s décor and a coin-operated TV but at least I had a bed for the night.

Though the blue sky had clouded over there were still people enjoying the end of a day on the beach; children running and paddling, a family playing cricket on the sand. Above them, the lower level of the two-tier seawall was lined with beach huts that looked like wardrobes. They were simple boxes with double front doors, mostly coloured in earthy pigments that echoed the nearby Jurassic cliffs. At the far end a few were more decorative including one pale turquoise hut with curtains behind small panels of glass giving the impression of a more sophisticated French *armoire*. Beyond these huts I followed in the footsteps of Jane Austen by taking a walk to the end of the Cobb. Made famous by its appearance in films of *Persuasion* and *The French Lieutenant's Woman*, this muscular structure had been acting as harbour wall and breakwater since the thirteenth century and still provided a superb vantage point to look back on the pretty town below the cliffs.

In the opposite direction there was another beach, pebbly but with a definite row of white huts. I wandered over and managed to catch Heather and Tony Payne before they packed up for the day. They offered me tea and a jam tart so I sat with them outside the hut Heather's father had put up fifty years earlier. Tony, who'd grown up in nearby Bridport, also had a beach hut in his youth but those at West Bay had long since gone. The couple's current home was Pinner in Middlesex but thanks to a wooden chalet above the beach they could spend the whole summer at Lyme and come to the hut every day. In the winter they went abroad for the sunshine.

'I like the name,' I said, pointing toward the sign above the door.

'We were the first to name our hut,' Heather told me. 'It must have been about three years ago. I was just looking out to sea and it came to me – "Gulls and Buoys".'

Their hut had also pioneered the subtle addition of colour on the tip of the gable and other hutters had followed giving a nice effect along the row.

'My dad did it for practical reasons. He put yellow on the gable so he could see it from the sea; he sailed directly out in a straight line from the hut to get to the best fishing ground.' Nowadays the colour had been changed to stripes of blue so that the grandchildren knew which hut to head for after swimming.

It was quieter here than on the main beach and Heather and Tony clearly loved it. Prices were rising but they weren't tempted to cash in.

'I wouldn't sell the hut even if I was down and out,' declared Heather.

'If you were down and out you'd come and live in it!' Tony joked confidently.

'Too right I would!' And we all knew she was serious.

The next morning I set out from Lyme Regis to do a day trip around the East Devon coast, starting in Seaton. The bay was full of water when I arrived, deep blue like the cloudless sky above. To the west a white headland rose from the end of West Walk, a vivid contrast to the local strata of red mudstone, which abruptly ceased at the same point. This deep red was the backdrop to a row of white wooden huts, their shed-like profiles made crisp by the strong sunlight and the ruddy cliff. I stopped to chat to the couple outside number twenty who were enjoying the relative security of their position on the prom. For ten years they'd had a hut on the beach, which they'd had to replace twice. According to them, the sea could pick up a hut whole so that the structure would float on the waves until the bottom gave in and it sank. They'd seen it happen. Sometimes bits washed up further around the bay and people would go and scavenge the timber; people like their next-door neighbours whose loft was floored with recovered beach hut panels! All the huts were safely stored inland during the winter months but storms could and did hit in the summer. As a result they'd decided it was best to be off the beach; the thirty-four white huts on the shingle looked safe today but who could tell.

At Beer, the next village along the coast, the main street turned into a slipway giving access to the beach through a faultline between two huge masses of chalk topped with velvety green vegetation. The only promenades were strips of black rubber laid over the flint pebbles, criss-crossing from the numerous beach huts past fishing boats and deckchairs to the sea. The huts were on two levels; running along raised platforms below the cliff and, in front, placed directly onto the beach. The different blocks of colour denoted different operators; Kenno's Blue and White Tea Hut was next to the blue and white huts, while green and cream belonged to Chapples, established 1923 and the oldest family-run business in Beer. It was easy to see that not much had changed on the beach since then because there wasn't really much that could change. Admittedly Mr Chapple was now hiring out self-drive motor boats but there were still Luggers scattered across the beach, working boat rigs that claimed an ancestry as far back as the Vikings. As for the tourists, they were sat outside the huts or in traditional stripy deckchairs fitted with head shades, lightly grilling themselves under the summer sun. And there seemed to be quite a lot of them too, all pleased to have found an unspoilt spot; a spot that was attached, moreover, to a picturesque Devon village with a shop stacked full of clotted cream products and rock flavoured with scrumpy cider.

Sidmouth was a different case again. The bus journey was beautifully scenic featuring thatched cottages and English country gardens as well as a good deal of reversing down roads which were barely wide enough for the bus let alone anything that tried to come the other way. When I finally got there the Sidmouth seafront proved to be a genteel mix of Regency terraces, Victorian hotels and a cricket pitch right on the front. The main beach was bare of huts but at Jacob's Ladder I found blocks of flat-roofed wooden type put up in 1997 which, I confess, were a little disappointing after the high architectural standards along the promenade.

I took my penultimate bus ride of the day and wandered through the charming centre of Budleigh Salterton accompanied by the faint babbling sound of a stream running in open channels towards the sea. At the beach a broken line of huts pointed east, their painted walls picking out all the colours of the landscape. Beyond them was a gently sloping headland of low mud-red cliffs, the red capped with green and, in the middle distance, an isolated group of tall trees. In the other direction were neat rows of smaller cream huts let on a seasonal basis by the Council. Outside one of these I stopped to talk to a couple who had moved down to the area seven years earlier. As I spoke to the woman my brain raced to try and think where I had seen her before while my mouth tried to maintain a normal conversation. I wanted to ask if she used to read the BBC news but that would have been impolite so we exchanged a bit of beach hut banter and I went on my way. People in Budleigh Salterton were probably too discreet to ask Sue Lawley for her autograph so I wasn't going to disturb her peace any more than was necessary. And it really was peaceful, a proper get-away-from-it-all kind of place.

Exmouth was my last stop, the sun slipping out of the sky as I stepped off another bus at the end of the Jurassic Coast. Only one hut was still open along what seemed to me the wrong side of the beach road. Instead of being next to the sand the huts here looked over the beach through a filter of moving traffic. Permanent buildings of rendered blockwork, they were painted cream with a tilting zigzag roofline that stepped backwards from projecting central huts. The lady in number six had got her bike out ready to cycle home but I caught her doing some final tidying. She had only had her hut for a year but was a true convert, to the extent that she couldn't remember the last time she'd cooked at home.

'I've got everything here. All I need to do is bring my fresh meat and veg.'

The road didn't seem to bother her and she didn't really come for the beach.

'You can't swim anyway because of the fast currents where the river meets the sea. I started off bringing down books and magazines and everything – haven't read a thing! There's too much going on, especially on Sundays when people come down to see me.'

She had recently celebrated her sixtieth birthday with a party in her beach hut in the rain but her favourite time was when she had the place to herself.

'I often come down at about seven thirty in the morning to watch the sun coming up. I just love it here.'

There was still enough light to see the other type of Exmouth huts, twenty chalets so-called to mark them out as larger than average. They sat on a grassy verge above the car park, a curving permanent block with the benefit of glazed windows but a distinctly 1980s municipal look. The gabled roofline was carried on brick piers in front of the chalets, peaking above each pair. In the gable, corrugated plastic filled the triangular space as if the design had been adapted from a small business unit on an industrial park. I crossed the road and found that they looked better from a distance. Beyond the beach, the lifeboat was on trials speeding across the river mouth in front of Dawlish Warren. I walked along the seafront, past the palm trees and the carpet beds of pink busy lizzies then felt hungry after a seagull flew past with half a chocolate muffin in its beak. I found a chip shop and ate a portion of the seaside staple before turning in for the night.

Next morning I set out to cross the Exe estuary, dawdling on a train down the river's near side past wading birds and abandoned boat hulls before changing at Exeter St David's for a faster intercity service along the other side towards Dawlish. This line, designed by Isambard Kingdom Brunel, followed the coast carrying me past Dawlish Warren, a former bungalow colony now devoid of huts, right onto the seafront at Dawlish. The station where I disembarked was literally on the beach, built as a bridge over the path from the town behind, so that on rainy days holidaymakers were often to be found taking cover under platform one. Beyond the harbour wall a great lump of rust-red rock formed a natural monument and, as if paying homage to it, the succeeding row of huts were stained the same colour. Where the row ended so did the wide promenade, giving way to the sands of Coryton Cove once designated for gentleman's bathing. Joyce Maggs, a ninety-year-old resident who grew up on the beaches here, recalled the paradox of a segregation, which meant that men had to walk along the women's bathing area to get to their own. Her grandfather had built the bathing pavilion on the town's main beach where boys went in one end and girls the other in order to learn to swim and dive. The railway line which had disappeared inside the beach hut cliff also emerged from the 242-metre long Kennaway Tunnel at Coryton Cove slightly putting the lie to the idea of a secluded space for male bathing. As if on cue, a distinctive 'de-dah' sounded to announce the next service hurtling briefly by before vanishing into another cliff-tunnel on its way to Teignmouth. This stretch of line was the most expensive on Brunel's Great Western Railway, a true feat of engineering that I was now going to experience for myself. It was spectacular riding so close to the high tide.

At Teignmouth I wandered along the seafront to where a dusky pink sandbank projected into the Teign estuary. Along its ridge were back-to-back huts, twenty-two facing up river and nineteen looking out to sea. Because of their vulnerable position these painted wooden huts were moved at the end of each season but along the river beach there were larger, more permanent structures. The first ten or so were built of timber and seemed to stretch back quite a long way from their front decks. In contrast to the sandbank this felt more like a working beach packed with little boats, crab pots and eel traps. Several signs advertised 'Live Eels' which seemed to be a speciality here. I walked along to where a full ferry was departing for Shaldon across the river mouth, and came across a short terrace of two-storey huts.

The owner of the only pink one was sitting outside having a cup of tea with the harbour master. He confirmed that these had originally been fishermen's huts.

'Mine's narrower at the back 'cos it started life as an upturned boat. When I bought it five years ago it was a tin shack and now it's essentially just breeze blocks.'

He'd had to pay quite a lot to get it because like more conventional-looking beach huts these double-deckers were usually passed through the generations. He'd done it up to make it more homely with bright curtains, a cooker downstairs and a TV upstairs.

'I sometimes do my net work up there. It's still a fisherman's hut really.'

'So do you have a boat?' I asked.

'Ahh,' he sighed, 'too many boats. I've got to get rid of some but its good to go out into Lyme Bay with a few lobster pots; sometimes I catch sand eels in the summer.'

Two doors down the row, a Canadian flag was flying above a tall, shabby white hut. If the crowded roofline was anything to go by this hut was owned by pigeon-fanciers.

'They must like it here,' I said to the bottle-blonde lady sitting in the doorway.

'It could be because of this,' she replied, reaching down to her side and pulling out a large plastic sweet jar filled with bird food.

'And what about the flag?'

'That's there to show our support for the Canadian government's fishing policy.'

'So is this a fisherman's hut rather than a beach hut?' I asked, peering behind into a gloomy interior that seemed to be full of rods and other paraphernalia.

'It's a beach hut alright.' And the conversation was over.

The Teignmouth huts proved an interesting mixture encapsulating the town's past as a fishing centre and early tourist resort. I wondered whether the bays of Torquay and Paignton would have huts worthy of the so-called English Riviera?

At the bottom of a steep and winding road I found Oddicombe Bay where concrete interwar chalets sat next to the vertical cliff railway. Above the shingle beach there was a café with upper sundeck and flat-roofed 'cabins' dated 1962. This was probably when the notice was screwed to the wall that read: 'Persons operating portable radios and gramophones are asked to control the volume thereof so as to cause no annoyance to others. A byelaw makes it a punishable offence to cause such an annoyance.' Latterly, it seemed there was also a risk that loud music might precipitate one of the all too frequent rock falls. The far corner of the beach was fenced off beyond a scarlet sign warning of 'serious geological problems'. I squinted upwards at the crumbling red cliff then looked back at the cordoned area within which a dozen white beach huts had been abandoned. This was their second year of exclusion; having been decommissioned they were now sitting ducks, waiting to cushion the rocky blow when it came.

Crescents of bright beach huts at Littlehampton, West Sussex

The author at Calshot Spit, Hampshire

Edwardian beach huts on a windy summer's day at Bournemouth, Dorset

Tim Baber's hut and headquarters of the Mudeford Sandbank News, Dorset

Blake's beach huts at Ventnor on the Isle of Wight used to be bathing machines and have been operated by the same family for more than 170 years.

Paignton beach huts reflected in a rock pool

Skeleton huts at Weymouth, Dorset. Lockers at the back of the huts are used to store the canvas wall panels when not in use.

A busy day on the beach at Beer, Devon

Looking down on the terraces of Tolcarne Beach huts at Newquay, Cornwall

The blue and white hut at Westward Ho! was given to Jez Harris as a birthday present.

A very British scene at Budleigh Salterton, Devon

All the huts at Woolcombe in Devon have girl's names. From left to right these three are called Marjorie, Katherine and Matilda.

I walked beside the shore past pretty Babbacombe then climbed the painfully steep Walls Hill. The views were magnificent. To the east I could see all the way back to Teignmouth, Dawlish and Exmouth. Directly to the west was the Mediterranean vision of Anstey's Cove, complete with aquamarine waves splashing against the sand and swimmers gathered around the hull of a solitary powerboat. Even the burnt out remains of a chalet block didn't detract from the idyllic tranquillity. This was, however, an enforced peace because the cliffs here were so unstable that the footpaths had been blockaded. Thankfully the chalets at Meadfoot Beach looked in less imminent danger, built into the curve of a lower, albeit rugged, promontory. As the waves of high tide sparkled in the midday sun a boy and girl took turns to launch themselves from the slipway into the water. It wasn't the south of France but the clear sea looked tempting enough to fool the willing. And from the western end of the bay I looked back at the horizontal row of hut doors and saw that their line was continued by an elegant Regency terrace, now converted into a hotel. With the blues of sea and sky and the middle ground of lush green trees Meadfoot made for a very attractive alternative to the foreign Riviera. Despite a few pavement cafés near the marina, central Torquay felt rather less Continental, with heavy tourist traffic rumbling and humming through the town. The funfair was in full swing and within spitting distance of the big wheel was another line of beach huts below the high sea wall at Corbyn Head.

Two-thirds of the fifty gabled huts rested on stilts, with different coloured doors and barge boards to offset their white wooden walls. Below the Grand Hotel I stopped to chat to a couple who'd had their hut since 1963. After a high tide and easterly wind the previous year they'd considered getting rid of it.

'But our family wouldn't let us!' said the lady.

Her silver-haired husband was sitting on the top of the steps dressed all in green; green polo shirt, green jumper, green shorts.

'I used to have a business in the town,' he said, 'so I'd come down for a swim at lunchtime. When the tide's out it's too rocky to swim but when it's in its like having you own lagoon in front of the huts.'

As he spoke the man had been squeezing brown pods of bladder wrack and rubbing the bubbly goo which seeped out onto his knees.

'It's very good for arthritis,' he disclosed. 'My mother used to use it, absolutely swore by it. And it's cheap – I just pick it up off the beach.'

Next morning I felt very much in need of something to ease my joints since I'd spent the night strung between the front seats of my parents' new camper van. They'd driven down from North Devon to join me and suggested I try out the third 'bed'. This amounted to a narrow piece of plastic sheeting fitted over two poles that slotted into fixings on the front doors. My attempts to climb into the thing were enough to send my poor mother into paroxysms of laughter and trying to get out was almost as bad. I was a bit too tall and a bit too grown up for this child's bunk but it put a new slant on the article I read next day about the over thirties who were moving back to the family home because of high house prices. Sharing a camper van with my parents was definitely going to be a one-off experience. And, as the whole vehicle moved every time I did, I felt sure they wouldn't be asking me to join them again anyway. The next night I stayed in a very comfortable B&B while they enjoyed the outdoor life without me.

This accommodation hiccough behind us, we set out in the van to explore Paington's beaches. Above the sea wall at Preston Sands there were white beach huts as far as the eye could see. Their doors and barge boards were all painted different colours, a particularly lovely vision when reflected in the giant rock pools near the cliff. On the barnacled walkway across the pools I met two young boys with fishing nets and such a pride in their catch that they eagerly showed me the tiddlers swimming around a big white bucket in the company of two crabs and a starfish. The burnt umber sand characteristic of this stretch of coast was coated with lime green seaweed that squelched pleasantly as I walked over it to the end of the hut line. There the rows were doubled up and a few were council owned, available to hire. Beyond them I spotted four scrap huts set back from the seafront. Knowing what lay in store for the disused few at Oddicombe I began to formulate a beach hut rescue plan.

My mind was whirring; wouldn't it be great to have a genuine beach hut in my garden? Of course, I really wanted one by the sea but after seeing so many, how would I choose where and how would I afford it? This way I could return home with the ultimate souvenir of my trip. Anywhere else in the country the logistical challenges would have been too great to even entertain the idea but didn't my parents have a great big camper van right here? It was beginning to feel like fate had brought them to help me effect the liberation of one of these poor, unloved huts. Mum and Dad were less enthusiastic but they humoured me as I made excited enquiries at the Tourist Information office. I got nowhere, but perhaps that was fate's way of helping me avoid disappointment; it would have been worse to get further down the line and only then realise that the camper van was too small and too full of stuff to transport a beach hut. With some regret I let the rescue idea go.

There were no huts along the town's main beach so we walked over the headland towards Goodrington where most of the huts were concentrated in the curve of the bay. People vied for space on the central sands and seagulls overhead vied for their rubbish. As we arrived a steam train chuffed its way behind the row of council huts and on the sand the Punch and Judy show was just starting. Joey the clown came on to introduce Mr Punch but the main character was having a wee wee. The kids loved it. Punch appeared, followed by Judy and a punk baby with red hair called Saturday ('they took one look at him and decided to call it a day!'). Judy got her stick out ready to hit Punch but asked first if this would be politically correct. With great disregard for this modern notion Punch shouted 'no' and then began hitting his wife *and* the policeman. The show was fast and witty, a clever adaptation of a traditional seaside entertainment. When it was finished I went back stage to meet Professor Mark Poulton, a man I felt sure would understand my love of beach huts.

Mark had decided to become a Punch and Judy man at the tender age of four after seeing the legendary Guy Higgins do his show at Weymouth.

'I left school at fifteen and did a summer season here then turned professional. I make my own puppets and being a puppeteer is my full time business.'

Now in his late twenties I guessed that it was hard work to make a living.

'Last year I nearly chucked in the beach shows. I don't charge much but people would walk past and say "50p, we don't need to pay we'll just stand and watch", then they'd go off and give their kids £5 or £10 to spend on the amusements. People fail to realise that at 50p this is good quality and cheap entertainment.'

Deemed a professor by dint of tradition, Mark was always working to make his show better while preserving the Victorian essentials. He told me that there had been a Punch and Judy show at Goodrington Sands for ninety-nine years. Next year would mark the centenary but it would also see the end of his licence. As it was one of only two professional beach shows still operating in England, I hoped that people would reach into their pockets so that he could continue to keep the show going and maybe inspire other four-year-olds to follow in his footsteps.

Home time was fast approaching when we reached Broadsands, the most rural of Paignton's beaches. I'd observed it everywhere, the point at which the exodus begins to occur, when people have had enough and are ready for their dinner. High tide was only half an hour away so most of the one hundred-odd huts were closed or closing. People were washing the red sand off their bare feet, deflating inflatables and packing towels and children into cars. We took a walk along the seawall then went off to find a fish supper in the port of Brixham.

Tuesday dawned and before we sped into Cornwall there was one last stop to make in South Devon. Plymouth was a bit short on beaches but under the Hoe where Sir Francis Drake played his famous game of pre-Armada bowls, green, yellow and red hut blocks stepped down a cliffside that had been moulded into a huge swimming complex with multiple pools, diving boards and a huge Art Deco lido. After a period of neglect the area was at last seeing some investment; restoration of the double-decker promenade was complete and there were diggers and workmen on the blue floor of Tinside Lido. The 1960s huts were well-used yet their permanent walls belied the struggle of a decade earlier when the council proposed demolition as a means of ridding itself of maintenance responsibilities. Outraged by this idea, Dessie and Jim Carnell proved to be a match for bureaucratic penny pinching, offering to take on the running of the huts in order to save them.

'They're only like small cupboards but they give such a lot of pleasure,' Dessie told me. 'When our daughters were young we used to come here all the time. Joanna's birthday was in Whitsun week and she had parties at the hut with everyone sitting along the wall eating jellies and sandwiches.'

Taking on the huts had clearly been a labour of love for the Carnells because it certainly didn't constitute the easy option. Jim ended up doing all the jobs, like the biannual re-painting. Within a year their commitment was justified by regular bookings and they'd since been able to hand the mantle to another hut couple. Muriel, a local character who, at the age of eighty-two, was renowned for her daily swims, had just returned to her hut from the sea and told me how she remembered floodlit bathing in the 1930s when an orchestra played above the lido. It seemed unlikely the council would be reinstating this musical accompaniment but their regeneration of one of the country's last surviving seaside lidos seemed to confirm Dessie and Jim's faith in the foreshore.

From Plymouth we took the Torpoint Ferry across the River Tamar into Cornwall. The road rose steeply towards Whitsand Bay where an unexpected colony of holiday chalets was pinned into the grassy slopes of Freathy Cliff like a vision of Nova Scotia or Newfoundland. It was sunny and the views out to sea were amazing but these exposed slopes probably looked less appealing in bad weather of the kind that had caused the Russian-built freighter Kodima to run aground earlier in the year. The ship was carrying Scandanavian pine, some 4,000 tons of which washed ashore along Whitsand Bay. This incident wouldn't be noteworthy except for the fact that some of the timber was subsequently turned into a beach hut under the cliffs of Rame Head. Students from Exeter School of Art had designed and built a three-storey hut *à la* Robinson Crusoe, managing to retain a temporary anonymity that delighted the national press. Their hut project was only accessible by sea but curious visitors had found hammocks and a note asking that any barbeque equipment be replaced after use. It was all deliciously Bohemian, not least because of its temporary nature. If the winter waves didn't get the hut the owner of the wrecked ship could still ask for his timber back!

The distances between Cornwall's hut sites were elongated by the county's craggy coastline and a paucity of roads, most of the latter being dense with holiday crowds driving down to get away from it all. At Looe, the brightly painted hulls of proud fishing boats glimmered in the sunshine but the last few hire tents that survived an arson attack in the late Eighties had been packed away above the beach kiosk. There had been no replacements and at Par, the once strong force of more than 200 wooden huts had dwindled to a mere eighteen hangers-on. My great aunty Sylvia, who'd had two huts here after moving from Southend, knew the price of such fires having managed to save just one blackened plate from her mother's anniversary dinner service after vandals torched her beach hut. Everything was quiet on the morning of my visit but the front of one hut had been smashed in as if to demonstrate that the yobs had not yet quit this playground. The other huts, in various colours and sizes, were scattered among grassy dunes behind the beach. Around them, bulging scarlet hips adorned wild rose bushes and insects hummed from the gorse and thistles. The beach's eastern backdrop was rolling fields and fuzzy hedges leading towards Gribben Head in the distance. On the other side was the less picturesque bulk of the china clay works, its steaming chimneys a reminder of this area's main export. Over the years, demand for china clay had pockmarked the landscape with huge craters, the most well-known of which was now home to the Eden Project, an ecological experiment and major tourist attraction housed in biospheres that looked like the spawn of some massive extra-terrestrial being.

I pushed on to Falmouth where Gyllyngvase Beach had lost all its huts but busy Swanpool Beach had recently acquired a dozen new ones. The row of unstained wooden sheds matched the grey-brown tone of the nearby cliff as well as the hefty mound of pale granite boulders whose job it was to break the force of oncoming waves. Lapping against the legs of happy children the clear water looked harmless enough but I wondered whether the huts would have to be moved come autumn. The blue summer skies would not last indefinitely and after nearly three weeks I was about to leave the south coast to make the last leg of my journey along the northern coast of Cornwall and Devon. Crossing the width of skinny Cornwall I was now headed for St Ives, the most westerly destination of my trip.

Three beaches awaited me. Near the railway station was Porthminster, where soft blonde sand spread out for half a mile in front of me and the buildings of the main town, made distinctive by their gold lichen-topped roofs, clustered to my left. The old wooden huts here were little more than changing cabins, with thin white fronts and equally thin doors painted dark green to match the verdant cliff behind. Their felted roofs sloped backwards from flat fronts, making a simple design that was surprisingly charming. I walked around the harbour past caricaturists, hair braiders and fishing tour touts trying to extract customers from the bustle of tourists and, on the way up Fish Street, towards Porthmeor Beach, passed little lanes dotted with craft shops and studios. The town's famously clear light continued to attract artists who might, one day, find a place for their work among the canvases at Tate St Ives. The curved gallery front sat above the crowded sands without condescension, its contemporary take on 1930s seaside architecture happily complimenting the double-decker hut blocks built against the cliff directly below it. These had the same shade of warm blue paintwork used on the second set of huts, where drying wetsuits were draped over the first floor railings and blue gingham curtains hung behind the glazed windows and doors. Despite all the mid-afternoon beach action, the huts were curiously quiet.

I meandered my way to Porthgwidden Beach, a sheltered little cove on the other side of the promontory known locally as The Island. At the rear of this arc of sand an old building with whitewashed stone walls served as the beach café with two tiers of permanent huts running from it. Windows divided into rectangular panes gave away the interwar heritage of the lower level whereas the huts on top looked to have been plonked there a few decades later. There were plenty of bronzed bodies reclining outside the huts. Passing the time of day with one man, I mentioned the enviably azure water that filled the bays. Though I'd meant it as a compliment he took the opportunity to complain about the high water rates through which residents paid to keep the sea clear. Campaigns like Surfers Against Sewage had been hugely successful in lobbying for proper treatment of human waste, instead of the cheap and well-established solution of pumping it out to sea and hoping for the best. The problem was that somebody had to pay for it. Sought-after Blue Flags, awarded by the European Commission since 1987, only went to beaches that met strict criteria for public health and good environmental stewardship so that the holidaymakers elbowing their way with me past the picture galleries and pasties, the fudge, rock and surf shops knew their stomachs would be safe after swimming at St Ives. All UK resorts have had to address the unpleasant question of sewage but Cornish rate-payers have more coast to look after than most. Thankfully, standards have changed so much that we are now able to take clean sea water for granted.

The next day I was in Newquay, Cornwall's surf capital. Whereas the St Ives coastline had been undulating, Newquay was rugged. Jamie Oliver had filmed an episode of 'The Naked Chef' while staying at Lusty Glaze and I couldn't help thinking how easily the beach's name might transfer to that of a novel culinary technique. At the bottom of sheer cliffs, flat-roofed cedar-red beach huts sat on low terraces alongside the National Lifeguard Rescue Training Centre and the holiday cottage where Jamie cooked up a feast for his surfing buddies. Every day the café fielded four or five enquiries from people wanting to rent one of the huts. I followed the flat sweep of pale sand towards Tolcarne Beach. Though the landscape felt intrinsically Cornish the bright white huts nestled into its eastern corner were decidedly Mediterranean-looking. There was something about the tiered arrangement, complete with palm trees, and the sun bleached paint on the doors; green in the top row, yellow one level down, then red, and at the bottom a shade of blue that was more reminiscent of Greek fishing villages than south-west England.

Both Lusty Glaze and Tolcarne were privately owned and had once been the property of Garfield Daniel. It was Daniel who, upon taking over in 1936, built the concrete terraces and cabins. Only the blue block of huts was still in this original material though; the others had developed a bad case of concrete cancer necessitating individual wooden replacements. It was also in the Thirties that surfing began to develop as a serious sport. Garfield Daniel was one of the pioneers and Jon, the current owner of Tolcarne Beach, showed me the orange painted strip of wood with one curved end and the initials 'G.D.' that had been one of his boards. It now took pride of place in the beach café.

Jon suggested I talk to Jean Cornah, a regular Tolcarne beach-goer from childhood, who I found relaxing outside her red hut. Thankfully the sunshine was as Mediterranean as the colour scheme because, though they say size doesn't matter, you wouldn't fit many people in one of these cabins if the heavens opened. The huts were a similar style to those at Porthminster Beach and since Garfield Daniel had started his beach business at St Ives this seemed more than coincidence. Unlike at Porthminster though, the stable doors were placed centrally with the upper half hinged to open upwards. Either side of the doors were narrow windows to let in light. Jean dug out some black and white photos and showed me her family at the hut in every decade since the 1930s. Before that her landlady mother had had a tent on the beach.

'My uncle's grandfather used to lead the horses that pulled the bathing machines on Great Western Beach. I've got a picture at home. Give me your address and I'll send you a photocopy.'

Great Western was the next beach around and it was onto these sands that residents of the Hotel Victoria could emerge by lift, travelling direct from any floor down through a hundred feet of rock. Until five years ago the lift ran on a telephone system clicking as it went. On the occasions when it got stuck people had to be manually wound up from the beach but a new electric replacement had made the hotel's unique selling point rather more reliable. Jean's uncle's grandfather must have ferried many a guest from the end of that lift tunnel into the sea in a bathing machine.

Another example of Victorian ingenuity bequeathed to modern Newquay was the suspension bridge built in 1900, a year after the Hotel Victoria, to connect the mainland to a stray lump of rock between Great Western and Towan beaches. Known as The Island, for that is what it became every high tide, the rock was privately owned and in 1910 a house was built on its summit. Previous owners included Sir Oliver Joseph Lodge, inventor of the spark plug! At Towan I was getting nearer the town centre and harbour. The double-decker hut block here was owned by the council but was being used for storage. As far as hut locations were concerned it couldn't compete with Tolcarne and had clearly given up trying. Instead it appealed to learner surfers who could test themselves in the tamer waves of Towan before graduating to north-west facing Fistral Beach where the surf was big enough to make it the site of international competitions. I walked through the busy town where a DJ playing in the window of a clothes shop vied with the tinny sounds of amusement arcades to attract a teenage audience displaying bare flesh in varying degrees of tannedness. The cool caché of surfing provided Newquay with an 'in' to the youth market that most other British seaside resorts could only dream of. And Fistral Beach was where they all hung out. A steady stream of boards and bodies were leaving as I arrived in the late afternoon but the sands were still packed. The lack of beach huts was no surprise because the concept was somehow at odds with all the activity here. Huts and boards represented the static and the dynamic in seaside pastimes and it was pretty clear which end of that spectrum I fell into.

With one day of the August Bank Holiday gone in a blaze of sunshine I woke up to yet more blue sky on Sunday. Widemouth Bay, two miles west of Bude, lingered in my childhood memories as a huge stretch of golden sand so I set out on the off-chance of there being huts there that I hadn't noticed at the age of six. And there were; at the end of the car park, just six of them, all green and gabled. Though the beach was busy, with little silhouettes of people at the margin of the shimmering tin-foil sea, only one hut was open. Three generations, children, parents and grandparents, were amusing themselves on and around the veranda.

'Usually the huts here pass from mother to daughter,' the grandmother told me, 'but my sister was offered it after her friend's daughter moved away. She wanted someone to use it and we'd been coming here since we were little.'

'Did there used to more huts?' I asked.

'Oh no, there's always been six. I remember them from before the war and there were six then.'

We talked until my own family turned up to accompany me on the home stretch of my trip.

We drove on to Bude where the annual jazz festival had endowed the town with a party atmosphere. People were spilling out of pubs; chatter and music filled the air. After lunch and a cooling drink from the bar we crossed the canal on Nanny Moore's bridge, a nice monument to the nineteenth century bathing attendant who helped ladies change in her makeshift tent then saw them safely dipped under the waves. Despite the crowded town both Summerleaze Beach, with its almost-camouflaged green huts and tidal swimming pool, and smaller Crooklets Beach next door, seemed relatively quiet. In the early Sixties the district council had advertised 'clean and well-kept huts' for hire at both sites in small, medium and large sizes. The permanent line of cream fronted huts that sashayed up the low cliff at Crooklets had been built by then too, qualifying under the 'large' heading. With the tide having exposed acres of yellow-ochre sand all the huts were miles from the sea so we found a nice spot about midway between the two to lay down our towels and rugs. Had I wanted to take up surfing this would have been a good beach to choose because it was home to the country's oldest Surf Life Saving Club. Founded in 1953, the club had been the subject of one of the BBC's earliest live outside broadcasts when locals were given the opportunity of being 'televised while bathing'. It was hardly Baywatch but it probably made good TV in 1954.

Come early evening we packed up our things, brushed the wet sand off our feet and joined the going home time throng. From being an observer of this phenomenon it was nice to be part of it not least because for once I actually was going home; not home where I lived but home where I grew up, back to North Devon.

The beach at Woolacombe had failed to make much of an impact upon my childhood because getting there involved traffic jams and bottlenecks around Barnstaple. Of course, everything is relative and perhaps this congestion was mild by city standards but it was exactly the sort of thing my parents had been escaping from in their move to the country. By the time my boyfriend and I arrived at Woolacombe on Bank Holiday Monday every campsite, hotel and B&B in the area had already disgorged their guests onto the broad sands. Parked cars streaked like a metallic ribbon along the cliff road, fracturing Exmoor's gradual descent into dunes and then sand. We drove right around the bay but even the double yellow lines had disappeared beneath bumper to bumper cars. This was the farewell finale of the school holidays and nobody wanted to be left out. After much despairing we found a parking spot near the town boundary and descended into the melee of people who, from the road, resembled nothing less than multi-coloured ants.

Entering through the official car park we were welcomed to Woolacombe Sands by an unusual signpost in the shape of a replica bathing machine made by the staff of Parkin Estates. As owners and operators of the beach since 1945, Parkin Estates built the huts and were responsible for their introduction thirty years ago. Each season they had to create an eight-foot high bank 300 metres long for the 'ladies' to perch upon. Unlike boats, I hadn't found any evidence that beach huts were given a gender by their owners; until now. As well as numbers every flat-roofed Woolacombe hut had a name and they were all female.

'They're very popular,' the woman in the beach office told me. 'We get people booking for the season from January onwards and they'll often ask specifically for Sarah or Mildred or whichever is their favourite.'

I walked along the row, past the doors painted either bright red, green, yellow or blue and paid my respects to Patricia, Gertrude, Jemima, Maureen, Myrtle, Florence and the rest of the girls. There was a Katherine but she spelt her name differently so I didn't feel compelled to give her any special attention. Inevitably there was a traffic jam leaving Woolacombe but with the beach behind us, heading back through a green valley dotted with sheep, I was glad to have found some more huts I'd never seen before.

Although it meant going back on myself I'd purposely saved the huts at Westward Ho! till last. This was my local beach; a beach that faced the Atlantic ocean with its exclamation mark but hid from the land behind a long pebble ridge. This was the beach I'd visited with my family, my friends and even my classmates on a geography field trip to measure its pebbles. In the village (because a village it had remained, despite the best efforts of speculators in the 1860s) I counted eleven wooden huts in the car park near the surf club to add to my running total. This would have been a disappointing finish but the huts along the promenade running west away from the bingo and chips provided just the right ending to my journey. They were of the traditional gabled type but each was slightly different from its neighbour and there were no rules about colour as spectacularly demonstrated by the orange hut with lime green shutters. Behind them were static caravans and a lushly wooded cliff; in front were more of those distinctive silver-grey pebbles and a big network of rock pools. As I kept walking I noticed that some huts were linked up to a nearby electricity line. This provided Jez Harris with power for his fridge. Like me, he'd grown up in Torrington but unlike me he loved surfing. His hut, painted bright blue on the bottom and white on the top, had been an eighteenth birthday present. Jez's mum had seen the hut for sale and changed her mind about buying a drum kit. She bought her son the hut so he could keep his board in it and over the summer he practically lived there. I admit it, I was jealous.

To ward off the green-eyed monster I kept walking towards the beginning of the cliff path where a ramshackle Victorian house had stood in a state of romantic decay for as long as I could remember. Behind it was a green surrounded by beach huts, which, by this point were quite some way from the beach. One of the many things I'd learnt from my trip was that this didn't matter at all. Hutters here could still hear the Atlantic breakers and smell the salt air while looking out to sea. And I was about to join them, if only briefly. By virtue of being friends with his niece, I'd managed to borrow the key to Tim Langdon's hut and headed back along the row to find it. Tim's hut had cream walls with racing green paintwork on the windows and door; the rusty padlocks were tricky to open but after some wiggling the clasps opened and I was in! I drew back the flowery curtains and looked around the homely interior complete with box seat, folding chairs and gas stove. I'd reached the end of my journey and there was only one thing to do. I put the kettle on and found the tea bags.

Chapter Fourteen
Here comes the Sun

I n September 1929 a unique event occurred on the beach at Eastbourne. Bathers went on strike. One hundred and fifty people caused a sensation on the front when they emerged simultaneously from their hotels and boarding houses dressed only in their bathing costumes and wraps. Converging on the Corporation Bathing Station the protesters found every hut occupied and proceeded openly to defy the rule of 'no hut, no bathe'. *En masse* they threw off their wraps and plunged into the sea – without paying a penny for the privilege. The police were called and the names of about forty of the 'offenders' were taken. It was a shocking day for the normally sedate resort of Eastbourne.

A decade earlier, the summer of 1919 had seen a rush to the coast, the collective exhalation of a war weary population. For thousands of people it was the first holiday opportunity for five years and the August scramble for lodgings found many willing to accept the makeshift accommodation of sofas in seaside living rooms or temporary beds placed in bathrooms. The extension of leisure time down the social scale that had begun with the Edwardians continued apace during the interwar years. By the end of the 1930s an annual holiday had become the norm for fifteen million people and the principal of paid leave was finally given legislative backing in the Holidays with Pay Act of 1938. It was a period of radical transformation in European society. Traditional industries faltered, there was an economic depression and yet spending at British seaside resorts was on the rise. Huge capital sums were invested in municipal improvements like parks and promenades and resort competition, spurred by newly dedicated advertising budgets, led to the construction of attractions such as lidos, pavilions and winter gardens that each claimed to be the biggest and best of their type. A lot had changed. As H. B. Brenan wrote in 1936: 'Before the war many villagers in central England had never seen the sea. Today, members of a Women's Institute in a Cotswold village…will visit Aberystwyth one year and Bournemouth the next as unconcernedly as thirty years ago they would have gone pickinicking'. Women discovered freedom between 1914 and 1918. And from 1920 onwards the new seaside scene that evolved was in large part due to a greater commingling of the sexes. The Eastbourne bathers strike happened because people's expectations had changed.

Although mixed bathing was now commonplace local government boards tenaciously clung onto the idea that beach behaviour must be subject to regulation. They allowed for personal preference by providing a choice between machines, huts, cabins and tents but bathers were supposed to pay and wait their turn as they always had. Resort authorities did not look kindly on people who tried to bypass the system. *The Times* of 10 August 1921 reported how at Broadstairs the District Council had taken action to stop the disagreeable practice 'popular among visitors who arrive on the sands with simply a macintosh [sic] covering their bathing costume.' Their only concession to complaints about the under-supply of changing tents was to allow school children to bathe 'directly from *certain* parts of the foreshore.'

'Mackintosh bathing' had begun before the war but it became an identifiable phenomenon during the Twenties. By this time leisure had become more democratic and the regulation of beach behaviour was no longer seen as a vote-winner for central government. When Colonel Day M.P. stood up in the House of Commons to ask for 'legislation forbidding undressing on beaches for bathing purposes' in 1927, his request was met with ridicule. The troubled Colonel wanted to make sure that the gravity of the situation was properly understood: 'Is the Home Secretary aware that in many cases large groups of people undress

The interwar fashion for sun-bathing led to shorter bathing costumes and a range of new products to assist the tanning process.

on the beach without any covering at all?' Home Secretary Joynson-Hicks dismissively remarked that 'I am quite sure that in any case of that kind the Hon. Member...would not be present.' Resorts were left to make their own moral judgements.

As a means to impel public scrutiny of the rules the Eastbourne strike was a novel tactic. Bathers were frustrated that the demand for changing huts was always much higher than the available supply, a situation which contributed to making the hire charge of eightpence per person seem unjustifiably dear. And their protest got results. The town council shrewdly took heed of proposals to improve existing bathing arrangements; more changing accommodation was provided and a victory – of sorts – was won after mackintosh bathing was permitted along the Grand and Royal Parades. Fearful of losing revenue, however, the council charged adults 6d. and children 4d. for the privilege of removing their mackintoshes on the beach. This was as far as they were prepared to go. According to the write-up in *The Times* on 4 February 1930 'an amendment that macintosh [sic] bathing should be allowed at all the stations was defeated by a large majority.'

Away from the big resort beaches attitudes were more relaxed and guesthouses that advertised the possibility of bathing for free clearly did so on the assumption that it would attract customers. In 1931, for example, the Highbury Boarding Establishment in Swanage offered guests the following enticements: 'Facing Sea. In an Excellent Central Position. Convenient for all Amusements. *Sea Bathing allowed from the House.* The Comfort of our Guests studied in every way.' With so many places chasing tourist income municipal authorities could not afford to be left behind. At the 1932 Conference of Health and Pleasure Resorts Alderman Spurgen of the host town, Folkestone, welcomed delegates from some fifty English and Welsh resorts but bluntly warned them to raise their game. He saw holidaymakers with cash in their pockets using Folkestone, once an exclusive destination, as a mere staging post on the way to France in search of liberty and an escape from British '"grandmotherly" government'. Thankfully the results of a questionnaire on mackintosh bathing suggested cause for optimism; resorts now generally viewed it as an amenity that ought to be permitted.

The same questionnaire also sought information on another new seaside habit when it asked whether 'sun-bathing was permitted on the front, and, if so, under what conditions'. Sunbathing represented the biggest challenge to existing norms of beach behaviour in the interwar years yet it appears to have been accepted with minimal fuss. There were two reasons for this – health and fashion – a combination strikingly reminiscent of the early days of sea-bathing two hundred years earlier. Ultimately, the search for sunshine would lead to the desertion of British beaches for the Spanish Costas but in the Roaring Twenties it inspired a vibrant, distinctly modern approach to the seaside and its architecture.

By the 1930s excessive modesty was a thing of the past. Here women are filmed dashing out of old bathing machines on a Jersey beach.

The health imperative came first with the key developments taking place in Europe. Adolf Just's 'air-and sun-bath cult' found nationwide appeal in Germany after it was launched in 1896. Other important elements of this outdoors-life philosophy included nudism, vegetarianism and hiking. Then in 1903, Dr Auguste Rollier opened the 'sunshine clinic', a medical centre to treat tuberculosis in the Swiss Alps. Two decades of practice and research later, Rollier published *Heliotherapy*, the text-book of the movement, in which he claimed that over eighty per cent of his patients had been totally cured using natural sunlight and sun-lamp treatment. In Britain, Dr Armstrong of the Royal Sea Bathing Hospital had also been working on a system of progressive exposure to ensure that TB patients got a healthy tan without the discomfort of sunburn. Dr Armstrong described tanning as 'Nature's barrier against an *excessive* dose of ultra-violet radiation in which sunlight is very rich.' UV rays were the new wonder-drug believed 'to encourage the production in the deeper layers of the skin of substances which promote health and raise the resistance of the body to bacterial infection.' His patients would begin with five minutes exposure on each part of the body. Day by day the dosage would be increased by five minutes so that an uninterrupted course of treatment – which assumed that the sun shone reliably in Margate – would give full protection against sunburn after about two weeks. Then the real cure could begin, involving months, sometimes, years of outdoor therapy.

But if pre-war patients at the Royal Sea Bathing Hospital could see the beach from their open verandas the link had yet to be drawn between sunbathing and the seaside. During World War I animal fats were extensively used in the manufacture of high explosives, causing a deficiency in the national diet, which, in turn, led to an increased incidence of rickets and tuberculosis. Codliver oil was distributed as a substitute but when demand fell away in the summer months scientists realised the role of sunlight in supplying certain nutrients. By the time Dr Saleeby became chair of the Sunlight League in 1924 there seemed a very real medical incentive to the League's goal of 'teaching the nation that sunlight is Nature's universal disinfectant, as well as a stimulant and a tonic.' To prevent diseases like rickets the League would lobby for the 'systematic use of sunbaths' and what better location could there be for this than the seaside? Dr Saleeby stated his belief that 'The beach is incomparable. It gives the child everything.'

Charities that raised money to take inner-city children for a week's seaside holiday would often solicit donations through the pages of guidebooks. Clearly aware of the new potency of the sun, literally as well as metaphorically, the National Society for the Prevention of Cruelty to Children (NSPCC) ran a campaign in the early Thirties with the aim of 'Making the Sun Shine.' In a one page ad with seven sentences of text the word 'sun' appeared five times. Those people who could afford a summer holiday were asked to think of those who couldn't. 'What a wonderful change when the sun breaks through! The world is brighter, the children happier, your holiday more enjoyable. The sun in the skies is beyond human control, but the sun of human happiness is yours to command. By dispelling the clouds of ignorance, neglect and ill-treatment the NSPCC is taking sunshine into little lives and paving the way to healthy, useful manhood and womanhood.' Harnessing the natural goodness of sunshine would improve the health of the nation as well as the individual.

The arguments were as compelling as they had been from eighteenth century advocates of sea-bathing. In both cases, however, the necessary ingredient to stimulate a widespread appeal was fashion. The far-reaching changes associated with sunbathing happened when a tan became something everyone wanted; no longer the preserve of medical practitioners and German nudists, a tan became aspirational. Revising the well-established physical aesthetic that equated brown skin with the labouring classes was a gradual process. By the end of the Victorian period outdoor pursuits like river boating, cycling, swimming and tennis had become increasingly popular with both sexes. Even the most well brought up lady could not handle a tennis racket and a parasol at the same time so catching the sun had to be accepted as an inevitable consequence of these new sports. The association of brown skin with the poorest manual labourers was also less tenable in a predominantly urban society. The poor now worked in factories and lived in slums; their habitual pallor and bowed legs were the result of living life *indoors*.

Of course, gradually moving the beauty goalposts does not explain the creation of an international trend. There had to be something more. In 1923, when Coco Chanel walked down the gangway of the Duke of Westminster's yacht 'brown as a cabin boy', she became the legendary 'inventor' of sunbathing. And whether or not the queen of couture truly deserves that accolade is largely irrelevant because, as a woman with the power to influence fashion, Chanel made sunbathing chic; a bronzed body became the latest accessory. Prince Jean-Louis de Faucigny-Lucinge thought it possible that Chanel had invented sunbathing simply on the basis that 'at that time she invented everything'. The prince was one of the first people to go to the summer Riviera when he and his young bride took a villa at Cannes in 1924. During the winter months the Côte d'Azur was full of English visitors and had been throughout the nineteenth century. Come the end of April, however, fashionable doctors quit Nice to return to London and their patients who'd enjoyed the warm air along the *Promenade des Anglais* packed up and followed them. The Mediterranean heat between May and October was deemed intolerable if not down right dangerous. As pioneers the Faucigny-Lucinges enjoyed an empty Riviera. 'It was delicious. We immediately started sunbathing, which was something new at the time. A lot of sunbathing, exaggerated sunbathing. It was a study, it took time, hours and hours of sunbathing.' Others soon followed in their fashionable wake and by 1930 Juan-les-Pins had become *the* place to be in summer. 'Already at nine a.m. the beach is covered by prostrate or reclining forms – since most of the clientele hope for a definite number of hours' grilling a day...they saunter down betimes in exotic pyjamas and wraps... and hit the horizontal on the narrow strip of burning, golden sand.' Every new day allowed for comment on a 'new and highly provocative crush... commenting languidly through sun-glasses and over foot-long cigarette holders on the limbage and the loinage and the torsage'.

Not everyone was a convert. Evelyn Waugh disliked how 'you rub on oil, and bits of sand and waste-paper adhere to you'. He was not among the lucky few able to achieve a consistent tan and commiserated with those who 'turn a mottled crimson, with white flakes in places as though you were afflicted with some noisome skin disease'. Worse than this, he was shocked by people's credulity: 'nowadays people believe anything they are told by "scientists", just as they used to believe anything they were told by clergymen.' In his opinion, there was no higher motive, no exalted moral purpose behind sunbathing. If only these people would be frank and say: 'We like to lie and cook in the sun because (a) someone told us it was fashionable; (b) it is rather fun seeing what our friends look like without their clothes; (c) it is comfortable to let our brains dry up completely so that we haven't got to bother about thinking.'

Waugh hated sunbathing but the consensus in its favour was such that he also had to admit that 'now and then I am forced to do it'.

The decadent hours of Riviera leisure were a long way from normal life as most people knew it – that was part of the attraction. Sunbathing and its associated apparel were adopted in Britain and if wearing the

Girls with bobbed haircuts pose outside a Brighton
bathing machine in 1926.

wide-legged trousers and vest tops of 'beach pyjamas' at Frinton-on-Sea was not quite the same as wearing them at Cap d'Antibes it must still have felt pretty exotic for the women who tried it. For those who couldn't afford the Mediterranean there was always Torquay, 'Queen of the English Riviera.' Palm-tree-lined promenades helped contribute to the impression of a resort enjoying mild winters and warm summers; enjoying them, moreover, in an atmosphere of elegance and luxury. In 1931 *The Times* was convinced enough to state that: 'Torquay is certainly the English equivalent of Cannes. There is no resort which, apart from a certain prim austerity in the administration of the licensing laws, comes nearer in character and amenities to the most progressive of Mediterranean towns'. Torquay Council spent large sums promoting this beguiling vision co-operating closely with the publicity department of the Great Western Railway. During the interwar period posters created by the railway companies captured and exploited the new aesthetic of streamlined, Art Deco inspired design. Joyfully coloured, these resort images often featured women in their bathing costumes.

Such images would have been inconceivable in the previous century. Even if the Victorians were less prudish than we've been led to believe, the fact remains that bare flesh was simply not fashionable. By 1914

the acceptance of mixed bathing had wrought important changes in
the status of the bathing costume. Now a more visible item of apparel,
moves were afoot to give it a more flattering shape which would not
be too revealing when wet. Unfortunately, as photographs from the
early twentieth century show, these goals were not always achievable
with the materials at hand. During the 1920s the ratio of bare skin to
bathing costume shifted year by year, for men as well as women, so that
a more recognisably modern form had been achieved by the end of the
decade. The one-piece suit was now made of figure-hugging machine-
knitted wool, often cut low at the back and with the sides scooped out
to help maximise tan-ability. In 1929 manufacturers Jantzen went so far
as to claim their newest women's model as the 'the suit that changed
bathing into swimming'. With shoulder straps instead of sleeves, shorts
cut just below the top of the leg and no overskirt, it created a sleek
silhouette. If the contemporary architect Le Corbusier wanted to make
the house a machine for living in, the bathing costume had finally found
functionalism and become a machine for swimming in.

And what better place to show off your new streamlined suit than
at the interwar lido? Between 1930 and 1939, 180 outdoor pools were
built in Britain. These buildings epitomised the spirit of the Thirties:
healthy exercise in the fresh air, sun worship, the mass cult of leisure
in which everyone could be a consumer, all wrapped up in the clean
forms of Modern architecture. The word 'lido' originally came from the
Latin 'Litus', meaning shore, but was borrowed from the Venice Lido,
another highly fashionable destination among the 'bright young things'
of the Twenties. The very name evoked a tempting sense of otherness.
However, with a limitless supply of bathing water on hand it might
seem strange that seaside resorts embraced this new leisure facility so
ardently. That they produced the behemoths of the day speaks volumes
about the intense competition to lure holidaymakers.

Scarborough was an innovator once again. Under the direction of
Harry W. Smith, the man also responsible for the bathing bungalows
described in chapter twelve, work began on the South Bay Bathing Pool

in April 1914. Smith had proposed the idea much earlier, arguing in 1900 that it would permit safe bathing at all times, even when the sea was rough, also that 'more commodious accommodation and comfort can be provided for the bather than is possible in a bathing van'. In addition the facility would earn revenue as a place to hold swimming galas and carnivals. Since the pool was cleverly intended to act as a buttress to the newly completed seawall, protecting the base of the cliff from erosion, construction work was allowed to continue after the outbreak of war and the pool was officially opened on 21 July 1915. Several thousand people were there to share in the Mayor's pride when, speaking of the town's newest amenity, he declared that 'I do not know where anyone could look to see anything approaching it'. And he was right – at the time no other town could boast of anything comparable. After the war Scarborough's example was rapidly taken up and improved upon, so much so that the South Bay Bathing Pool was soon looking out-of-date. In 1933 modernisation work included the construction of a thirty-three-foot high reinforced concrete diving stage, a must-have item for any lido and one of the totems of the Modern architectural aesthetic. Pools elsewhere in the country were now setting the agenda.

The Blackpool Open Air Baths opened in 1923 with tiered seating for 3,000 spectators and dressing rooms for 574 bathers, built along a concourse that measured a third of a mile. By the end of its first full season more than half a million people had paid to go through the domed entrance into what was said to be the largest swimming pool in the world. Proof that voyeurism was a significant part of the pool's appeal came from the fact that only 94,403 of those were actually bathers. Down south the St Leonard's Bathing Pool, built in 1933 by Sidney Little, Borough Engineer to the resort of Hastings, was a vast concrete arena on the waterfront; 2,500 spectators could sit around the D-shaped pool, there was a gymnasium underneath and a rooftop sun terrace above. There was even underground car parking. The following year another relatively small resort, New Brighton near Liverpool, banked on a lido to turn its fortunes around. As with many of these Depression era con-

struction projects, a key aim was to provide employment for the unem-
ployed – there must have been lots of them in New Brighton to justify
the expense of creating one of the largest lidos ever built in Britain,
occupying a prime seafront site of four-and-a-half acres. And still the
peak had not been reached. In an attempt to move out from under the
shadow of its near neighbour Blackpool, Morecambe unveiled the ultimate lido complex, a place for entertainment and events as much as
for swimming and sunbathing. In July 1936 the queue of people waiting
to attend the opening of the Super Swimming Stadium stretched for a
mile. Of an overtly Modernist design, the building rose from reclaimed
land at a cost of £130,000 and after 1945 became synonymous with the
Miss Great Britain beauty contest it hosted. Ultimately, the scale of
these edifices made them unsustainable and not one of the above has
made it into the twenty-first century.

But what did all this mean for the traditional bathing machine? It
might be imagined, and it has generally been assumed, that the 1920s
saw the end of wheeled changing rooms. Surely the above mentioned
craze for sunbathing should have seen these antiquated contraptions
off our beaches? Well, actually, no. There were plenty of people
who, like Evelyn Waugh, lacked the youthful figure or the modern
inclination to bare all in praise of the sun god. Not everyone wanted
to strip off in public. Well into the 1950s family groups photographed
on the beach included members of the older generation sitting upright
in their Sunday best. When Hannen Swaffer, a reporter for *The Daily
Herald*, went to the seaside in 1931 searching for 'the New England', he
found a lot to remind him of childhood holidays as well as an increasing
Americanisation. 'If you see the New Margate,' he wrote, 'you see a
town transformed by moving pictures.' It was August high-season and
'in the midst of all the revelry at Margate, while girls in bright-hued
bathing suits pushed about an enormous rubber ball in a bathing pool,
an Old Inhabitant rather deplored the change'. He missed the bathing
machines. 'Ah, the bathing machines may have been old-fashioned,
but very modest people would still prefer them,' the Old Inhabitant

Outdoor exercises at the vast St Leonard's Bathing Pool built in 1933.

told Swaffer, 'especially if they are a little over-sized. They don't like parading themselves while people sit around the pool, staring, waiting to see the next one come out.' At Margate, the place where rows of bathing machines had once stood was turned into 'a wonderful bathing pool to which young women walk down in trousers – scores of them... They wore them as though it was their right. They were proud of their legs.' This new body confidence belonged to the younger generation and perhaps that explains the disparity between bather and spectator numbers at lidos.

If Joseph Longland had had his way the transition from bathing machines to man-made sea-water pools would have happened much earlier. As Surveyor to Worthing Local Board of Health, Longland published a pamphlet in 1867 in which he opined that 'the old Bathing Machines are in themselves a disgrace to the present age.' He felt certain everyone would agree and in order to be rid of this seaside nuisance once and for all, Longland proposed to create an alternate facility of 'swimming lakes, which will be cleaned and refilled by high tides'. On a two-and-a-half acre site of Worthing's seafront Longland envisaged separate pools for ladies and gentlemen each connected by a 'Conservatory Promenade' to a central building with Turkish baths and a public hall for concerts and balls. Had it been built, Longland's complex would have combined similar facilities to those at interwar lidos with the iconic architecture of the Crystal Palace by creating glass covered passages or 'crystal ways' to link the bathing and entertainment elements of his scheme. There *was* disillusionment with the bathing machine in the nineteenth century so it might just have worked. Campaigners for tent and mixed bathing fought a rear guard action against these vehicles in the latter years of Victoria's reign. A *Punch* poem of 1883 mockingly asserted that ''Tis a deer-cart, a fish-van, or something between; Oh, a hideous hutch is the Bathing Machine'. And yet they could still be found on British beaches *after* the Second World War.

In a 1936 article Osbert Lancaster exhibited an unusually positive view of the Victorians that was uncharacteristic of his day. He praised the nineteenth century expansion of seaside resorts and wrote of 'that admirable invention the bathing machine', asking: 'why, oh why, did we ever forsake it for that wretched substitute the stationary hut?' Even by that time not everywhere had. Just a couple of years earlier a gentleman of my acquaintance called Dick Thomas had been introduced to the ocean courtesy of a bathing machine at Exmouth. In the time-honoured fashion he and his Mama were pulled into the waves by a horse; he can still remember the smell and the cold of it. Another publication of 1936, *The Seas and Shores of England* by Edmund Vale, described how at the Lincolnshire resort of Skegness 'bathing vans with their horses follow the tide'. At Aldburgh in Suffolk, the same author observed that 'bathing operations are conducted from machines of the most portentous type, each having double cabins. They are lowered by gravity down the steep shingle upper-works of the beach and raised by capstans'. Although it called them old-fashioned, a holiday guidebook was still listing bathing machines at Aldburgh for the 1939–40 season. Even Lancashire's holiday Mecca still had two 'bathing van proprietors' listed in its commercial directory for 1938, on the same page as the 'Lido Swimming Pool (Blackpool), Ltd'. In May the following year Blackpool Council politely declined an offer to buy up Mr W. H. Smith's remaining '17 bathing machines, a small patrol boat, harness for two horses, 200 towels and 300 assorted bathing costumes.' By that time it could hardly have been viewed as a wise use of tax-payers' money. Second World War coastal defence work did for most other surviving machines, like those at the Devon resort of Budleigh Salterton, which fell under the soldiers' axe.

Remarkably, a few hung on to be brought out after hostilities ended. There is always a chance that the 1947 Ward Lock guidebook for Woolacombe was suffering from editorial oversight in its reference to the availability of bathing machines but there can be no such doubt about Britain's last operational examples. There is a certain irony in the fact that Llandudno, one of the first places to permit mixed bathing, was also the last to dispose of its bathing machines. In 1958, William Jones, the last

Going for a swim from a beach hut that began life as a bathing machine.

of the bathing machine proprietors decided to retire at the age of 80. His wheeled wooden huts, which were still being hauled in and out of the sea until 1946, were sold off at £4/10s each for use as garden sheds.

So, after some two centuries of service, bathing machines had finally had their day. Post-war author Christopher Marsden was categorical about the best place for them: 'A few, with rusting wheels and gaping boards, must still be about: one ought to be rescued, for the Victoria and Albert Museum.' Did some serious, possibly bespectacled London curator rush down to the seaside with a big crate and orders to preserve a bathing machine? Not that I'm aware of. But in a country where 'make do and mend' had been instilled in the collective consciousness like a mantra, bathing machines did offer possibilities for recycling. With their wheels removed some stayed on the sand and became beach huts. Many more moved into gardens and onto allotments from where they still resurface from time to time. Like the Pettman's machine, used for seventy years as a shed and breeding hutch for rabbits, now in the care of Margate museum or the Eastbourne machine turned potting shed lovingly restored by Julian Martyr of the Langham Hotel. Slightly more quirky re-uses include the Scarborough machine turned into the attendant's hut at the North Bay putting green or, in Norfolk, the former Overstrand machine that still serves as one of the 'terminal buildings' at Northrepps International Airport!

Proud of its seaside heritage, Weymouth has two Georgian bathing machines on display and I went to track them down. I'd been told that one was a replica parked along the promenade though look as I might I couldn't find it. John Thadeus Delane, editor of *The Times*, had no such problem in 1852 for on the sands, 'In the midst of a cluster of modern bathing machines is carefully preserved one of primæval form surmounted by a crown bearing the following inscription: "The machine of the great and good King George III., the friend of the poor, the patron of Weymouth".' Delane thought it an odd monument: 'Fancy preserving for sixty years such a trophy of his prowess!' The royal machine was apparently in regular use until 1914, still in its place of honour at the extreme right of the line, obvious on account of its octagonal shape and pyramidal roof. Within a decade the machine's magic had worn off. A don from New College, Oxford remembered seeing it for the last time in 1923: 'it had been removed from its wheels, and, along with its fellows, had been degraded to some mean use, apparently a tool shed, which I was sorry to see, for I had thought Weymouth would have had more regard for this relic of its royal patron.'

My first glimpse of the replica machine inspired similar feelings of regret. There it was, behind a fence, behind a main road, behind the Marina. Consigned to the Council works depot awaiting repair, its location seemed that bit more ominous as, when I walked in, a rubbish truck pulled out. The men in high-visibility waistcoats, whose permission I asked to look at the machine, were clearly not used to such requests but good-naturedly let me get on with it. What was most striking about the vehicle was its huge chassis; the wheels, which were as high as my shoulders, were quite separate from the changing hut, which sat entirely on top of a central platform. Overall it looked heavy, unwieldy and, even by bathing machine standards, the design was old-fashioned. Small

A 1920s birthday boy with his grandfather outside the beach huts at Aldwick beach, Worthing.

wonder Delane was bemused by retention of the real thing. Yet its pedigree was good and at Weymouth Museum I was allowed behind the scenes to go and see the *bona fide* Georgian machine that had served as a model. In this scene the replica was a pale, bald and flabby George III forever poised in his decent toward the static waves. The octagonal machine he stepped from was one of those auctioned off in 1916. It was bought by Mr Clifford Chalker who removed the wheels and turned them into candlesticks before converting the main part into a summerhouse. In 1930 it was dismantled and put into store where it remained until being donated to the museum in 1971. Whether as a replica on the promenade or on display with mannequins, the bathing machine has indeed become a museum piece.

While mobile modesty machines were becoming a thing of the past, interwar resorts were investing in a higher standard of permanent beach-side changing rooms. They had to, because lidos had prioritised design, hygiene and comfort for everyone. Southport's Sea Bathing Lake, for example, offered two-storey male and female changing blocks which were considered highly advanced when they opened in 1928: the cubicles were pitch-pine, lined with six feet of terrazzo tiles then buff bricks up to the ceiling. They could even boast central heating. However the traditional system, which also adhered on the beach, of taking a cubicle as both a place to change and a place to leave one's clothes, had to evolve in order that the capacity of these pools could actually be realised. It was this false limit on the number of swimmers that had so inflamed opinion in Eastbourne and the lidos were not about to wait for a strike to prompt action when more people also meant more return against their massive construction costs.

From the mid 1930s lidos began to adopt more efficient storage solutions. The modernisation of Margate Lido in 1935, eight years after it first opened, saw the changing rooms redesigned and 2,000 smart galvanised steel and white enamelled lockers installed. These were fitted with coat hooks, trinket bowls, mirrors and ashtrays. Even more ingenious was the *Hyg-Gard-All* – essentially a wire basket fixed below a coat hanger – patented by James Sieber. When full of clothes the *Hyg-Gard-All* basket was handed over to an attendant thereby freeing up the changing cubicles. Thanks to this system it was possible for 1,440 people to enjoy Weston-Super-Mare's Bathing Pool at the same time!

This invention might have been used as a substitute for mackintosh bathing but there is no evidence that it was. Perhaps by this time resort authorities had finally decided to relax their morals in line with public opinion. Their efforts went instead to updating designated 'bathing stations' and providing more bungalow type accommodation for day use. Around the country interwar blocks sprang up that copied the Scarborough model, applying a nice bit of mock-Tudor timberwork to decorative gables, but stylistic variation also led to architecturally interesting buildings that are only now beginning to be recognised as an important part of our seaside heritage. Whether we're looking at the crescent shaped Neo-Classical colonnade of changing cubicles at Sandbanks, near Poole in Dorset, or the two-storey, flat-roofed chalet block with sinuous curved ends and crittal windows at Cromer in Norfolk, all these structures reveal something about the spirit of their age – perhaps none so uncompromisingly as the West Marina chalet block at St Leonards-on-Sea. Sidney Little, the 'Concrete King' and Borough Surveyor of Hastings, built ninety huts in a two-tier structure next to his Bathing Pool. Ornamental features were pared down to the absolute minimum in line with Modern architectural tastes and flat roofs doubled-up as sun decks. The building was massive in its simplicity, partly due to its secondary function as a component of the sea defences protecting the flood plain behind. Yet, in this most monolithic of beach hut blocks, all 'mod-cons' were provided; every occupant had their own electricity and water supply, there was a telephone for residents' use located in the caretaker's chalet and – the unique selling point – at the rear there were built-in garages. Even though car ownership was on the increase no other beach huts in the country incorporated this sensible luxury.

In 1914 there were just 140,000 motor vehicles on British roads. This figure had shot up to 1.5 million in 1930 and doubled to 3 million in 1939, a third of which were now private cars. The summer roads to the sea were jammed in a way they'd never been before and there were real disadvantages to this transport revolution. Sidney Little was well before his time in providing underground parking on Hastings seafront and below the St Leonards Bathing Pool but it was a problem all resorts had to face. In St Ives, the picturesque homes of Cornish fishermen were sacrificed for a car park in Pudding Bag Lane and a guidebook to Lyme Regis ruefully pointed out that there was now a car park on the site of the Assembly Rooms visited by Jane Austen. In 1939 Blackpool built a multi-storey car park with 1,000 spaces. Guest houses and hotels felt the change too. Holidaymakers who came by train were a captive audience; when they came by car they stayed for less time, exploiting the ability to tour from town to town. New coastal settlements, away from the railway lines, also developed because of the new motoring habit.

A look at the interwar coastline of Lincolnshire gives a taste of the different holiday communities established during the period. In 1936 the first Butlin's Luxury Holiday Camp opened at Skegness; the family chalets, like a town of inland beach huts, were solidly booked right through the season even before the camp was finished. A little further up the coast, the quiet sandy beach at Chapel St Leonards attracted motorists who would pitch their tents on the shore or camp, from the 1930s, in timber huts built along the sand dunes. Somewhere in between these two holiday choices, of communal amusement and individual freedom, was the aptly named 'Bohemia' plotland at Sutton-on-Sea. Along the sea wall were beach huts and behind these a collection of makeshift bungalows, railway carriages and old army huts jostled for space among the dunes. The most characteristic structures of this impromptu assembly were the circular, corrugated iron huts known by locals as 'rusty pork pies' and more endearingly by temporary residents as 'Osocosies'. One of these was even turned into a dance hall; the exterior cladding was removed to expose a criss-crossed trellis frame that was decorated with hanging baskets. It looks idyllic in old postcards but there were no proper sanitary arrangements and the poor drainage was considered an acute health hazard. Other interwar plotlands suffered similarly but whereas Peacehaven, Jaywick and Canvey Island survived and evolved, Bohemia was regulated out of existence by the district council. From 1939 innumerable other small coastal hut communities were literally swept away by the defending home army.

Holiday camps became the biggest post-war success but the appeal of beach huts has proved to be more lasting. In the Twenties and Thirties they were really coming into their own. No records exist for the number of beach huts in existence during the interwar period but with their purpose as a 'home from home' firmly established demand was certainly on the increase. By the end of the 1920s towns like Southwold and Frinton-on-Sea had got the long lines of huts for which they're now so famous. The stretch of coast around Bournemouth and Poole was covered with countless cabin and huts, so much so that in 1941 a guidebook described the bungalows rising in tiers east of Boscombe pier as a scene 'reminiscent of some Mediterranean hill town.' Whereas at lidos and municipal bathing stations the changing cabins were just

TYPE OF BEACH BUNGALOW.

A drawing of the new beach accomodation from *Southwold: A Guide to Assist the Visitor in the Enjoyment of a Holiday*, 1932.

that, the beach hut offered a more relaxed option. Its popularity was a true sign that the sea had moved on from being the domain of regulated, medically-inspired bathing by isolated individuals to a focus for shared family enjoyment. Owners would often be local, the hut a summer-time extension of their house and sometimes a useful extra source of income when let to holidaymakers. Mrs Betty Aston was born in 1920 and grew up in Herne Bay, Kent. 'At the bottom of Lane End they had a row of big huts you could spend the day in. We had one of those for a couple of years and, of course, the family spent the whole day down there.' While Betty played, paddled and bathed with other children her parents 'just read or dozed.' At Preston Sands, near Paignton in Devon, Glenda Hopkins and her family had a tent in the 1920s and upgraded to a more substantial wooden hut the following decade. She remembered how 'tea at the hut' was popular by the mid-Twenties: 'White lace tablecloths, often hand-embroidered, graced foldaway tables, tea in matching china cups and saucers with thinly sliced bread and butter, homemade cakes and biscuits to eat.' In the last years before the war she wore a knitted swimming costume, just like all the children, hers with a rabbit on the front: 'I can still remember the feel of the itchy thick wool next to my skin.' Glenda's mother loved the beach, loved her hut and had many friends who shared her passion. Their children all grew up together. Somehow huts have always managed to foster the sense of a beach community.

The Second World War brought different communities to the coast. In the first three days of war Blackpool took in 37,500 evacuees from nearby industrial cities. Men in uniforms appeared to close up the south coast, blowing up piers, swathing beaches in barbed wire and planting mines. Government ministries took over seaside hotels and civil servants, not holidaymakers, walked along the prom. If the British did not keenly feel their status as an island nation already then Winston Churchill's speech on the 4 June 1940, after the evacuation of Dunkirk, reinforced the strategic importance of our sea edges. Churchill committed to fight in France, on the seas and oceans, on the landing grounds, in the fields and streets and hills but his speech is memorable for one phrase in particular. Our beloved seaside, our favourite holiday resorts were the new front line. 'We shall fight on the beaches' said Churchill, and that's the bit we remember more than sixty years later. In place of fun and frivolity, a seriousness and sense of purpose descended on the coast. As historian James Walvin has put it, 'The gaudy, painted face of seaside England soon peeled and weathered – or was reduced to the greys, greens and browns of a nation at war.' Even if ordinary people could have saved their petrol rations and snatched time out of their long working hours, would they have been able to reconcile the wartime seaside with their sunnier pre-war memories?

It is perhaps indicative of the role beach huts had come to play in people's vision of a seaside holiday that official War Damage Commission records include a file dealing with reparation for destroyed huts. Their status was subject to debate because it was not clear whether they were actual 'buildings' or, if they were moved for winter and were not individually rated, they ought to share the same classification as cara-

Relaxing outside a 1940s beach hut.

vans. A claimant whose hut at Tankerton, Kent, had been damaged by the explosion of a mine on the nearby beach estimated the value of his property to be around £35. Assessors in the case of some seventy three huts at Sandown, Isle of Wight, which were damaged by enemy action in August 1940, quoted the cost of rebuilding a hut there to be just £15, based on 1939 prices. From the point of view of modern prices it is interesting to see it recognised that huts had been sold before the war for substantially more than the actual structure was worth: 'The value was really in the position and a large part of the figure...paid was in effect the premium of the rental of the site.' Perhaps most unfortunate among the claimants was a man who had carefully removed his hut from Hayling Island early in the war, dismantling it for storage at his Portsmouth factory premises. The factory had been burnt out during an air raid when some sections of the hut were damaged. What sections were left were used, without the owner's knowledge or consent, to board up the site. Many, many worse things happened on the home front between 1939 and 1945 but for people to bother, under these terrible circumstances, to seek compensation for lost beach huts suggests that these structures held both an important sentimental as well as a monetary value.

Since the mid-eighteenth century the number of seaside visitors had reached new peaks in every generation. When the summer season began in 1945, just a few weeks after the German surrender, the crowds were record breaking. The first Wakes holiday that July witnessed a staggering number of people heading for Blackpool – in just one day 102,889 people travelled by train to the resort. It's the sort of figure that seems inconceivable now but in the immediate post-war decades the seaside was a crucial and attainable escape from the continuing privations of austerity Britain. Almost everyone who could afford a holiday boarded a train bound for the coast. The 1938 Holidays with Pay Act had had little time to exert its positive influence before the war but by 1945 some eighty per cent of the workforce was paid for their leisure time. Holidaymakers photographed at Margate in July 1948 may have had to huddle under makeshift shelters made from deckchairs but they were alive and they were by the healing sea. The 1950s saw a gradual rise in prosperity so that, even with continued scarcity and rationing, people flocking to the resorts had more money to spend than ever before. This was the heyday of the British seaside. It was the beach hut's heyday too and if we now picture a golden age of the bucket and spade holiday then this is it. We feel nostalgia for a period that, in hindsight, looks more innocent, more genuine and less commercialised than our own. The current renewal of interest has turned the beach hut into a symbol for this simpler way of life.

But after extreme popularity came the British seaside's fabled slide into obsolescence. Our sunshine was no longer bright enough to compete with the Mediterranean variety; planes and package deals saw to that. So, when Paul Theroux observed beach hut owners on his 1982 trip around the coast he saw them as relics of a nearly departed age. In *The Kingdom by the Sea*, Theroux described the huts, or 'shallys', at Hove as 'fitted out for tea and naps...It was not unusual to see half a fruitcake, an umbrella, and an Agatha Christie inside, and most held an old person, looking flustered'. Inhabitants had lived through the war and were trying, in their dotage, to hang onto a seaside that nobody else seemed to care for. He made these people sound sad; melancholic but also rather pitiful. 'The shally people were old-fashioned,' he said,

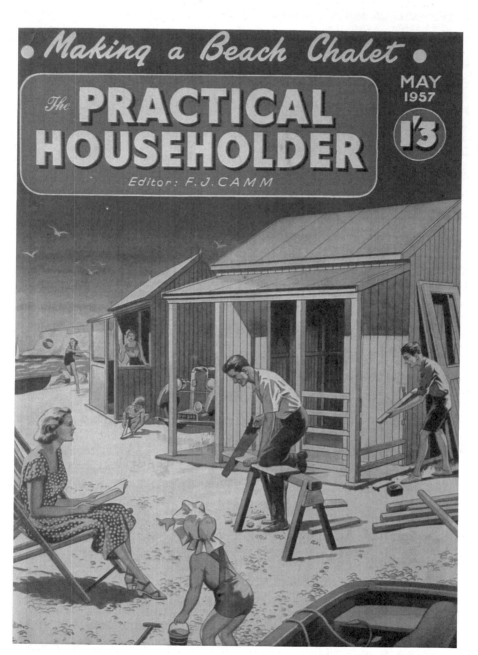

Beach huts were often do-it-yourself projects and their popularity after World War II inspired magazines like *The Practical Householder* to provide tips for easy construction

Two British institutions come together in the ritual of tea time at the beach hut seen here in the 1950s.

'they actually were the inheritors of the bathing-machine mentality...' But they weren't. These people were more likely to have been the Bright Young Things of the Twenties, the first generation to strip off on the sands, the first generation that could really stick two fingers up to the bathing machine. By the early 1980s, however, they were captured by Theroux living out their last days in a kind of holiday camp-cum-nursing home – but without the sense of community. There was no nostalgia but bad nostalgia. The American traveller made beach huts his poster child for the decline of the British seaside holiday. And maybe he was right – I was only six at the time so who am I to say. Except that year my family and I had two holidays in England, both near the sea. My parents eschewed the big resorts; we went to north Cornwall and to Staithes, a picturesque fishing village on the Yorkshire coast. My younger brother and I made sandcastles, raced oncoming waves, licked melting ice-cream from the sides of orange cornets, caught crabs and generally had a good time. We didn't feel the gloomy shadow of domestic tourism going down the toilet – which is not to imply the problems were invented but merely to suggest that the foreign holiday diaspora was not absolute. Beach huts have endured in the places they have because there continued to be a demand. The current strength of demand is new and Paul Theroux could hardly have been expected to foresee *that*. My coastal trip uncovered the stories of people who remained true to their beloved huts despite the seaside downturn at the end of the twentieth century. It is these people who bring my history up-to-date and, with a new generation of enthusiasts, they are the ones who will ensure beach huts have a future. Where Theroux found a marked lack of community spirit among beach hut owners, I found the reverse.

Epilogue

I pushed the door open and walked into a brightly lit room. Tables had been arranged end-to-end in rows across the space, all of them adorned with architects' models. Though it was an impressive sight my initial wonder turned towards panic at the scale of the task it represented. I was in Mablethorpe to help judge Bathing Beauties, an architectural competition to re-imagine beach huts for the twenty-first century. Sent in from all over the world, there were nearly 250 designs laid out in front of me, some embracing the traditional gabled shape, others rejecting it entirely. It was clear that the competitors had enjoyed themselves, playing with ideas and materials to turn the humble beach hut into a work of art. From among this quirky range of modern versus eco-friendly, unconventional versus seaside-themed, we had the difficult task of selecting the designs that would be built along the Lincolnshire coast. In a coastal area that had seen better days, the beach hut had been chosen to stand as a beacon of regeneration evoking a more prosperous past while simultaneously looking to the future. For a type of structure that had previously been viewed as ephemeral this was a pretty grandiose claim – but it was a claim that was being taken seriously.

In the opening decade of the twenty-first century, beach huts were swept up in the property boom becoming an indicator of the 'good life' as prices hit £90,000 at Southwold and £100,000 at Poole. On Mudeford Sandbank, sellers could literally name their price and someone would come forward willing to pay. It was a heady expression of desire outstripping supply and even if such values aren't sustainable in the long term they nonetheless reflect a genuine rediscovery of the British seaside that the local authorities in Lincolnshire hope to harness with Bathing Beauties. It is a paradox of global warming that only when our coastline is threatened by rising sea levels are we beginning to realise just how precious it is. Cheap air travel may have encouraged millions of us to holiday abroad over the past few decades but when everyone can afford it the caché wears off; staying at home has become cool thanks to a kind of inverse snobbery, something which can only be good for domestic tourism, for the environment and for the future of beach huts.

I had hoped to get around all Britain's huts but I missed some in England and didn't have time to visit Scotland and Wales, though I could have found a smattering in both places. The 20,000 or so that I did see on my journey demonstrated that huts and chalets were pretty much the same thing and, whatever they were called, they shared with sheds the wonderful ability to inspire sentiments of true devotion in their owners. But not all of them were loved; a few, like the first ones I saw at Seaton Carew, were derelict and since my trip there have been some sad losses. The Queen's beach hut, built for the royal family on the Earl of Leicester's Holkham Estate in the 1930s, was torched by arsonists in August 2003, leaving only a leaning chimney stack and the charcoaled remains of a wooden veranda. Just as wilful was the demolition in 2006 by Hastings Borough Council of Sidney Little's West Marina chalet block, dating from 1933. Despite strong protests from chalet users *and* proposals from a major architect's firm to restore the Modern concrete building to its former glory, the council would not be swayed and the only example of beach huts with built-in garages has gone forever. Seaford's post-war chalet blocks have also been pulled down though those at least have been replaced by a cheery row of wooden huts. The same is true of some of the Edwardian bathing bungalows in Scarborough's North Bay. Their condition had deteriorated over the years but thankfully the threat to the better preserved examples beside the South Bay has been met by a Grade II listing from English Heritage that will safeguard them for future generations. A 1920s chalet block at Weymouth, threatened by development plans for the 2012 Olympic sailing, has also been recognised as historically important enough to merit listing.

Holding on to the best of the past is important and at Boscombe in Dorset, the 1950s Overstrand Building has been brought back to life in spectacular style amid claims of offering the 'best beach huts in the world'. Designers Wayne and Gerardine Hemingway have given the three-storey hut block a retro revamp that includes a new penthouse as well as thirty-one surf pods. Bournemouth is not a well-known surf resort but with the creation of Europe's first artificial surf reef it is aiming to rectify that. The traditional bucket-and-spade seaside is shifting up a gear. And there is no reason why beach huts shouldn't also move with the times. Their design hasn't really changed much since the earliest bathing machines nearly three hundred years ago. Yet the Bathing Beauties competition proves that there is huge scope for new ideas: the stripy and curvaceous 'Jabba', described by its architects as 'a contemporary re-interpretation of the cave', is available to hire among the sand dunes of Mablethorpe; 'Come Up and See Me' is a giant glass of gin and tonic masquerading as a beach hut on the promenade while 'Halcyon Hut' plays with the traditional form using thin strips of cedar wood interspersed with acrylic so that light filters through the walls and roof to create a cabin that is both solid and fluid. At sunset the effect is superb.

So, after a long history, beach huts look set to remain a crucial feature of our coastal landscape. And one day I'll have my own. Writing a book was supposed to pay for it but prices have gone up so much that I'll need to pen several best-sellers before I get there! Then, of course, there's the problem of where I would buy. But perhaps location doesn't matter because, at the end of the day, it's the people that make the huts. Whichever community I end up joining, I know the other owners are likely to be as obsessed as me so I should fit right in.

Picture Credits

Every attempt has been made to secure the appropriate permissions for materials reproduced in this book. If there has been any oversight we will be happy to rectify the situation and a written submission should be made to the Publishers.

Illustrations are taken from the author's collection with the following exceptions where permission has been kindly granted by:

North Yorkshire County Council Libraries pp. 23, 103
Kent County Council, Margate Library p. 28
Norfolk County Council, Library and Information Services pp. 29, 148, 196
P.J. and S.P. Berry pp. 34, 65
Margate Museum pp. 36, 76
Royal Pavilion & Museums (Brighton & Hove) pp. 63, 198
Suffolk Record Office, Lowestoft branch, Ref: 1300/72/43/29 p. 100
Kent County Council, East Kent Archives Ref: R/U2 446/F p. 102
Mr F. L. Pettman p. 110
Kodak Collection at the NMeM / Science and Society Picture Library p. 114
Ivor Slocombe pp. 116, 140, 205
Zoe McLintock, Tunnels Beaches Ilfracombe p. 199
Royal Photographic Society Collection at the NMeM / Science and Society Picture Library p. 299
Southwold Press p. 312
Gail Durbin p. 317

All colour photographs were taken by the author.

Bibliography

AA Book of the Seaside (London: 1972)

A Journey from London to Scarborough in Several Letters from a Gentleman there, to his friend in London (London: 1734)

A Description of Blackpool in Lancashire frequented for Sea Bathing (Birmingham: 1789)

'A Ballad of Bathing', *Punch* (14 July 1883) p. 23

'A Summer Holiday', *The Graphic* (16 August 1930) pp. 260–61

Adams, J. Howe. 'Bathing at the Continental Sea-Shore Resorts', *The Cosmopolitan*, 19 (1895) pp. 131–45
 – 'Bathing at the American Sea-Shore Resorts', *The Cosmopolitan*, 19 (1895) pp. 316–29
 – 'Bathing at the English Sea-Shore Resorts', *The Cosmopolitan*, 19 (1895) pp. 395–404

Adamson, Simon H. *Seaside Piers* (London: 1977)

An Appeal to Common Decency and the Law of the Land Against the Practice of Bathing in Situations Exposed to Public View (London: 1818)

Anderson, Janice and Edmund Swinglehurst. *The Victorian and Edwardian Seaside* (London: 1978)

'At the Seaside', *The Cornhill Magazine*, 32 (1875) pp. 414–26

Austen, Jane. *Lady Susan, The Watsons, Sanditon* edited with an introduction by Margaret Drabble (Harmondsworth: 1974)

Baedeckers Belgium and Holland (Leipsic: 1885, 1894, 1897, 1901, 1905, 1910, 1931)

Baedeckers Northern France: Handbook for Travellers (Leipsic & London: 1889)

'Bathing Machines', *Notes and Queries* (1886) pp. 67, 135, 214, 295, 394, 477; (1893) pp. 346, 415; (1894) pp. 93, 157, 478; (1904) pp. 130-31, 230.

'Bathing Machines - A Quaker Invention', *Journal of the Society of Friends Historical Society*, 4 (1909) pp. 176–77.

'The Bathing Machine', *Punch* (1 September 1883) p. 97

'The Bathing Machine: A convenient contraption' (http://www.bognorregisheritage.co.uk/bmachine/bathmachine.htm, accessed 2 June 2002)

Beardwood, Lynette. 'FANY at the Western Front: War Tales 1914–1919' (http://www.fany.org.uk/history/ww1/ww1_page_03.html, accessed 11 January 2005)

Bebb, Prudence. *Life in Regency Scarborough* (York: 1997)

Blume, Mary. *Côte d'Azur: Inventing the French Riviera* (London: 1992)

Boulogne-sur-Mer: Bathing Town and Ville de Plaisance (Boulogne: 1857)

Beresford, G.C. *Schooldays with Kipling* (London: 1936)

Berry, Sue. *Georgian Brighton* (Chichester: 2005)

Borough of Worthing. *Byelaws...with respect to Public Bathing* (Worthing: 1901)

Boyce, Benjamin. *The Benevolent Man: A Life of Ralph Allen of Bath* (Cambridge, Mass.:1967)

Braggs, Steven and Diane Harris. *Sun, Fun and Crowds: Seaside Holidays Between the Wars* (Stroud: 2000)

Brenan, H. B. 'The Visitor', *Architectural Review*, 80 (July 1936) pp. 14–16

Brent, John. 'The World's Bathing Places', *Munsey's Magazine*, 27 (1902) pp. 549–57

Brighthelmstone Directory (Brighton: c1790-1800) Brighton Local Studies Library

Brodie, Allan and Gary Winter. *England's Seaside Resorts* (Swindon: 2007)

Burke, Edmund. *A Philosophical Enquiry into the Origin of our Ideas of the Sublime and Beautiful* (1759) (facsimile reprint Menston: 1970)

Burney, Fanny. *The Early Journals and Letters of Fanny Burney, Vol. 1 1768-1773*, ed. Lars E. Troide (Oxford: 1988)

Clegg, K. 'The Diary of a Schoolboy on holiday in Filey 1908' (Filey: 1998)

Clements, Peter. *Lowestoft: 200 Years a Seaside Resort* (Lowestoft: 1994)

Colmer, Michael. *Bathing Beauties: The amazing history of female swimwear* (London: 1977)

Commandant De Gerlache De Gomery. *Belgium in War Time: The Unconquerable Soul* (London: 1918)

Connolly, Joseph. *Beside the Seaside* (London: 1999)

County Borough of Blackpool, 'Minutes of the Proceedings of the Council – General Purposes Committee' (24 May 1939)

Corbin, Alain. The *Lure of the Sea: The Discovery of the Seaside in the Western World, 1750 – 1840* (Cambridge: 1994)

Cowley, Phil. *Harwich and Dovercourt in Old Picture Postcards* (1993)

Crosby, G. *The Excursionists' Guide to Scarborough* (Scarborough: c1860)

Darby, Michael. 'The First Bungalows', *Country Life* (3 August 1978) pp. 306–09

'Dawlish', *Exeter Flying Post* (13 November 1871) p. 7

Defoe, Daniel. *A Tour Through the Whole Island of Great Britain* (1724-26) (London:1986)

Delane, John Thadeus. *John Thadeus Delane: Editor of The Times, His Life and Correspondence*, Vol. 2. (London: 1908)

Dexter, Walter. *The England of Dickens* (London: 1925)

'Diary of Their Majesties' Journey to Weymouth and Plymouth', *Gentleman's Magazine*, 59:2 (1789) pp. 951–52, 1047

Dutton, Geoffrey. *Sun, Sea, Surf and Sand – The Myth of the Beach* (Melbourne: 1985)

Eastbourne Gazette. 'Bathing Charges Sensation: will the Corporation act?' (18 September 1929) p. 1

Everitt, Sylvia. *Southend Seaside Holiday* (London & Chichester: 1980)

'Extract from a Letter from Miss Peggy Dripping at Margate, to Miss Polly Teacaddy in Aldersgate Street,' *The Times* (20 September 1791) p.3

Fagg's New and Improved Safety Bathing Carriage, Prospectus (c1893 National Archives)

Fearon, Michael. *Old Filey Remembered* (Beverley: 1994)

Ferry, Kathryn. *Beach huts and bathing machines* (Oxford: 2009)

Fisher, Stephen ed. *Recreation and the Sea* (Exeter: 1997)

Fryer, Peter. *Mrs Grundy: Studies in English Prudery* (London: 1963)

Gerard, Francis. *Picturesque Dublin* (London: 1898)

Gershlick, Janet. *Southwold Beach Huts* (Southwold: 2003)

Granville, A. B. *The Spas of England and Principal Sea-Bathing Places* (2 vols, 1841) (Bath: 1971)

Gray, Fred. *Designing the Seaside: Architecture, Society and Nature* (London: 2006)

Green, Rod. *Beach Huts* (London: 2005)

Hannavy, John. *The English Seaside* (Princes Risborough: 2003)

Hardy, Francis H. 'Seaside Life in America', *Cornhill Magazine*, 1 (1896) pp. 605–19

Hardy, Dennis and Colin Ward. *Arcadia for All: The Legacy of a Makeshift Landscape* (London: 1984)

Hart, Harold W. 'Walter Fagg's broad-gauge line: notes concerning a Folkestone invention', *The Journal of Transport History*, Third Series, (March 1981) pp. 69–74

Hawthorne, Julian. *Hawthorne and His Circle* (New York & London: 1903)

Hern, Anthony. *The Seaside Holiday: The History of the English Seaside Resort* (London: 1967)

Holyoake, Gregory. 'Benjamin Beale's Bathing Machines', *Bygone Kent*, 1 (August 1980) pp. 457–62.

Hope-Moncrieff, A. R. *Where Shall We Go: A Guide to the Health and Holiday Resorts of Great Britain*, 14th ed. (London: 1899)

Hopkins, Glenda. 'Six Decades at the Beach Hut' (Margate Museum files: unpublished MS)

Horn, Pamela. *Pleasures and Pastimes in Victorian Britain* (Stroud: 1999)

Horwood, Catherine. 'Girls Who Arouse Dangerous Passions': women and bathing, 1900–39', *Women's History Review*, 9 (2000)

Howell, Sarah. *The Seaside* (London: 1974)

Illustrated Times, 'By the Seaside, No I - The Sands at Ramsgate' (23 August 1856) pp. 136–39
    'By the Seaside, No II – Scarborough' (23 August 1856) p. 140
    'By the Seaside, No. III – Portobello' (30 August 1856) pp. 153–54
    'By the Seaside, No. IV – Bournemouth' (30 August 1856) p. 156
    'By the Seaside, No. V – Margate' (13 September 1856) pp. 189–90

Inglis, Andrea. *Beside the Seaside: Victorian Resorts in the Nineteenth Century* (Melbourne: 1999)

James, Hawkins Francis. 'The Family Album for the use of Hawkins Francis James Esq. open to the contributions of all charitably-disposed persons among his family and friends,' (MS Diary of holiday in Ramsgate 1828 (East Kent Archives R/U2 446/F1)

Jones, Ivor W. *Llandudno: Queen of the Welsh Resorts* (Cardiff: 1975)

Kilvert, The Rev. Francis. *Kilvert's Diary 1870–79*, Chosen, Edited and Introduced by William Plomer (London: 1978)

King, Anthony D. *The Bungalow: The Production of a Global Culture* (New York: 1995)

Klijn, Pat. 'Postcard Collecting Themes: Beach Huts and Bathing Machines', *Picture Postcard Monthly*, 197 (September 1995) pp. 32–33

Lancaster, Osbert. 'The English at the Seaside', *Architectural Review*, 80 (July 1936) pp. 8–14

Lansdell, Avril. *Seaside Fashions, 1860-1939* (Princes Risborough: 1990)

Lamplugh, Lois. *A History of Ilfracombe* (London: 1984)

Laver, James. *Victorian Vista* (London: 1954)

Lenček, Lena and Gideon Bosker. *The Beach: The History of Paradise on Earth* (London: 1998)

Letters from Bine Overman at Ostend to Messrs. Francis Cobb & Son, Margate, July-November 1785 (East Kent Archives EK/U1453/B5/4/105 1-4)

Lewis, Rev. John. *The History and Antiquities, as well Ecclesiastical as Civil, of the Isle of Thanet, in Kent* (London: second ed. 1736. See copy in Society of Antiquaries Library for additions by James Theobald)

Lindley, Kenneth. *Seaside Architecture* (London: 1973)

Longland, Joseph. *Pastimes with Neptune: A Design for Improving Sea Bathing at Worthing* (Worthing: 1867)

Maitland, Peter. 'The Architect', *Architectural Review*, 80 (July 1936)

Manning-Saunders, Ruth. *Seaside England* (London: 1951)

The Margate Guide (London: 1785)

Marsden, Christopher. *The English at the Seaside* (London: 1946)

Maupassant, Guy de. *Pierre et Jean* (Oxford: 2001)

McManus, Blanche. *The American Woman Abroad* (New York: 1911)

Mickleburgh, Tim. *Glory Days: Piers* (Shepperton: 1999)

Miller, John (ed.) *The Best of Southwold* (Stroud: 1998)

Murray, Amelia M. *Letters from the United States, Cuba and Canada* (London: 1856)

Neave, David. *Port, Resort and Market Town: A History of Bridlington* (Hull: 2000)

Pearce, Caroline. 'Bude: Part II', *The Englishwoman's Magazine* (May 1852) pp. 269–74

Pearson, Lynn F. *The People's Palaces* (Buckingham: 1991)
Piers and Other Seaside Architecture (Princes Risborough: 2002)

Pimlott, J. A. R. *The Englishman's Holiday: A Social History* (Hassocks: 1976)

Piscator. *The Bath and the Beach or All About Bathing* (London and Brighton: 1871)

Pococke, Richard. *The Travels Through England of Dr. Richard Pococke successively Bishop of Meeth and of Ossary, during 1750, 1751 and later years* (London: 1888)

Pope, Anne (ed.) *Herne Bay Holiday Town: Remembering 1920s–1960s* (Canterbury: 1995)

Powers, Alan. *Farewell My Lido* (London: 1991)

Pritchard, Edward William. *Observations on Filey as a Watering Place; or A Guide for Visitors* (1853) (facsimile with introduction by K. Clegg, Filey: 1998)

Reeby, Janet. *Taking the Waters at Weymouth: Sea and Spa* (Weymouth: 1995)

Reach, Angus B. 'The Sea-Side and the Summer Sea-Siders', *The British Journal*, 2 (1852) pp. 106–110

The Scarborough Mercury, 'North Side Transformation: The Bungalows' (16 June 1911) p. 3
– 'Peasholm Park and North Bay Bungalows' (21 June 1912) p. 6
– 'Birth of the Bungalows' (2 November 1956) p. 3

Scheveningen-on-the-Sea: Guide to the Famous Watering Place (The Hague: 1895)

'Sea-Bathing: The Eighteenth Century Style', *The Times* (9 June 1933) p. 15

Searle, Muriel V. *Bathing Machines and Bloomers* (London: 1977)

Sitwell, Osbert and Margaret Barton. *Brighton* (London: 1935)

Sharp, Evelyn. 'How to Dress in the Water', *The Guardian* (26 May 1906)

Smith, Janet. *Liquid Assets: The lidos and open air swimming pools of Britain* (London: 2005)

Smith, Sam. 'Bathing Machines', *The Architectural Review*, 36 (July

1964) pp. 65–67

Smollett, Tobias. *The Expedition of Humphry Clinker* (Oxford: 1998)

St Clair Strange, F. G. *The History of the Royal Sea Bathing Hospital* (Rainham: 1991)

Swaffer, Hannen. 'Swaffer at the Seaside: The New England- But the Old Ramsgate', *The Daily Herald* (3 August 1931) p. 6
  'Swaffer at the Seaside: The New England on the Sands' (4 August 1931) p. 6

Sweet, Matthew. *Inventing the Victorians* (London: 2001)

Tickner, Lisa. 'Vanessa Bell: *Studland Beach*, Domesticity, and "Significant Form"', *Representations*, 65 (1999)

The Times, Letters to the Editor
  'Ramsgate and Margate Bathing', 29 September 1841, p. 6
  'Ramsgate Bathing', 30 September 1841, p. 5; 1 October 1841, p. 7
  'Bathing at Ramsgate and Margate', 2 October 1841, p. 7
  'Bathing at Scarborough', 5 October 1841, p. 7
  'Bathing at Ramsgate', 10 October 1842, p. 3; 25 August 1846, p. 3
  'Bathing at Gravesend', 16 August 1842, p. 6
  'Bathing at Brighton', 7 September 1846, p. 7; 10 September 1846, p. 8
  'Bathing at Broadstairs', 15 October 1847, p. 7
  'Sea Bathing at Brighton,' 4 September 1850, p. 8
  'A Defence of Dover Bathing', 21 August 1856, p. 5
  'The Bathing at Dover', 22 August 1856, p. 12
  'Scarborough Bathing', 1 October 1863, p. 7
  'Sea-Bathing in England and France' (John Hulley), 6 August 1864, p. 10
  'Decent Bathing', 8 August 1864, p. 12
  'Bathing at Lowestoft', 25 September 1865, p. 12
  'Bathing at Eastboroune', 28 September 1865, p. 10

'Bathing at Sheerness', 16 July 1866, p. 11

'Bathing at Aberystwyth', 13 September 1866, p. 10; 17 September, p. 9

'The Bathing Accident at Boulogne', 26 September 1879, p. 8; 27 Sept 1879, p. 10

'Sea-Bathing at Home and Abroad', 24 August 1871, p. 6; 25 August 1871, p. 3

'Sea-Bathing', (Jabez Streeter), 28 August 1871, p. 12

'Rules for Bathing', 4 September 1882, p. 8

'Bathing Regulations,' 11 August 1899, p. 10

'George III's Bathing Machine', 29 June 1933, p. 15

The Times, 'A Bathing Predicament' (5 August 1843) p. 7

'Suicide of a Young Lady in a Bathing Machine' (4 August 1856) p. 10

'A Lady Drowned while Bathing', 8 June 1867, p. 9

'Dangers of Sea Bathing', 22 August 1873, p. 4

'Bathing Regulations at Southend', 8 May 1912, p. 7

'Mixed Bathing', 22 May 1912, p. 13

'Sea And Spa: Broadstairs Bathing Rule', 10 August 1921, p. 6

'Bathing Facilities at Eastbourne', 30 October 1929, p. 20

'Bathing at Eastbourne: Regulations Relaxed', 4 February 1930, p. 11

'Bathing at Bournemouth: What is "Regulation Costume"', 4 May 1932, p. 11

'British Health Resorts: Bathing Restrictions', 3 June 1932, p. 20

'New Dress Designs for Men: "Popular Bathing Slip"', 4 March 1933, p. 9

'The Seaside', *The Illustrated London Almanack from 1853*, pp. 37–38

'The Sea-side Resorts of the Londoners', *Chambers Edinburgh Journal*, 515 (1853) pp. 305–09

The South Coast Quarterly, 1 (June–August 1899)

Turner, E.S. *Taking the Cure* (London: 1967)

Thoreau, Henry David. *Walden* (1854) (Oxford: 1999)

Theroux, Paul. *The Kingdom by the Sea* (London: 1983)

Towner Art Gallery. *The Modesty Machine: The Seaside Bathing Machine from 1735* (Eastbourne: 1992)

Travis, John F. *The Rise of the Devon Seaside Resorts, 1750-1900* (Exeter, 1993)
    'Continuity and Change in English Sea-Bathing, 1730–1900: A Case of Swimming with the Tide', in S. Fisher ed., *Recreation and the Sea* (Exeter: 1997)

Tuohy, Ferdinand. 'The New Bronze Age', *The Graphic* (23 August 1930) p. 298

Vale, Edmund. *Seas and Shores of England* (London: 1936)

van Leeuwen, Thomas A.P. *The Springboard in the Pond: An Intimate History of the Swimming Pool* (Cambridge, Mass.: 1999)

Wales, Tony. *Bognor Regis* (Stroud: 1997)

Walker, Kenneth. *Clacton-on-Sea in Old Photographs* (Stroud: 1995)

Walton, John K. *The English Seaside Resort: A Social History, 1750-1914* (Leicester: 1983)
    'The first Spanish seaside resorts', *History Today*, 44:8 (August 1994) pp. 23-29
    'The Seaside Resorts of Western Europe, 1750-1939', in S. Fisher, ed., *Recreation and the Sea* (Exeter: 1997)
    The British Seaside: Holidays and Resorts in the Twentieth Century (Manchester: 2000)
    "The Queen of the Beaches: Ostend and the British from the 1890s to the 1930s' , *History Today*, 51:8 (August 2001) pp. 19-25

Walton, John K. and James Walvin, eds., *Leisure in Britain, 1780-1939* (Manchester: 1983)

Walvin, James. *Beside the Seaside* (London: 1978)

Wansey, Henry. *The Journal of an Excursion to the United States of North America in the Summer of 1794*, (1769) (facsimile reprint, New York: 1969)

Ward, Wilfred. *The Life of John Henry Cardinal Newman Based on his Private Journals and Correspondence*, Vol. 1 (London: 1912)

Waugh, Evelyn. 'This Sun-Bathing Business', *Daily Mail* (5 July 1930) p. 8

Weightman, Gavin. *The Seaside* (Devizes: 1993)

Wey, Francis (trans. Valerie Pirie). *A Frenchman sees the English in the 'Fifties* (London: 1935)

Whittaker, Meredith. 'The Earliest Bathing Machines in Scarborough', *Scarborough Evening News* (23 December 1980).

Whyman, John. *The Early Kentish Seaside (1736–1840)* (Gloucester: 1985)

Woodruff, C. H. 'The Making of Margate', *Home Counties Magazine*, 4 (London: 1902)

Yonge, C. M. 'Victorians by the Sea Shore', *History Today*, 251(1975) pp. 602–09

Index

Page numbers in italic refer to illustrations

C

G

H

M